THE JACOBITE WARS

THE JACOBITE WARS

Scotland and the
Military Campaigns of 1715 and 1745

John L. Roberts

POLYGON
AT EDINBURGH

© John L. Roberts, 2002

Polygon at Edinburgh
An imprint of Edinburgh University Press Ltd
22 George Square, Edinburgh

Typeset in Bulmer by
Hewer Text Ltd, Edinburgh, and
printed and bound in Great Britain by
Antony Rowe Ltd, Chippenham, Wilts

A CIP Record for this book is
available from the British Library

ISBN 1 902930 29 0 (paperback)

CONTENTS

THE AUTHOR

Dr John L. Roberts, who died in November 2000, was a well-known Highland geologist. A graduate of Edinburgh University, he obtained a PhD in geology at the University of Liverpool, researching the metamorphic rocks of the South-west Highlands, on which he later published over twenty papers. He was a lecturer at universities in Saudi Arabia and Lebanon, and travelled widely, before returning to Britain to take up a post at Newcastle University. There, he taught geology for twenty years before taking early retirement in 1986 to live in the far north of Sutherland.

Subsequently, John devoted his energies to writing books. He was a highly skilled geological and landscape photographer, as demonstrated in his two photographic field guides, *The Macmillan Field Guide to Geological Structures* (Macmillan Reference Books, 1989) and *A Photographic Guide to Minerals, Rocks and Fossils* (New Holland, 1998). His *Highland Geology Trail* (Luath Press, 1998) was written to inform the interested amateur about the rocks underlying the scenic grandeur of the North-west Highlands in all its diversity.

Geology is a historical science, allowing us to look into 'the abyss of time' and examine 'a succession of former worlds', in the words of John Playfair and James Hutton. It was perhaps a natural extension of John's lifelong study of the rocks of the Highlands that he developed a strong interest in the human record of the area. He was the author of three earlier books on Scottish history, published by Edinburgh University Press: *Lost Kingdoms; Feuds, Forays and Rebellions*; and *Clan, King and Covenant*. Together, these volumes cover the period from the early Middle Ages up to the Glencoe Massacre. During the last year of his debilitating illness, John completed work on the text of *The Jacobite Wars*.

PREFACE

The Jacobite Rebellions of 1715 and 1745 have long been regarded as romantic episodes in the history of Scotland, wreathed admittedly in myth and legend, but with negligible political significance. Until quite recently, they attracted little attention from serious historians. Instead, the lives of the Old Pretender, James Edward Stuart, and more especially of his son Charles Edward Stuart, the Young Pretender, famous as 'Bonnie Prince Charlie', have provided a rich source of inspiration for countless works of artistic imagination. Indeed, the Romantic Movement seized on the figure of Bonnie Prince Charlie as the epitome of a truly tragic hero, second only to Mary, Queen of Scots, while celebrating the rebellion he led in 1745 as one of the most dramatic episodes in Scotland's history.

Both in character and in career, Charles Edward Stuart provided the perfect materials for myth-making. With his audacity and undoubted charisma, he seemed to have embodied Romanticism's exaltation of vision and emotion at the expense of reason. Furthermore, Charles's spectacular defeat against the forces of the Hanoverian Establishment gave him the additional allure of nostalgic melancholy. Seventy years after Culloden, Bonnie Prince Charlie's place in the Scottish pantheon was secured by Sir Walter Scott, who had become preoccupied with cultural nationalism, refashioning Scots history into imaginative accounts more akin to folklore than to historical fact.

The retrospective glorification of Charles Edward Stuart has generated so many idealised half-truths and popular misconceptions that it is now difficult to realise how close the Stuarts came to actually overthrowing the Hanoverian regime during a period when it was particularly vulnerable. The aim of this book is, therefore, to provide a clear and demythologised account of the military campaigns waged by the Jacobites against the Hanoverian monarchs, set against a background of Scottish political, religious and constitutional history.

It can be argued that, if the Prince had been a less 'romantic' figure, less attentive to the voice of his own assumed genius and more amenable to reason, he might have succeeded in exploiting the weakness of George II, changing the course of British history rather than merely dominating Scottish mythology. Conversely, the strength of his political challenge may have been possible only for someone reckless enough to brush aside military realities for a passionate cause.

It was only by the force of his personal magnetism that Charles Edward Stuart managed to instigate the 1745 Rebellion at all and to persuade his Scottish adherents to rise in rebellion on his behalf. Acting on impulse, he arrived in Scotland, accompanied by a paltry handful of ageing courtiers, but bringing with him no promise of French men and arms to back up his initiative. Having captured Edinburgh in a whirlwind campaign to make himself the master of Scotland, Charles then needed all his overweening self-confidence to keep up the momentum of the 1745 Rebellion by invading England and advanced as far south as Derby, where he briefly posed a major challenge to George II. However, at Derby he was overruled by the natural caution of his commander-in-chief, Lord George Murray, so that the campaign came to nothing, despite the threat of a supportive French invasion.

Curiously enough, the 1715 Rebellion would also never have happened without individual initiative, when John Erskine, sixth Earl of Mar, raised the Jacobite standard a year after the death of Queen Anne, the last of the Stuart monarchs. Hardly a dashing figure, 'Bobbing John' lacked Charles's charisma, and proved himself utterly incompetent as a military commander in the field. Consequently, the 1715 Rebellion never really threatened the security of Great Britain under the new regime, despite widespread support for it in Scotland. Indeed, it may well be argued that Mar only intended to exert political pressure on the Whig ministry that came to power in 1714 by allying himself with the interests of the Tory party in England. Another leader of the 1715 Rebellion might well have exposed the Hanoverian government's weakness under the Whigs even without French support, which was unlikely given that Britain and France were at peace with each other.

It is, therefore, hardly surprising that later Whig historians have dismissed the Jacobite Rebellions of 1715 and 1745 as politically insignificant, once the Jacobite cause had effectively died with Charles Edward Stuart in 1788. British historians have only recently come to emphasise the danger faced by the Hanoverian regime during those years of political and religious turbulence. Not only did the exiled Stuart dynasty attract support at home, especially from within the Tory party, but it could also look to France and Spain as its natural allies on the Continent. France in particular was quite prepared to supply men and arms to restore the Stuarts, or even to invade England on their behalf, whenever this seemed to be in the

French interest. Although French threats never materialised, they were taken very seriously at the time, especially in 1745, when Britain, under George II, was fighting France in the War of the Austrian Succession. One historian has recently described the 1745 Rebellion as being the greatest crisis to face Great Britain in the eighteenth century.

Scots historians have also tended to discount the true significance of the Jacobite Rebellions of 1715 and 1745, but on quite different grounds. Indeed, it is difficult to know quite what to make of Jacobitism from a Scottish perspective, bearing in mind the religious divisions that then existed within the country. Both rebellions occurred within the context of the 1707 Act of Union and took on all the trappings of a national crusade to restore Scotland's independence, especially in 1715. James Edward Stuart promised consistently to break the Union between Scotland and England if he ever ruled over Great Britain. However, the 1707 Act of Union had also guaranteed the survival and status of the Presbyterian Church as Scotland's national Church. Since the Jacobite cause was committed to restoring a Catholic dynasty to the throne, it was anathema to the Presbyterians, who were dominant in the Scottish Lowlands, south of the River Forth. Instead, Jacobitism attracted not just the wholehearted support of the Catholics, a very small minority in the country, but also the staunch backing of the Episcopalians, who were then predominant, not only in the Scottish Highlands but throughout the country to the north of the River Tay.

However, after the crushing defeat of the Jacobites at the Battle of Culloden, the Episcopalian Church was suppressed so effectively that, by the time the penal laws against it were repealed in 1792, only four Episcopalian bishops and forty clergy were left. By then, the national identity of Scotland had been firmly associated with Presbyterianism for many years and remained so, especially during the nineteenth century, so that Jacobitism could no longer claim to be a national movement. Indeed, once Scotland took on the identity of North Britain, the image of Jacobitism was reduced to the melancholy nostalgia of 'a noble cause nobly lost', stripped of real political significance, especially after the Celtic Revival of the nineteenth century had virtually rewritten Scotland's history. By then, the Jacobite cause was firmly linked to the fate of the Jacobite clans, brutally suppressed by 'Butcher' Cumberland in the aftermath of his victory at Culloden, so bringing to an end the clan system.

Once the failure of the Jacobite rebellions had been taken as evidence that they had never seriously threatened the Hanoverian government, it was then only a short step to the Whig interpretation of the period, in which 'England, and subsequently the other kingdoms of the British Isles steadily, nigh inexorably progressed towards the constitutional, Parliamentary democracy of the present day', to quote David Szechi. Such an interpretation assumed that no persons in their right minds could have supported the exiled dynasty, except for the basest of motives, unless they were the self-deluding dupes of the Catholic Church in Rome.

However, this view belittles the commitment of the Jacobites, faced with formidable difficulties if they were to overthrow what was originally a foreign dynasty during the sixty years after the 'Glorious Revolution' of 1688–9. To oust the Hanoverians, the Jacobites needed external support. Countries such as France or Spain would consider launching a sea-borne invasion of England or Scotland only in the event of war with Britain and this intervention would succeed only if control of the sea had already been wrested from the British navy. In addition, any sea-borne invasion of the British Isles would always be very vulnerable to the weather. Thus, the Jacobites needed a particularly favourable conjunction of circumstances to overthrow the Hanoverian regime. Given that these circumstances never arose during the four uprisings of 1708, 1715, 1719 and 1745, another school of historical thought takes the pessimistic view that the Jacobites could never have overcome the 'power of inertia, the Revolution settlement, and the British state'.

By contrast, yet another historical interpretation holds that Jacobitism actually came within a hair's breadth on a number of occasions of overthrowing the Hanoverian government and that it was a genuine political movement with mass support. This interpretation implies that the Hanoverian regime after 1714 was not the monolithic entity envisaged by Whig historians, which relied on the safeguards of parliamentary democracy for its legitimacy. On the contrary, contemporary British government had shaky foundations, dependent on a less than popular German dynasty for its authority. Political vulnerability would then explain the furious government reaction to the 1745 Rebellion, especially in the Scottish Highlands, and the ferocity of its retribution, remembered in the laments of popular Scottish culture.

Note. Dates are given throughout the text according to the old-style Julian Calendar, which was used in Great Britain until 1752. These dates lag 11 days behind the new-style Gregorian Calendar, introduced on the Continent by Pope Gregory XIII in 1592. The New Year is taken to start on 1 January rather than 25 March.

Outline Map of Scotland Showing Places of Significance
in the Jacobite Campaigns of 1715 and 1745

Map showing Route of Jacobite Army in 1745–6

Places associated with Flight of Charles Edward Stuart, April–September 1746

Chapter One

ORIGINS OF THE JACOBITE MOVEMENT

Jacobite: An adherent of James II of England after his abdication, or of his own son the [Old] Pretender; a partisan of the Stuarts after the revolution of 1688 [Latin *Jacobus*: James]
Note: James II of England ruled over Scotland as James VII.
Quoted from the Oxford English Dictionary

The Jacobite Movement in England and Ireland

The Jacobite movement had its origins in the 'Glorious Revolution' of 1688-9, when William of Orange replaced James VII of Scotland on the throne of Great Britain. The change in dynasty itself had been triggered by the politically inept behaviour of James VII who ruled as a Catholic king over a Protestant country at a time of religious persecution in France. During his brief reign, James not only had shown excessive favour to his fellow Catholics, but he also had seemed oblivious of the limits to religious toleration that his other subjects were prepared to accept. He had offended them in particular by using the royal prerogative to allow Dissenters and, indeed, Catholics to take public office. Moreover, he had purged the municipal and other corporations that elected members to the House of Commons in a blatant attempt to influence the results of the Parliamentary elections of 1688.

The crisis came in the summer of 1688 with the birth of his son, James Edward Stuart. The likelihood that the new heir to the throne would be brought up a Catholic was enough for the leading politicians of the time to issue an invitation to William of Orange, the staunchly Protestant ruler of the Netherlands, who was not only the king's nephew but also his son-in-law through his marriage to James's daughter Mary. They apparently hoped that William would persuade James to moderate his policies, turning a blind eye to the probability that William only accepted their invitation so that he could depose the king as the ally of Louis XIV of France and then be able to ally Britain with Holland at the head of a grand coalition to contain the territorial ambitions of France. Thus, the religious and political freedoms of the British people were hardly uppermost in William's mind when he invaded England in November 1688 with an army of 14,000, whatever the views of subsequent generations of Whig historians.

Although James prepared to meet force with force, his position was fatally weakened by defections from his own army, particularly among his leading officers. Even his commander-in-chief, John Churchill, afterwards the first Duke of Marlborough, deserted him. The king abandoned armed resistance once local revolts had erupted throughout the country in support of William and entered instead into negotiations with his son-in-law. But the talks made no headway and, in December 1688, James fled the country to France and the protection of Louis XIV.

Once William had effectively seized power, elections were held in England to a Convention Parliament in January 1689. This Parliament then passed the Declaration of Rights, requiring the monarch to rule with the consent of a freely elected parliament. The absolute power previously claimed by the Stuart dynasty, according to the Divine Right of Kings, was finally curtailed. The king would now need the agreement of Parliament in order to suspend legislation, levy taxation or maintain a standing army in peacetime. William implicitly accepted these restrictions on his exercise of arbitrary power when he accepted the Crown of Britain on behalf of himself and his wife, Queen Mary. However, he proved to be an energetic and autocratic ruler who clashed repeatedly with Parliament, which was determined to preserve its own hard-won liberties. Nevertheless, the tensions within the country were not enough to actively fuel Jacobitism until the accession of George I in 1714.

In March 1689, James VII landed in Ireland where Richard Talbot, newly created Earl of Tyrconnel, still ruled as Lord Deputy on his behalf. Ireland was already divided on religious grounds, since Protestantism had taken root in Ulster after its 'plantation' by lowland Scots over the previous century. It took a large and efficient army under William of Orange to defeat James at the Battle of the Boyne in July 1690, although the Jacobite army was reinforced by several thousand French troops. However, hostilities continued for another year until the signing of the Treaty of Limerick. Its military articles allowed the Irish troops in the service of James VII to go abroad into exile, an opportunity taken by more than 10,000 in what became known as the 'Flight of the Wild Geese'. Significantly, these Irish exiles included the descendants of what remained of the Catholic gentry in Ireland from pre-plantation times. They were mostly native Irish in origin, but others were from old English families who, by-and-large, were still Catholics and whose forebears had lived in Ireland for centuries. Many of these exiles took service with Louis XIV, forming the Irish Brigade of the French army. Others entered into the commercial life of the countries where they settled, especially in subsequent generations. Along with other exiles from England and, more especially, from Scotland, they were the backbone of Jacobite support on the Continent for more than fifty years.

The 'Flight of the Wild Geese' inevitably left the Protestant Ascendancy dominant in the affairs of Ireland throughout the eighteenth century, especially after 1691, when Westminster passed an Act preventing Catholics from sitting in the Irish Parliament in Dublin, stripping them of all political influence. The Irish Parliament thus became a 'Protestant Parliament for a Protestant People'. It passed a series of penal laws against the wishes of William, which benefited the Protestant settlers from plantation times at the expense of the few remaining Catholic landowners. As a consequence, the exodus of Catholic gentry continued for decades and Jacobitism went into almost total eclipse in Ireland.

The Jacobite Movement in Scotland

In Scotland things were quite different. Within twenty years of the 'Glorious Revolution', the Parliament in Edinburgh would be abolished by the 1707 Act of Union. Before then, after the flight abroad of James VII, elections would be held in March 1689 to a Parliamentary Convention in Edinburgh. The Convention offered the Crown to William and Mary and then passed the Claim of Right. This was a far more radical document than its English equivalent, the Declaration of Rights, although both documents made the royal prerogative subject to the consent of a freely elected parliament. James was seen as having forfeited his kingdom by his exercise of 'arbitrary despotic power', which had subverted the 'fundamental constitution of this Kingdom [of Scotland]' by violating its laws and liberties. Catholics would now no longer be eligible to hold public office, while episcopacy was condemned as being an 'insupportable grievance and trouble to this nation . . . contrary to the inclinations of the generality of the people ever since the Reformation, they having been reformed from Popery by Presbyters, and therefore [episcopacy] ought to be abolished'.

In fact, 200 Episcopalian ministers had already been expelled by force from their livings in the 'rabbling of the curates' over the winter of 1688–9, especially in the Presbyterian heartlands of south-west Scotland. Further expulsions occurred in 1689, after many more clergy refused to abandon their earlier oath of allegiance to James as the rightful King of Scotland. As they also refused to swear allegiance to William and Mary, they became known as 'non-juring' Episcopalians. The Episcopalian Church survived, especially north of the Tay, where it was well established both among the

Highland clans and also the conservative families of the north-east of Scotland. In the Highlands, the Presbyterian faith had taken root only among the clans that came under the influence of the Campbells, Earls of Argyll, or the Gordons, Earls of Sutherland.

In June 1690, William was forced to restore Presbyterian government to the national Church, against his own sense of religious tolerance. Otherwise, what had now become the Scots Parliament would refuse to vote him the revenues he urgently needed for the Nine Years War with France. This conflict had broken out in May 1689 with the landing of French troops in Ireland in support of James. In October 1690, when a meeting of the Church's General Assembly was called for the first time in nearly forty years, it was dominated by still-surviving ministers who had been expelled from their livings in the 1660s for refusing to accept the establishment of an Episcopalian Church under Charles II.

Out of nearly 1,000 parishes in Scotland, only 180 ministers and elders attended this meeting and they all came from the Lowlands, south of the River Tay. So constituted, the General Assembly proceeded to rid the Church of 'all inefficient, negligent scandalous and erroneous ministers'. This purge of Episcopalianism would take more than twenty-five years to complete, and a further thirty until it was all but rooted out in the aftermath of the 1745 Rebellion. Until then, the Presbyterian Church flourished only in the Lowlands of Scotland, giving its reluctant support to William and his successors. Meanwhile, Episcopalianism survived in the north of the country, among the Highland clans with their military traditions, and the conservative families of the north-east Lowlands around Aberdeen.

The close identification of the Jacobite cause with the non-juring Episcopalians simply reflected their shared values. Jacobites were nearly all staunch Episcopalians, apart from a small number of Roman Catholics; likewise, Episcopalians were, politically, nearly all Jacobites, convinced the Stuart dynasty had a God-given right to rule over them. Scotland was, therefore, dangerously divided.

In the constitutional and religious settlement that followed the accession of William and Mary, the leading Scottish magnates played what can only be described as an ambivalent role. Only John Graham of Claverhouse, created Viscount Dundee by James VII, remained loyal to his former sovereign, raising the Jacobite standard on his behalf in April 1689, a month after James himself had landed in Ireland. After mustering an army from among the Jacobite clans of the Great Glen, he inflicted a heavy defeat upon the government forces at the Battle of Killiecrankie on 27 July 1689. However, this proved a pyrrhic victory for 'Bonnie Dundee', who was killed at the head of his troops. Deprived of his charismatic leadership, the rebellion ran out of steam, although it was not until 1 May 1690 that the Jacobite forces were decisively defeated at the Battle of Cromdale.

Nevertheless, the Jacobite clans remained a threat to the new regime and John Campbell of Glenorchy, first Earl of Breadalbane, undertook to pacify the Highlands. After more than a year, he succeeded in getting the rebel chiefs to agree to submit to the government, although they insisted that they could not swear allegiance to William and Mary without the consent of James VII, now living in exile at Saint-Germain in France. This consent was not received until shortly before the government's final deadline of 31 December 1691. The delay provided Breadalbane's rival, Sir John Dalrymple of Stair, with the ideal excuse, as Secretary of State for Scotland, to launch a punitive expedition against the MacDonalds of Glencoe, whose aged chief Alasdair MacIain had failed to submit before the agreed deadline. The notorious massacre at Glencoe was carried out by two companies from the Campbell, Earl of Argyll's regiment of the standing army, making it appear that the Campbells had taken revenge upon their ancient enemies of Clan Donald. In fact, the atrocity was driven by Dalrymple's own insecurity as a former holder of high office under James VII. He felt compelled to prove his loyalty to the new regime and hated the Highland clans with their alien way of life with an intensity that can only be described as paranoid.

King William was deeply implicated in the Glencoe Massacre, having signed and countersigned the secret orders from Dalrymple authorising it. The public outcry following the Massacre gave the Jacobites a propaganda victory and eventually a Commission of Enquiry was set up to investigate the affair. However, its members were appointed by William himself, trying to safeguard his own reputation. Unsurprisingly, the Commission glossed over the king's involvement in the affair, although the Scots Parliament subsequently placed the blame squarely with Sir John Dalrymple of Stair, causing his political downfall.

In an attempt to placate Scots opinion, William then approved legislation allowing Scotland to set up an overseas trading company, comparable to the East India Company of London. Known as the Company of Scotland, its very name suggests that all the hopes of the Scottish nation were invested in its success. Its catastrophic failure was part of a chain of events that culminated in the Act of Union of 1707. Despite its title, the Company of Scotland was actually based in London and drew on the commercial and financial expertise of the English capital. However, it clearly threatened the monopoly long enjoyed by the East India Company and confidence in the venture collapsed when the English Parliament objected to its very existence. Yet, despite the obstacles placed in its path and the lack of any official support, the huge sum of £400,000 was raised over the next six months in Scotland, said to represent half of all the capital available to the nation. It was an extraordinary gamble that Scotland took and lost, leading to the country's demise as an independent nation.

By summer 1698, an expedition had set sail under sealed orders for the isthmus of Darien (now Panama) in Central America, aiming to establish a trading colony in what was Spanish territory. The settlers were ill equipped and without adequate provisions, and, after only eight months, those who survived disease and starvation abandoned the colony in the face of Spanish and English hostility. By then, another expedition had left Scotland, only to capitulate in humiliation when Spanish forces besieged the colony. The venture ended in utter disaster. Only one of the five vessels that had originally left Scotland managed to sail back home to safety and nearly half the colonists lost their lives. Almost all levels of Scottish society had invested heavily in the venture and many were now threatened with bankruptcy.

Parliaments in Conflict: Legislative Background to the Act of Union

On the Continent, the Nine Years War with France had ended in 1697 with the Treaty of Ryswyck and Louis XIV had been forced to recognise William of Orange as King of Great Britain, ruling over the country 'by the grace of God'. This temporarily quashed any Jacobite hope that James VII might be restored to the throne with French help. Curiously enough, William then let it be known that he was prepared to recognise James VII's son, James Edward Stuart, as his lawful heir, provided he was allowed to rule in peace until his own death. James VII spurned the proposal, on the grounds that the boy would be brought up as a Protestant. This left the throne open to Princess Anne, the younger sister of William's wife Mary. William repeated his proposal again in 1700, after the death of Anne's last surviving son. However, James once again turned down the chance that his son might peacefully succeed William of Orange on the throne of Great Britain.

After this rebuff, the English Parliament passed the 1701 Act of Settlement, requiring the sovereign to be not just a Protestant but also more specifically an Anglican. The Act set aside the legitimate rights of fifty-seven claimants to the throne, who were descended in one way or another from James VI of Scotland. Instead, it guaranteed the succession to Sophia, Electress of Hanover, a granddaughter of James VI, and to her descendants, should William or Princess Anne die without any heirs, as looked likely. The Act eventually brought Sophia's son George, Elector of Hanover, to the throne of Great Britain in 1714 as George I. No such Act was passed by the Scots Parliament, offended that it had not even been consulted over a matter of such constitutional importance.

After Queen Anne had succeeded William of Orange in 1702, the English Parliament at Westminster declared war against France, again ignoring the Scots Parliament. This marked the outbreak of the War of the Spanish Succession, following the death of Charles II of Spain without heir in 1700. The war was waged by a grand Protestant alliance of Britain, Holland and the Holy Roman Empire of Germany against the Catholic monarchies of France and Spain. James VII had already died in 1701, leaving his thirteen-year-old son James Edward Stuart to succeed him as the claimant to the throne, later to be known as the 'Old Pretender'.

The Scots Parliament reacted to the Act of Settlement by passing the 1703 Act of Security against the wishes of Queen Anne and her ministers in London. This stipulated that the Crown of Scotland should only be offered to Sophia, Electress of Hanover, and her heirs, if the full sovereignty of the Scots Parliament was guaranteed. Indeed, the Act was intended to 'secure the honour and sovereignty of this crown and kingdom [of Scotland]; the freedom . . . and power of [its] Parliaments; the religion . . . and trade of the nation, from English, or any foreign influence'. The threat of force was implicit in the 1703 Act of Security since all Protestant men of fencible age in Scotland were to be trained in defence of the kingdom. It was followed by the even more belligerent Act anent [about] Peace and War, which specified that no successor to Queen Anne could declare war without first consulting the Scots Parliament.

This defiant show of national independence by the Scots infuriated the English Parliament, which promptly entreated Queen Anne to fortify and garrison the Border strongholds of Carlisle, Berwick and Newcastle, to raise a militia in the northern counties of England and to dispatch regular troops north to guard against a Scottish incursion. Then, in February 1705, the Alien Act was passed by the English Parliament. This was nothing less than an ultimatum. By Christmas Day 1705, the Scots Parliament must either accept the Hanoverian succession by repealing the 1703 Act of Security, or else be in negotiations for the union of the two Parliaments; otherwise all Scots not domiciled in England would be treated as aliens and all imports from Scotland banned. This last clause threatened the economic interests of the Scottish nobility and other landowners, since much of their income was derived directly or indirectly from the export of cattle, linen and coal to England.

The Union of England and Scotland under a single parliament had been contemplated ever since James VI of Scotland had succeeded to the throne of England. But it was only in the turbulent years after the 'Glorious Revolution' of 1688–9 that the proposal made any headway, receiving further impetus after Queen Anne came to the throne in 1702. By then, the Darien disaster had demonstrated the virtual impossibility of Scotland pursuing colonial and trading policies overseas in competition with the economic interests of England. Many Scots came to realise that union with England was almost essential for Scotland's prosperity. Otherwise, there was little prospect of access to England's colonial markets, guarded so jealously by such monopolies as the East India Company of London.

The Act of Union was carried through the Scots Parliament by John Campbell, eleventh Earl and second Duke of Argyll, who, in April 1705, was made Queen's High Commissioner to the Parliament in Edinburgh. In September 1705, it was agreed that commissioners should be appointed to negotiate a Treaty of Union with England. However, because these commissioners were nominated by Queen Anne, the twenty-five articles of the Treaty of Union eventually agreed between the two countries on 23 July 1706 were hardly to the liking of the Scots.

The two countries were to be united as one kingdom, under the name of Great Britain, and ruled by a single parliament at Westminster. Although the Scots would have preferred a federal union, preserving the identity and independence of the Scottish nation, the Act of Union was finally passed by the Scots Parliament on 16 January 1707, despite violent rioting in Edinburgh, Glasgow and elsewhere in the country and the widespread display of popular opposition to the Treaty. Among the Act's statutes, a clause finally establishing the Presbyterian Kirk as the national Church of Scotland was especially significant. This clause was introduced as a concession after several thousand Presbyterians had burnt the articles of Union at Dumfries on 20 November 1706. The Act of Union was almost immediately ratified by the Parliament at Westminster and the Scots Parliament was adjourned. It would not meet again until 1 July 1999, nearly three centuries later. Before his death in 1701, James VII had already instructed his son James Edward Stuart not to contemplate any such union between Scotland and England. Now the repeal of the 1707 Act of Union became an established tenet of Jacobite policy.

The Failed Invasion of 1708

The popular outcry in Scotland against the 1707 Act of Union may well have convinced Louis XIV of France that the time had come to play the Jacobite card, especially as James Edward Stuart was now nearly twenty years of age. In fact, after Marlborough's victories at Blenheim (1704) and Ramillies (1706), the French king had already dispatched Colonel Nathaniel Hooke to Scotland to assess Scottish support for a French invasion aimed at restoring the Stuart dynasty. However Hooke's glowing report of Jacobite sentiment among the Scots, largely gained at second hand, was mostly wishful thinking. And so it proved in 1708, when Louis finally authorised a naval expedition to land James Edward Stuart upon the shores of Scotland.

French preparations were substantial enough to demonstrate that the expedition was no mere diversionary tactic. A fleet of five warships, together with more than twenty frigates, mostly French privateers, assembled at Dunkirk during January and February 1708. When the fleet finally set sail on 6 March 1708, 5,000 French troops were aboard the ships in twelve battalions, with enough arms to equip another 13,000 men. However, the two Frenchmen in command of the expedition itself had no interest in its success. Marshal de Matignon had to be bribed with the promise of honours before he would even accept command of the troops, while Admiral de Forbin told the French king to his face that the whole scheme was just a 'forlorn hope'.

James, Duke of Berwick, evidently said much the same thing to Louis XIV. He was the natural son of James VII of Scotland by Marlborough's sister Arabella Churchill, making him an elder half-brother to James Edward Stuart. Now a Marshal of France and an outstanding general, he was the natural leader of any such expedition, since he enjoyed the full confidence of the French king. But he evidently knew nothing of the plans, arriving back at Versailles from service in Spain only a few days after the invasion force set sail.

The French fleet sailed north from Dunkirk through the North Sea, intending to land James and his forces on the southern shores of the Forth to a pre-arranged signal. The expedition seemed to be accident prone from the start, having been delayed because James had gone down with an attack of measles and, barely recovered, had come on board at the last moment. The icy waters of the North Sea were stormy and James and his attendants were all horribly seasick. The fleet sailed too far north through faulty navigation, missed the original rendezvous and eventually anchored off Crail at the mouth of the Forth. A small party went ashore at Pittenweem but they were met by only a handful of James's supporters, and the French commanders refused James's desperate pleas to be landed. By now, it was clear that the Jacobite promise to Louis XIV that 'the whole nation will arise upon the arrival of its king' was an empty boast.

Next morning, sixteen men-of-war under Admiral Sir George Byng arrived off the Firth of Forth, after pursuing the French fleet north from Dunkirk. A running battle then began as the French ships sailed north towards Buchanness, chased by Byng. He then returned to Leith, in case the French fleet had doubled back south. In fact, it sailed right round the north coast of Scotland to arrive back in Dunkirk, after losing several ships in atrocious weather to the west of Ireland. The whole expedition had proved an utter flop, although it did cause panic in London with a run on the Bank of England, demonstrating the vulnerability of the government in London to the Jacobite threat.

On landing, James had planned to issue a 'Declaration to the Scottish Nation', urging the loyal people of his ancient realm of Scotland to break the Union with England. A free Parliament would then be called in Edinburgh to decide upon the constitution, especially with regard to the Church. However, he only attracted the support of some gentry in Stirlingshire, whose 'erratic journeyings' were later judged as hardly significant enough to make them guilty of treason. Otherwise, the country remained quiet, as might have been expected in the Lowlands. The Presbyterian majority to the south of the River Tay had a vested interest in the 1707 Act of Union, which had finally guaranteed the very existence of the Presbyterian Church of Scotland, established by law as the national Church. They were not likely to rise to restore a practising Catholic to the throne of a Protestant country.

Equally, the great magnates could not be expected to rally to the Jacobite cause, at least not for the time being. After all, only a year previously, it was the peers of the realm, supported by the gentry and the burgesses, who had pushed through the 1707 Act of Union against much popular opposition. They had especially benefited from its financial provisions, which had granted compensation to the shareholders of the now-defunct Company of Scotland, wound up under the Act itself. Indeed, the original capital invested in the Company was repaid to all its shareholders with interest at 5%, amounting to the grand sum of £232,884 sterling. All levels of society benefited but the great magnates gained most of all, since they had invested the largest sums in the Company of Scotland.

Nevertheless, the government acted swiftly in the aftermath of the failed invasion, arresting all those Scots suspected of Jacobite sympathies, including the Dukes of Atholl and Gordon, the Earls of Aberdeen, Breadalbane, Erroll, Nithsdale and Strathmore, and the Earl Marischal. They eventually obtained their freedom by finding financial security for their future conduct, with payments varying between £3,000 and £5,000. Several Highland chieftains, such as Sir Ewan Cameron of Lochiel, Alan MacDonald of ClanRanald, Coll MacDonald of Keppoch, Alasdair Mac-Donald of Glengarry and Robert Stewart of Appin, were also taken into custody at the same time.

On his return to France, James Edward Stuart took service with Louis XIV, like his father before him. At the Battles of Oudenarde (1708) and Malplaquet (1709), he, therefore, found himself facing the very country-men he claimed as his own subjects. James distinguished himself with great courage, especially at the Battle of Malplaquet, where he charged twelve times at the 'enemy' lines with the Maison du Roi, (the king's bodyguard).

Afterwards, the two armies faced one another indecisively for more than a year. By July 1710, James was a familiar figure to the enemy troops serving Queen Anne in the Allied army. Soon it looked as if they might even declare their loyalty to him, since they cheered and waved their hats whenever he was seen riding along the French lines on a white charger.

As Sir Charles Petrie commented in *The Jacobite Movement*:

It has rightly been said that this was the moment of all others when an almost bloodless revolution and restoration might have taken place, and had James possessed the initiative of his elder son [Charles Edward Stuart] he would have paid a surprise visit to the British camp, in which event the course of history might well have changed; but James III was not Bonnie Prince Charlie, and . . . much water, and not a little blood, had to flow . . . before the succession to the three crowns [of England, Scotland and Ireland] was finally settled.

Eventually, James returned to Saint-Germain in September 1710 after his spell of active service in the French army, while his cause seemed to gain hold at Westminster.

Whigs and Tories, and Fluctuations in Jacobite Hopes

By now, more than twenty years had passed since the 'Glorious Revolution.' Throughout much of this time, politics at Westminster were dominated by the ministers of the Crown, supported by members of what is best described as the Court Party. These ministers could belong to any party, or none, for William of Orange had liked capable men as his ministers, regardless of their politics, so long as they served his interests. In fact, power had often been shared between aristocratic Whig and Tory politicians, whose fluctuating fortunes under the Crown's patronage make the politics of this period so complex.

The political differences between the Whigs and the Tories first arose in the late seventeenth century in reaction to the Exclusion Crisis of 1679–81. Parliament had tried to bring forward legislation to exclude James, Duke of York and the younger brother of Charles II, from succeeding to the throne of Great Britain on the grounds of his Catholic religion. Supporters of this legislation were branded Whigs by their opponents, a derogatory name derived from the Scots word *Whiggamore*, originally applied to the extreme Covenanters who launched the Whiggamore Raid of 1648 against Edinburgh. First used in Scotland, the name came to denote a strict Presbyterian opposed to the religious settlement of 1660 under Charles II. Once James VII lost his throne in the 'Glorious Revolution', what was now the Whig party became the bitter opponents of the Jacobite cause, especially after the accession of George I in 1714.

The politicians who supported James, Duke of York, in the Exclusion Crisis were branded Tories. This was even more pejorative a term than Whig, derived as it was from the Irish word *Toraighe*, meaning 'a pursuer'. It was applied in the seventeenth century to those Irish Catholics who had turned to banditry and cattle-thieving after being dispossessed of their land by Protestant settlers. Subsequently, the Tory party in England came to represent the landed interest and, especially, the minor gentry, who gave their support to 'Church and King'. Even so, any sentimental attachment they felt for the Stuart dynasty was qualified by their support for the established Church of England.

Until the elections of 1710, Parliament itself was dominated largely by the Whigs. Then popular discontent with the War of the Spanish Succession, coupled with the heavy burden of taxation needed to finance it, as well as a perceived threat to the Anglican Church, returned the Tory party to Westminster, boosted by the support of staunch Jacobites in the country. Robert Harley had come to power under Queen Anne as her chief minister and Lord High Treasurer. However, his influence was undermined by the intrigues of Henry St John, soon to be created the first Viscount Bolingbroke, who served as Secretary of State. He eventually brought the War of the Spanish Succession to an end by negotiating the Treaty of Utrecht between Britain and France in July 1713.

The peace itself forced James Edward Stuart into exile from Saint-Germain and he took up residence at Bar-le-Duc in the Duchy of Lorraine, then part of the Holy Roman Empire. Until France declared war against Britain in 1744 during the War of the Austrian Succession, James could expect little or no French military help. Even so, the last few years had seen a revival of Jacobite hopes. Before the elections of 1710, the new administration under Robert Harley had actually sounded out James, Duke of Berwick, acting through an intermediary. They discussed the possible succession of James Edward Stuart to the throne of Great Britain upon the death of Queen Anne, while the Old Pretender wrote an elegant and impassioned letter to his half-sister around this time, appealing to her better nature in recognising him as her heir. He was certain that she would prefer the succession of her own brother, the last male of their line, to the Duchess of Hanover, the remotest of their relations.

Queen Anne, however, gave little or no sign that she was prepared to recognise James as her rightful heir while he remained a Catholic, and the 1701 Act of Settlement remained a formidable barrier to his restoration. Indeed, the Tory party as a whole would accept James only if he was prepared to renounce his Catholic religion to become an Anglican. This he steadfastly refused to do, saying nevertheless that 'all the just securities that can reasonably be asked for your religion, liberties, and properties I shall be most willing to grant'. But his word was not good enough for a nation that saw his return as simply the first step in converting the country to Catholicism.

As Sir Charles Petrie has written:

The Jacobites were prepared to accept James on any terms, and the Whigs would not have him at any price . . . The choice, in effect, still seemed to be between George [son of Sophia, Electress of Hanover], who had nothing to recommend him except his religion, and James, to whom the only objection was his religion.'

Moreover, the Treaty of Utrecht had finally thrown George, then still the Duke of Brunswick, into the hands of the Whigs, since the peace brokered by Bolingbroke between Britain and France did not include the Dutch republic or the Holy Roman Empire, of which Hanover was a part. Indeed, George I came to regard all Tories with hatred for the part they had played under Bolingbroke in betraying their continental allies at the Treaty of Utrecht. He would rule over the country after 1714 more as the Elector of Hanover than as the King of Great Britain. Indeed, his command of the English language was so poor that he had to talk to his ministers in French.

Equally, James's absolute refusal to turn Anglican made the Tory party, and especially Bolingbroke, wary of restoring him to the throne. In later years, Bolingbroke wrote with hindsight: 'The Tories always looked at the restoration of the Stuarts as a sure means to throw the whole power of the Government into their hands. I am confident they would have found themselves deceived.' He reacted at the time by trying to take the power of the government in his own hands, while passing legislation to cripple the opponents of the Tory party. However, time was not on Bolingbroke's side. It was only on 27 July 1714 that he finally persuaded Queen Anne, as she lay dying in Kensington Palace, to dismiss his arch-rival Robert Harley, Earl of Oxford. On her death, just five days later, he still had not been confirmed in power. She had refused to countenance Bolingbroke as her chief minister, perhaps repelled by his dissolute and drunken life, and his over-worldly cynicism. Instead, two days before her death, she had promoted Charles Talbot, first Duke of Shrewsbury, to the post of chief minister, apparently at Bolingbroke's suggestion. If so, it was a serious error of judgement on his part since, when Queen Anne died early on 1 August 1714, Shrewsbury acted quickly to proclaim George the King of England, Scotland and Ireland. Just five weeks previously, George had become Elector of Hanover on his mother's death. Power had now passed from the Tories since George, while still only heir to the throne, had already collaborated with the Whig party to appoint a Council of Regents, which ruled over the country immediately after Queen Anne's death.

Chapter Two

OUTBREAK OF THE 1715 REBELLION

During the months immediately after the accession of George I in August 1714, there was no great display of popular feeling against the change of dynasty. As Bolingbroke wrote afterwards:

> The thunder had long grumbled in the air; and yet when the bolt fell, most of our party appeared as much surprised as if they had had no reason to expect it. There was perfect calm and universal submission throughout the whole kingdom.

Aware that 'the Crown would belong to him who was first there to seize it', James Edward Stuart had hurried from exile in the Duchy of Lorraine when he heard of Queen Anne's death, intending to cross the Channel at once. However he received neither any French encouragement, nor the messages of support he had expected from England or Scotland. Instead, the Marquis de Torcy, acting as the Foreign Minister of France, ordered him back to Lorraine. George I landed at Greenwich on 18 September 1714 and, a few days later, made a triumphal entry into London, to be crowned King of Great Britain on 20 October.

Early in 1715, a general election was called, sweeping the Whigs back into power. In Scotland, James Graham, first Duke of Montrose, now acting as its Secretary of State, so manipulated the elections that forty out of forty-five seats in the Commons, and nearly all the representative peers in the Lords, were returned as supporters of the Whig ministry and the Hanoverian regime. Meanwhile, the Tories were ruthlessly purged from their official positions in England, in a ban that would last for the next forty-five years until George III came to the throne in 1760. As Evelyn Cruikshanks has emphasised in *Political Untouchables: The Tories and the '45*, the ban attacked the very foundations of Tory society. Even if the Tory knights of the shires did not want places for themselves under the Whig administration of George I, they certainly wanted positions for their relations and dependants. Bolingbroke wrote later: 'If milder measures had been pursued, certain it is that the Tories would never have embraced Jacobitism. The violence of the Whigs forced them into the arms of the Pretender.' From then on, the only effective opposition to the new regime would come through the use of force, real or threatened.

The exclusion of all Tories from public office inevitably caused unrest, although disturbance only spread throughout the country after the general election of March 1715. The French ambassador reported that the Tories were 'moved by a violent rage at their exclusion from office' and he warned that the country was 'heading for civil war which they regard as their only resort'. Threatened with impeachment, Bolingbroke fled the country to become Secretary of State to James Edward Stuart. His place as the potential leader of a Jacobite rebellion in England was taken by James Butler, second Duke of Ormonde. Butler began to plan an uprising in the West of England, coupled with local insurrections in Scotland and the North of England, but he too fled to France when the government sent troops to arrest him. Yet another attempt at rebellion was made by George Granville, Lord Landsowne, but this also foundered, although in Oxford the rebels held out for several weeks against government troops.

Discontent Mounts in Scotland

In Scotland, powerful resentment had been building up against the Hanoverian regime ever since the Act of Union in 1707, at least among the nobility and the landed classes. Although the peerage had pushed the Act through, supported by only a bare majority of lesser gentry and burgesses in Parliament, they had effectively disenfranchised themselves. Hardly a year later, the Privy Council of Scotland was abolished for short-term political gain, leaving a vacuum of political power at the heart of government in Scotland, where it had always acted as the ultimate guardian of public order, especially in the Highlands. Instead, far greater powers were given to Justices of the Peace on the English model, so threatening the exercise of political power by the Scottish nobility through the system of heritable jurisdictions.

Moreover, although the Act of Union had allowed the Scottish peers to elect sixteen of their number to the House of Lords in 1710, these elections had been manipulated by the government by means of the 'King's List'. The eldest sons of Scottish peers had no vote and were debarred as well from sitting for the shires and burghs, unlike their English counterparts. Claims of Scottish nobility to hereditary seats in the House of Lords had also been rejected.

Scottish anger had been further fuelled by judicial decisions made at Westminster undermining the independence of the Scottish legal system, contrary to the Act of Union. In particular, the barbaric provisions of the English law of treason had been extended to Scotland in 1709. The measure had been opposed by nearly all the Scottish Members of Parliament, and the government had been forced to make some concessions to Scottish opinion, albeit in legal terms applicable more to England than to Scotland. Then, in 1711, an Episcopalian minister called James Greenshields had appealed successfully to the House of Lords against his conviction for defying the Presbyterian authorities in Scotland, so overturning a ruling by the Court of Session in Edinburgh. By now, it was clear that the Parliament at Westminster was quite prepared to breach not just the spirit of the 1707 Act, but also its legal provisions. Given its majority at Westminster, England could now ignore independent Scottish institutions.

In matters of trade, Scotland had hardly benefited at all from the Union, since Scottish merchants were now exposed to the full rigours of English competition. Only the droving of black cattle from the Highlands to market in England had led to any increase in trade, apart from in smuggling. Moreover, after the abolition of the Scottish treasury and the extension of the powers of the English exchequer to Scotland, the collection of customs and excise had come under boards of commissioners, whose mostly English officers operated locally in the burghs where they were deeply resented. When, in 1712, the Tory government at Westminster proposed to levy the same duty on malt in Scotland as in England (again in violation of the Act of Union), a crisis between the two countries was reached.

Supported by all Scottish factions at Westminster, James Ogilvie, first Earl of Seafield, introduced a motion to the House of Lords seeking to dissolve the Act of Union, although he had been prominent among its original architects. Among Scottish grievances he cited were: 'the dissolution of the [Privy] Council, the Treason Act, the incapaciting [of] the peers–but above all our many taxes, especially the Malt Tax Bill, and the ruin of our trade and manufactories.' The Lords divided equally, with fifty-four peers voting on either side, and the motion was only defeated by four votes, cast by proxy.

Further discontent had arisen when Westminster passed the 1712 Act of Toleration in the aftermath of the Greenshields affair. It sought 'to prevent the disturbing of those of the Episcopal communion, in that part of Great Britain called Scotland, in the exercise of their religious worship, and in the use of the Liturgy of the Church of England'. The Act allowed Episcopalians in Scotland to attend their own services, if held by ministers ordained by a Protestant bishop. It required these ministers to take the Oath of Allegiance, while renouncing their support for the cause of James Edward Stuart in an Oath of Abjuration. They were required to pray during divine worship for Queen Anne and Sophia, Electress of Hanover, as the lawful heir to the throne. This Act was anathema to the strictly Presbyterian established Church of Scotland, especially as the Act of Union had specifically guaranteed its independence as the national Church. The Presbyterians suspected the Act of Toleration was intended to weaken their established Church, opposed as it was to the Jacobite cause, rather than to allow freedom of worship to the Episcopalians, who were sympathetic to the claims of James Edward Stuart. Indeed, the Act was only passed because the Parliament at Westminster was now dominated by the Tory party with its landed interests and High Anglican principles. The Act of Patronage of 1712 had been equally offensive to the Presbyterians, restoring 'the patrons to their ancient rights of presenting ministers to the churches vacant in that part of Great Britain called Scotland'.

However, whatever their qualms, Presbyterians in Scotland could not easily abandon the Union, which guaranteed the existence of their established Church. They, therefore, found themselves in an uneasy alliance with the Whigs, reluctantly supporting George I's regime. Even if they had believed James Edward Stuart when he protested he was willing to allow freedom of conscience in religious matters, they still regarded Episcopalian government of the Church as an 'iniquity'. Presbyterians might protest about the Union, but they still held fast to their anti-Episcopalian principles as staunch Whigs.

Scottish Presbyterians evidently agreed with most Englishmen that religion was ultimately more important than hereditary principle, accepting that James Edward Stuart had disqualified himself from succeeding to the throne by virtue of his Catholic faith. As Bolingbroke protested after fleeing to France: 'England would as soon have a Turk as a Roman Catholic for King.' But to many other Scots, disillusioned with the Union and grieving for their lost national identity, sovereignty now counted for more than religion. England might easily enough abandon the Stuart dynasty that had barely reigned there for a century; Scotland, for the most part, still retained its traditional loyalty to a monarchy that had ruled over the nation in the direct line since 1371 and whose antecedents lay deep in Scottish history. Therefore, as the events of 1715 unfolded in Scotland, the Jacobite Rebellion began to take on the appearance of a national movement. Only committed Presbyterians stood apart in their reluctant acceptance of the Union. Had they taken to arms in defence of their religion, the 1715 Rebellion would have become civil war.

From Dissatisfaction to Rebellion

When armed rebellion against the Hanoverian government finally broke out in Scotland, the rather improbable leader who emerged was John

Erskine, sixth Earl of Mar of his line. Mar had actually acted as Secretary of State for Scotland in the Tory ministry before the death of Queen Anne and, no doubt, had hoped to continue in this office under George I. In a letter to his brother a week after the change of dynasty, he had written, 'Though I say it who should not, I can make as good terms with the other side for myself as any of them', so demonstrating the ease with which he could change sides and earning his nickname of 'Bobbing John'. He then wrote an effusive letter to George I at the end of August 1714, reminding him of the service he had performed in championing the Act of Union in 1707 and assuring him of his undying loyalty if granted office in the new Whig ministry.

Unwisely, George I did not even bother to acknowledge Mar's loyal address. Instead, the king ordered him to return his seals of office as Secretary of State for Scotland, which were then granted to James Graham, first Duke of Montrose. Despite this rebuff, Mar lingered in London for nearly a year. Then, on 15 July 1715, he received a letter from James Edward Stuart, pressing him to act for him in Scotland by raising the Jacobite standard in the Scottish Highlands.

Mar did not act on this demand until 6 September and may have finally decided to throw in his lot with the Stuart dynasty only after George I had publicly snubbed him at a levee on 1 August, celebrating the first anniversary of his accession, when it became obvious that Mar had no hope of preferment under the Hanoverian regime. Slipping out of London in disguise that evening, Mar sailed next day from Gravesend on board a collier bound for Newcastle, taking with him Major-General George Hamilton and a few personal servants. After reaching Newcastle, the small party embarked with John Spence of Leith, who landed them at Elie on the south coast of Fife.

Once in Scotland, Mar spent his first nights at the house of Thomas Hay, seventh Earl of Kinnoull, contacting known Scottish Jacobite supporters in a stream of letters. He then set out for his estates in the north, accompanied by Hamilton and Kinnoull's son, John Hay of Cromlix. After stopping at various places to drum up more support, they finally arrived at Braemar, where Mar had intended to lodge with John Farquharson of Invercauld who, however, promptly decamped during the night with all his arms. Although Mar now wrote to his brother in Edinburgh that he was 'living here upon my own estates peaceably', he actually spent the next week organising a great deer hunt, (probably commemorated in the name of a hill at the head of Glen Quoich, called Carn Elrig Mor, meaning the Hill of the Great Deer Trap). This event of 27 August was, in fact, a front for a council of war of Jacobite leaders. They held a further meeting on 3 September at Aboyne, after Mar had visited his estates at Kildrummy, where many of his own tenants had to be threatened with force before they would join him.

Given the political and religious divisions within the country, support for the 1715 Rebellion would come not just from the Jacobite clans of the Scottish Highlands, but also from the Episcopalian heartlands, especially the north-eastern Lowlands of Scotland, north of the River Tay. These rather diverse factions shared a common belief in the Divine Right of the Stuarts to reign over the country. Protest at the violation of this hereditary principle in favour of George I and his successors was voiced by the Gaelic poets, one of whom declaimed at the time of the 1745 Rebellion:

Oh slender the string George, that you harped on for the three kingdoms; guileful the Act which cloaked you as King over us; there are more than fifty people closer in blood and claim than you in the continent . . . It is not permissible for us to turn aside from, or suppress our temporal King. For, from the moment he was first conceived, he was the true, rightful heir. No difference of faith, or even lack of faith, may draw us away; without lawful authority, it is a treacherous thing for us to renounce him.

The hierarchical Episcopalian Church still held James VII to be the legitimate head of the Church of Scotland while he lived and, even after his death in 1701, was not prepared to recognise Queen Anne when she came to the throne in 1702. Only after the death of 'Bonnie Prince Charlie' in 1788 did the remnants of the Episcopalian order in Scotland finally submit to George III, when the clergy were instructed by their few remaining bishops to pray for him, using the English Book of Common Prayer.

There is little doubt that Jacobite supporters were in a majority throughout Scotland as a whole, if we accept the figures given by the Reverend Robert Patten from Allendale in Northumberland, who accompanied the Jacobite forces south to Preston. Patten later estimated that a total of 30,000 men could be raised for the Jacobite cause, a figure which tallies with that given by General George Wade in 1724. By comparison, the nobility who supported the Hanoverians could muster only 10,000 men. In fact, the large numbers of men cited by Patten never took the field in 1715. Nevertheless, far greater numbers appeared in arms for James Edward Stuart than for King George. Indeed, the Hanoverian army under the command of John Campbell, second Duke of Argyll, was so short of volunteers that it was forced to rely on enlisted men and their professional officers, as well as 6,000 Dutch auxiliaries. North of the Forth, almost all the nobility supported the Jacobite cause, apart from the Duke of Argyll and the Earl of Sutherland, along with a number of lesser gentry, chiefly from around Inverness, all staunch Presbyterians.

Farther south, the two sides were more equally balanced. However, many of the Lowland nobility probably only adopted the Hanoverian cause out of expediency, forced to ally themselves with the strictly Presbyterian local gentry and their tenants. Certainly very few were active in containing the uprising, preferring to remain on the sidelines. As a result, the Lowlands south of the Forth supplied far fewer men to the Hanoverian cause in 1715, compared with the 14,000 'fencible men' who had answered a similar call to arms in support of King William in the summer of 1690. Indeed, local Lowland militias were loath to serve more than the statutory requirement of forty days.

Accordingly, as Bruce Lenman has argued in *The Jacobite Risings in Britain, 1689–1746*, Mar's rebellion in 1715 was never just a Highland affair, nor even an atavistic struggle between the Highlands and the Lowlands, contrary to popular myth. Rather, the conservative or even archaic traditions of Highland society may be seen to have predisposed the Jacobite clans to rise in support of the Stuart dynasty. Audrey Cunningham, in her account of *The Loyal Clans*, follows Donald Gregory (whose book, *The History of the Western Highlands and Isles of Scotland*, was published in 1836) in suggesting that such support was founded upon the natural loyalty of a patriarchal society to their rightful sovereign. Just as a chief's authority over his clansmen rested ultimately upon his claim to be descended from the illustrious progenitor of the clan itself, so the Stuart kings had a hereditary right to rule over the country as the fathers of their people. Yet the ties of kinship binding together a clan were largely between its chief and his leading gentry as the common descendants of a distant ancestor. Clansmen could rarely lay claim to that ancestry.

By the first two decades of the eighteenth century, these ties were gradually weakening under commercial and economic pressures which had their origins a century earlier in the Statutes of Iona, imposed on the Highland clans by James VI of Scotland. Indeed, in the Lowlands, clan chiefs were now largely assimilated into society, sharing the same beliefs in property and economic progress as its landed classes. Alasdair MacDonald of Glengarry said, after the failure of the 1715 Rebellion, that he did not so much resent King George himself, but the power given to his ministers in London, including such Whig politicians as 'King Townsend, King Stanhope, King Walpole, etc'. No doubt, such attitudes were just as common among the Lowland aristocracy, who were often Jacobites at heart.

In fact, the Highland clans were divided on religious grounds in exactly the same way as the rest of Scottish society. Allan Macinnes, in *Clanship, Commerce and the House of Stuart*, analyses the Highland clans in detail, identifying eight as predominantly Presbyterian, all of which supported the Whig government and the Hanoverian succession. The most important was that of the Campbells, Earls of Argyll, now elevated to a dukedom in reward for their services to William of Orange. They exercised supreme power and influence throughout the first half of the eighteenth century as the political agents of the Whig government in Scotland. Archibald Campbell, third Duke of Argyll, was even known as the 'King of Scotland' for his astute management of Scottish affairs. Farther north, such Whig clans as the MacKays, the Gunns, the Rosses and the Munros shared the same Presbyterian religion as the Gordons, Earls of Sutherland.

Another six clans were predominantly Catholic and they all joined the 1715 Jacobite Rebellion. Apart from the Gordons, Earls of Huntly (now created the Dukes of Gordon), they included the MacDonalds of Clanranald, Glengarry and Keppoch, the Chisholms of Strathglass and the MacNeills of Barra. Several other clans, such as the MacGregors of Glengyle, the Frasers of Lovat, the MacDonalds of Sleat, the Farquharsons, the Grants of Glenmoriston and the Camerons of Lochiel, were partly Catholic. However, altogether they never made up more than a fifth of the fighting strength of the Jacobite clans.

The popular image of the Jacobite clans as largely Catholic was itself a product of Whig propaganda. Most were, in fact, non-juring Episcopalians. They had embraced their faith in the decades following the restoration of Charles II in 1660, while rejecting any accommodation with the Presbyterian establishment after the religious settlement of 1689. The hierarchy of Episcopalian Church government had features in common with the traditions of Highland society.

Twenty of these Episcopalian clans gave their whole-hearted support to the Stuart cause in 1715. Another five clans, the Frasers, the Grants, the MacLeans of Lochaline, the Campbells of Cawdor and the Murrays, Dukes of Atholl, were divided in their allegiance. This left eleven clans that took no part at all in the conflict, although they too were mostly Episcopalian. Apart from the Sinclairs of Caithness, the MacLeods of Raasay and the MacQuarries of Ulva, they were all close neighbours of the pro-Hanoverian and all-powerful Dukes of Argyll, which explains their reluctance to act. They included such clans as the Lamonts, the MacLachlans, the Mac-Naughtons and the MacNabs, and they were nearly all of mixed denomination, being partly Presbyterian.

Nearly all these Episcopalian clans had a long-standing history of allegiance to the Stuart monarchy, dating back to the Civil Wars of the 1640s. However, their actions then had been driven more by their enduring hostility to the Campbells, Earls of Argyll, whose chief was the most important of the Presbyterian leaders of the Covenanting movement, than by any innate loyalty to the Stuart dynasty itself. Given their military traditions, they would now form the fighting strength of the Jacobite army, not just in 1715, but also thirty years later in 1745, making up its front line in nearly every battle fought in these two campaigns.

Those Highland clans who shared the same religion as James Edward Stuart and gave him their support were, therefore, a small minority. However, their ranks were augmented by such Catholic families in the north-east of Scotland as the Keiths, Earls Marischal and, especially, the Dukes of Gordon. Their commitment to the Jacobite cause was doubtless reinforced by the refusal of James VII to sacrifice his faith for his Crown in 1689 and by his use of the royal prerogative in 1687 to set aside the penal laws against Catholics. The appointment of Thomas Nicholson as the first Vicar-Apostolic of Scotland in 1694 represented an important advance on the previous decades of sporadic Catholic evangelicalism, mostly by Gaelic-speaking missionaries from Ireland. Catholic communities were revived, as a result, in the remoter parts of the Highlands and Western Islands. Found in a broad swathe from the north-eastern fringes of the Grampian Mountains to the Outer Hebrides, they included such mainland districts as Strathglass, Glengarry, Lochaber, Knoydart, Arisaig and Moidart, and the islands of Barra, South Uist and Benbecula in the Outer Hebrides.

The Standard is Raised

This, then, was the political background in Scotland when the Jacobite standard was raised by the Earl of Mar on 6 September 1715 at Braemar. The dignity of the ceremony itself was upset when the gilt ball on top of the standard fell to the ground, an event considered to be an ill omen by the watching Highlanders. Mar made a speech, regretting his own part in pushing through the Act of Union in 1707 and now admitting it to be a mistake.

At Westminster, the Parliament passed an Act for Encouraging Loyalty, often known, quite mistakenly, as the Clan Act. This required all 'suspected . . . persons, whose estates or principal residences are in Scotland, to appear at Edinburgh, or where it shall be judged expedient, to find bail for their good behaviour'. Twenty-one peers and forty-one gentry were summoned but, of these, only two surrendered themselves, whereupon they were promptly arrested. This action hardly encouraged loyalty to the Hanoverian regime, forcing those remaining at liberty into the Jacobite camp, including the eighty-year-old John Campbell of Glenorchy,

Earl of Breadalbane. He persuaded a doctor and a minister to sign a medical certificate, claiming that he was too ill to travel to Edinburgh, as he suffered from an alarming array of illnesses, such as 'coughs, rheums, gravels, stitches, defluxions and disease of the kidneys'. Nevertheless, he managed to join Mar at Perth on 20 September 1715. Others made similar excuses or simply ignored the summons.

By now, the government in London was seriously alarmed. It had already ordered three regiments of infantry from Ireland which had arrived in Edinburgh on 24 August. Meanwhile, Major-General Joseph Wightman, as the commander-in-chief in Scotland, had ordered all the regular troops in Scotland to Stirling, where they had begun to muster towards the end of August, amounting to barely 1,000 men. Then John Campbell, second Duke of Argyll, was ordered north to replace Wightman as commander-in-chief of the government forces in Scotland. Argyll wrote back to London, assessing the deteriorating situation thus: 'If the enemy think fit to act with the vigour that men of commonsense would, in their circumstances, the handful of [Hanoverian] troops now in Scotland may be beat out of the country.' Indeed, Mar was now ready to march south from Braemar and his forces would soon capture Perth.

On the night of 14 September, Argyll reached Edinburgh where a botched attempt to seize the castle for James Edward Stuart had failed a few days previously. He inspected its defences and then spent the next week calling up all the forces he could muster. But, by the end of his first week in Scotland, he still had only 1,600 men, mostly ill-trained and poorly equipped. Against them was a Jacobite army apparently consisting of several thousand of men. By 21 September, Argyll thought the situation so dangerous that he wrote south to say that he was surprised that:

> his Majesty's Ministers still persist to think this matter a jest, and that we are in a condition to put a stop to it. Give me leave to say, Sir, that if all of us who have the honour to serve his Majesty here are not either knaves or cowards, we ought to be believed when we tell you that this country is in the extremest danger.

Three days later, he wrote again, begging for yet more troops: 'I must end with insisting on considerable reinforcements, for without it, or a miracle, not only this country will be utterly destroyed but the rest of his Majesty's dominions put in the extremest danger.' Only sheer incompetence on Mar's part seemed likely now to stop the Jacobite cause from triumphing in Scotland.

Capture of Perth

In mid-September, Mar had marched south from Braemar, passing through the Spittal of Glenshee before reaching the village of Kirkmichael in Strathardle, where he halted for a day or two. At this point, he probably commanded only a few hundred men under John Farquharson of Inverey, together with a party of Gordons under the young Earl of Aboyne. However, numbers were growing quickly. At Kirkmichael, they were reinforced by 300 cavalry under the joint command of the Earl of Linlithgow and Lord Drummond, together with 500 foot soldiers from Atholl (mostly Murrays, Stewarts and Robertsons). They were commanded by William Murray, Marquis of Tullibardine, whose father, the Duke of Atholl, remained loyal to the government, while his two younger brothers Charles and George Murray and his uncle Lord Nairne, supported the Jacobites. Whether this actually reflected a real division in loyalties or simply a family arrangement intended to preserve the Atholl estates whatever happened is a matter for debate. Many other families were similarly divided with their younger sons joining Mar's army, while the eldest son and heir remained at home, giving his nominal support to the government.

Meanwhile, the city magistrates in Perth were sufficiently alarmed by the proximity of Mar's forces at Kirkmichael, only thirty-five miles north, to appeal for help to the Duke of Atholl who sent 200 men to defend the city. They also turned to the Earl of Rothes, Sheriff and Lord Lieutenant of Fife, who started to raise a local militia. However, Colonel John Hay of Cromlix now seized the initiative for the Jacobites. While recruiting in Fife, he was approached by Jacobite sympathisers from Perth, who offered to deliver the city to him. On 14 September 1715, Hay entered the city from the north with around 200 horsemen, after crossing the River Tay. The Athollmen promptly switched sides and the local militia from Fife, hearing of the city's capture, 'threw down their arms and ran'. On 22 September, the Jacobite forces in the city were strengthened by a party of Robertsons under their chief, Alexander Robertson of Struan.

The scale of the Jacobite uprising under Mar now became apparent as James Edward Stuart was proclaimed king throughout the north-east of Scotland at places as far apart as Inverness, Forres, Gordon Castle, Aberdeen, Brechin, Montrose, Dundee, Perth and Dunkeld. Mar finally entered Perth itself on 28 September 1715, after a leisurely journey from Kirkmichael by way of Moulinearn and Logierait. He had apparently spent much of the intervening time writing a 'barrage of letters, declarations and manifestoes to all and sundry'.

Chapter Three

MARCH SOUTH TO PRESTON

Delays, Raids and Indecision as Mar Prepares for Battle

In his authoritative account, *The Jacobite Rising of 1715*, J. C. M. Baynes comments that Mar would have made an admirable chief of staff to a more forceful commander-in-chief. As it was, Mar spent the next six weeks in Perth without taking any decisive action against the forces that Argyll was mustering at Stirling. To be fair to Mar, all the men he had been promised took nearly a month to arrive in Perth and, even then, the Highland clans from the west had not appeared. However, on 6 October, his forces in Perth were boosted by 700 MacIntoshes and Farquharsons under the command of William MacIntosh of Borlum. Old Borlum (as he was known) was the uncle of the young chief Lachlan MacIntosh of MacIntosh, Captain of Clan Chattan, and was later described as a 'tall, raw-boned man, about sixty years of age, fair complexioned, beetle-browed, grey-eyed, [who] speaks broad Scots'. The MacIntoshes had 'come out' for King James on 15 September and had captured Inverness in his name.

On the same day, Alexander Gordon, fifth Marquis of Huntly, arrived with 500 horsemen and possibly 2,000 foot soldiers, far too many to be quartered immediately in Perth. His horsemen were in two squadrons: one of heavy cavalry ridden by the gentry from his Lowland estates in Aberdeenshire; and the second of small long-tailed ponies mounted by his Highland tenants. To Huntly's fury, the ponies' untidy appearance was much mocked; with rough blankets as saddles and ropes for reins, they were hardly bigger than their riders. Many gentry from the surrounding counties of Aberdeen, Kincardine, Forfar and Angus also swelled Mar's army. On 24 September, Argyll reported that: 'There are every day numbers of Horse composed of gentlemen and their servants, who go over to join their army, all extremely well armed.' They included more than 360 cavalry, commanded by James Carnegie, fifth Earl of Southesk, and John, Master of Sinclair, together with several hundred foot soldiers, under the command of James, Earl of Panmure, and Lord Ogilvie. Finally on

7 October, George Keith, tenth Earl Marischal, brought in 300 cavalry and up to 500 foot soldiers.

On the morning of 2 October, Mar heard that a ship had entered the harbour at Burntisland, carrying munitions for the Earl of Sutherland. After some hesitation, he ordered Sinclair to mount a large raiding party of eighty horsemen and a hundred foot soldiers. Fifty baggage-horses would carry back the anticipated booty of 3,000 muskets and a large stock of ammunition, while another 500 men were to be sent to Kinross to guard their return from ambush by government forces.

Sinclair left Perth around 5 p.m. for a rendezvous outside Burntisland. There, he found that the ship was lying offshore, waiting for its captain to come aboard. The town and harbour were quickly taken and the vessel itself successfully captured by a flotilla of small boats. Once aboard, Sinclair was disappointed to find only around 300 muskets, a bag of flints, two or three barrels of gun-powder and some boxes of cartridges. Then his men made off looking for drink, apparently leaving Sinclair to load the baggage-horses himself.

Next morning, the baggage-train left Burntisland but, at Auchtertool just a few miles north, most of the foot soldiers disappeared to loot and plunder. When the raiding party finally returned to Perth, it was a dishevelled procession. Sinclair's own cavalry led the slow baggage-train of heavily laden horses; next came several hundred foot-soldiers, mostly drunk and 'festooned in stolen clothing, bags of meal, bottles of wine and other loot'; followed by a 'pitiful host of people whom they had plundered, begging for the return of their belongings'. Despite its disorganisation and the small haul of arms, the whole episode did greatly boost the morale of Mar's forces, although it was said to be a 'strange use of cavalry to capture a ship'.

This success encouraged the Jacobites to invade Fife with 4,000 men. They took possession of all the towns lying along its south-eastern coast and eventually held all of Fife. By then, only the Lowlands south of the River Forth remained under the effective control of the Hanoverian government, apart from the far north and the Campbells' territories in Argyll.

Mar was now in a position of strength but the expedition to Burntisland had done little to address his shortage of arms and money. Originally, he had hoped for substantial supplies of arms and men from France, where twelve ships were ready to sail in August 1715, laden with 12,000 muskets, 18,000 swords, 4,000 barrels of gun-powder, 12 field-guns with ammunition and 2,000 troops. However, Louis XIV had died on 21 August and the Duke of Orleans had been made Regent to the five-year-old Louis XV. Orleans had been persuaded to order the unloading of the ships by John

Dalrymple, second Earl of Stair and British ambassador to France, on behalf of George I. Louis XIV had also promised James Edward Stuart £100,000 but had died before it was paid–just one more piece of the bad luck that seemed to dog the Jacobite cause. Mar was reduced to raising money to pay his troops by ordering all the Jacobite landowners in his army to levy 'twenty shillings on every hundred pounds Scots of valued rent' on their own tenants. However, little money was raised, despite repeated orders, after which Mar sent soldiers out to collect it.

One such tax-gathering expedition ended in near disaster through bravado and the chaotic indiscipline which had also characterised the raid at Burntisland. Between 300 and 400 officers and men were to collect taxes in Dunfermline but detoured to Castle Campbell near Dollar, just ten miles from Stirling, so alerting the government forces in the castle. At Dunfermline, 'all the gentlemen of the horse separated into alehouses and taverns, and after[wards] most went to bed', leaving only two sentries posted. Early on the morning of 24 October, 200 government dragoons rode into Dunfermline and captured seventeen or eighteen of the officers and their servants, who had run out into the streets at the commotion. Other officers hid until the dragoons had left and then:

> every one run in different way: some left their horses sticking in dunghills, in the streets, and others, when their horses fell in any narrow lane with jostling, or making too great a haste to get away, left them on the spot, and came to Perth on country horses, and said they had their horses shot under them; others run to Burntisland, some to different places of the country, some got under beds, others up to garrets, and most of this when the enemy was gone.

The foot soldiers in the Abbey escaped attack but, without any officers to give them orders, they stayed put until the dragoons had left the town. They then marched off to Burntisland, before returning to Perth.

Crossing the River Forth: the Jacobite Army Divides

Before the abortive expedition against Dunfermline, Mar had briefly taken the initiative by making plans for a strong Jacobite task force to cross the Firth of Forth, probably to reinforce the Jacobite uprising that had already broken out in Northumberland. Early in October, Sinclair had been dispatched under sealed orders to reconnoitre the coastal villages and small towns in the East Neuk of Fife but had found that three men-of-war and a number of smaller vessels were patrolling the waters of the Firth of Forth for the government. Moreover, Argyll was clearly alert to the danger, having already given orders to clear all craft from the Fife coast. However, these orders had been largely ignored, as Sinclair found when he travelled east along the coast from Wemyss to Crail, proclaiming King James and looking for all available boats.

By 9 October, enough boats were ready to carry more than 2,000 men across the Forth and Mar acted. Borlum was given command of the task force and was to prove the ablest of all Mar's commanders, a 'brute beast who was as obstinate as a mule and as savage as a tiger'. He apparently left Perth on the evening of 9 October, with 500 men, to occupy Burntisland as a diversionary tactic. Marching across Fife under the cover of darkness, they took the town unopposed. In response, Argyll ordered a blockade of the harbour by the men-of-war in the Firth of Forth, unaware that the crossing would be made over twenty miles farther east.

Marching overnight, the rest of Borlum's forces reached the East Neuk by the morning of 12 October. They lay low during the day and began to embark that evening, so that half were already across the Forth long before the following dawn. They landed in East Lothian at North Berwick, Gullane and Aberlady after crossing more than fifteen miles of open sea. The boats had then returned undetected to the East Neuk before daybreak, so that it was only when Borlum entered Haddington that afternoon that the Hanoverian authorities in Edinburgh realised they had been fooled.

Alerted to the danger, the government's men-of-war still lying off Burntisland were ordered to intercept the flotilla of small boats that set sail the next evening, carrying the other half of Borlum's forces. However, they only captured one fishing-boat with forty men on board. Several other boats were driven north-east to the Isle of May, where 400 men landed and started to quarrel. They eventually returned to Perth, after managing to get off the island when the wind changed, blowing the Hanoverian men-of-war out to sea.

By the morning of 14 October, Borlum had mustered all his forces in Haddington after a well-executed, if hazardous, operation, which took Argyll completely by surprise. It seems that Mar now expected Borlum to march south 'to join the noblemen and gentlemen of the South of Scotland and North of England then in arms for the King [James]', who, on 6 October, had already raised the Jacobite standard in Northumberland. He may well have been following a 'grand plan', since he wrote on 21 October: 'I hope all is pretty right again, but it was an unlucky mistake in Brigadier MacIntosh, in marching from Haddington to Leith.' Borlum had probably received information from Jacobite sympathisers in Edinburgh, suggesting that the city might surrender if surprised. Accordingly, he marched towards the city with a force now around 1,500 strong. But, on reaching its outskirts early in the afternoon of 14 October, Borlum made instead for the port of Leith. There his forces seized the Old Citadel, built to guard the harbour in Cromwell's time, after overwhelming the town guard.

By now, Argyll knew of Borlum's advance upon Edinburgh. He immediately sent 300 dragoons, as well as 200 foot soldiers mounted on heavy farm-horses, and arrived himself in the city at 10 p.m. that evening. Next morning, he and his forces marched out of Edinburgh, followed by the Edinburgh Volunteers. At Leith, he demanded that the Jacobite forces in the Old Citadel surrender but they refused. Argyll now realised that Mar could attack his forces in Stirling so he returned to Edinburgh, abandoning any attempt to lay siege to the Old Citadel at Leith.

Meanwhile, Borlum saw little point in holding Leith. He, therefore, slipped away with his forces during the evening of 15 October, taking advantage of the ebb tide to march along the shore eight miles east to Seton House. Forty of his men were so drunk on looted brandy that they were caught next day by government troops, after squabbling along the way. However, Borlum had also sent a message to Mar by boat from Leith. To allay suspicion, he ordered his cannon to fire upon the vessel as it left the harbour and the captain of a man-of-war standing off Leith let it pass, evidently thinking it had escaped from Borlum.

Next day, Mar left Perth for Auchterarder with most of his troops. By the evening of 17 October, his cavalry had reached Dunblane, five miles north of Stirling, although the infantry lagged far behind. Even so, Mar's advance caused great alarm in the government camp at Stirling, where Lieutenant-General Thomas Whetham sent three urgent expresses in quick succession to Edinburgh. Warned of the danger, Argyll arrived back in Stirling on the evening of 17 October, with 200 dragoons and fifty foot soldiers. But, oddly, Mar decided to retreat to Auchterarder the next day, before taking all his forces back to Perth.

Why Mar should withdraw from such a position of strength is difficult to understand, except that he admitted that his forces had left Perth 'before the provisions were ready for us', only to find that 'all the country around Stirling . . . was entirely exhausted by the enemy so that there was nothing for us to subsist on there'. Clearly, if Mar had moved against Stirling just a few days earlier, when Borlum was ready to cross the Forth, the outcome might have been very different. By attacking Argyll in a pincer movement, Stirling could well have fallen to the Jacobites, giving them control over all of Scotland south of the Forth. But Mar apparently never thought of these tactics, however obvious to hindsight, unwilling to take the offensive until backed by the Highland clans under General Gordon of Auchintoul, which were only recently mustered at Strathfillan. Moreover, Mar seems to have lost contact with Gordon, admitting later that he 'had no account of General Gordon as I expected, and the soonest I could expect him at the

Heads of Forth was two days after that, and I could not think of passing [the River] Forth till I was joined by him'. In fact, Gordon and his forces were marching west from Strathfillan to attack Inveraray just as Mar reached Dunblane with his cavalry.

Apparently Mar had a grand strategy in mind which he insisted on following, refusing to adapt it to a changing situation. Otherwise, he would surely have sent a message to Gordon on 16 October before leaving Perth, ordering him to march the thirty miles from Strathfillan south to Stirling. Backed by Gordon's force of between 1,000 and 2,000, Mar could well have defeated the government army under Argyll in the third week of October.

Argyll's abrupt departure for Stirling on 17 October took the pressure off Borlum and his forces at Seton House. They had spent two days strengthening its fortifications and searching the surrounding countryside for food. Next day, they were briefly threatened by a government force of 500 who, however, all withdrew to Edinburgh after finding Seton House too well defended. On 18 October, after Mar had received a message from the Jacobite rebels in Northumberland begging for reinforcements, he ordered Borlum to take all his troops south. At Kelso, having crossed the Lammermuir Hills, Borlum finally joined forceso with the Jacobites rebels, Thomas Forster and William Gordon, Lord Kenmuir, who had already raised the standard in Northumberland.

Rebellion in Northumberland

After Parliament had issued a warrant for Thomas Forster's arrest on 20 September, he had escaped north to Northumberland. At first he had taken refuge at Bywell House on the River Tyne, where a bungled attempt was made to arrest him. He, then, had gone into hiding, meeting up a few days later with several other Jacobite sympathisers active in the county, including James Radcliffe, third Earl of Derwentwater, and a cousin of James Edward Stuart, who was also under threat of arrest. On 6 October, the group had raised the Jacobite standard at Greenrigs, north of Corbridge. As Forster's Jacobite party rode across country towards Rothbury, its numbers had swollen from around 50 to 150, mostly country gentlemen with their servants and tenants. Leaving Rothbury on 7 October, the small army had stayed in Warkworth, before riding north to Alnwick on 13 October and then turning south toward Morpeth the next day, hoping that Newcastle would declare itself for King James. By now, it consisted of 300 men, mostly from the Scottish Borders.

The delay proved fatal. The government had already rushed two regiments north, under Lieutenant-General George Carpenter, to reinforce Newcastle and local volunteers had also been recruited to defend the city, a total of around 1,200 foot and horse. Jacobite sympathisers, such as Sir William Blackett, were arrested and the Tyne keel men, who loaded London-bound ships with coal from their barges, declared their loyalty to the government.

The Jacobite forces now turned west from Morpeth to reach Hexham on the evening of 15 October, where they camped near Derwentwater's mansion of Dilston Hall for the next three days. By now, Thomas Forster had learnt that Newcastle was completely under government control, while two ships sent with supplies from France had failed to make contact with Forster's forces near Holy Island and sailed away north. His only good news was that William Gordon, sixth Viscount Kenmuir, had arrived in Rothbury from the Scottish Borders, with 180 followers. Since Carpenter was now threatening to advance against him from Newcastle, Forster withdraw north with his forces and, by the evening of 19 October, was back in Rothbury, his starting-point nearly a fortnight earlier. Hearing that Borlum was marching south through the Borders with much-needed reinforcements, he ordered a rendezvous with him at Kelso on 22 October.

This amalgamated Jacobite army of Highlanders and Border gentry idled away the next four days in Kelso, giving the government time to mobilise against them. However, on 27 October, the news that Carpenter had already reached Wooler from Newcastle with around 1,000 men galvanised the Jacobite commanders into holding a council of war. Once again the government had the initiative, while the Jacobite camp was arguing. The Scots gentry from the Borders wanted to march west to seize Dumfries, Ayr and Glasgow, so that virtually all of Scotland would then be held for King James; Argyll's forces could then be defeated in Stirling in a pincer movement. However, Forster and nearly all his Northumbrian followers aimed to capture Carlisle before marching south into the Catholic stronghold of Lancashire.

Borlum argued that they should stand firm and attack Carpenter as he advanced from Wooler; after all, Carpenter had half their number of troops and they were mostly untrained raw recruits. Moreover, the Jacobites could fight on ground of their own choosing. With hindsight, this strategy would almost certainly have led to a Jacobite victory, greatly enhancing their reputation as a fighting force and, no doubt, attracting a great many more recruits. The Jacobites could then have held all of southern Scotland and the government forces at Stirling could have been defeated by the combined forces of Borlum and Mar. Then, and only then, would it have been sensible to consider invading the North of England. However, Borlum's arguments were disregarded and eventually a compromise was agreed to withdraw south-west along the Scottish Border towards Carlisle, where a final decision could be made.

On 27 October, the Jacobite forces marched out of Kelso towards Jedburgh, leaving the field to Carpenter. Tensions in the Jacobite ranks mounted and the Highland forces threatened to mutiny, asserting that 'they would fight if they [their officers] would lead them on to the enemy, but they would not go to *England*'. Otherwise, they would march back north to join the other Highland clans then advancing against Inveraray. Only with difficulty were Borlum's Highlanders finally persuaded to continue the march towards Carlisle. If a decision was then taken to invade England, they would consider themselves free to abandon the whole enterprise and return home. The Jacobite forces occupied Hawick for the night, before marching next day to Langholm, where the fateful decision was finally made to march south into Lancashire.

Forster became commander-in-chief as soon as the Jacobite army marched into England on 31 October 1715, after crossing the Scottish Border at Longtown. By 7 November, the Jacobite forces had reached Lancaster by way of Appleby, meeting no opposition on their march south, except at Penrith, where the local militia scattered at their approach. But equally, there was no flood of eager Jacobite volunteers, although the Jacobites were still expecting to sweep through the south of Lancashire on a tide of popular feeling against King George. On 9 November, the cavalry under Forster reached Preston, where the abrupt departure of two troops of Hanoverian dragoons at their approach seemed to augur well for an unchallenged Jacobite advance south. The foot soldiers marched into Preston the next morning.

The intention was to leave Preston for Manchester on Saturday, 12 November. However, while 'the gentlemen soldiers from Wednesday to Saturday minded nothing but courting and feasting', Hanoverian forces were rapidly closing in on the town and Forster only received news of their approach on the afternoon of 11 November as he issued orders for the next day's march.

Forster had had a close watch kept on the movements of Carpenter's forces at his rear and, therefore, knew that Carpenter had left Durham on 7 November and was now trailing Forster's army south from Carlisle. But Forster had been lulled into a false sense of security by the over-confidence of the Lancashire gentry in their sources of information. On 12 November, he was, therefore, shocked to hear that a second government force under General Sir Charles Wills was advancing to attack him from Wigan to the south.

Wills's army consisted of six regiments of dragoons, the foot regiment of the Cameronians and 600 militia soldiers from North Lancashire. Meanwhile, Forster's numbers had been swollen by probably over 1,000 Jacobite sympathisers from Lancashire, mostly Catholic gentlemen and

their servants. Borlum was cynical about their fighting abilities, saying
bluntly to Forster: 'Look ye there, Forster, are yon fellows the men ye
intend to fight Wills with. Good faith, Sir, an ye had ten thousand of them,
I'd fight them all with a thousand of his dragoons.' A contemporary
account describes how:

> a more uncouth and unsoldierlike body had never before appeared in
> the field than these Lancashire rustics; some with rusty swords
> without muskets, others with muskets without swords, some with
> fowling pieces, others with pitchforks, while others were wholly
> unprovided with weapons of any sort.

When Forster finally realised the enemy's strength and his own weakness, he went to pieces, leaving his commanders to organise the defence of
Preston while he took off to bed, drunk. However, by the following
morning, he had recovered sufficiently to reconnoitre the approaches to
Preston from the south. Crossing the bridge over the River Ribble, just
south of the town, he met a vanguard of Hanoverian dragoons, advancing
from the south. Forster ordered the hundred Highlanders guarding the
bridge under Lieutenant-Colonel John Farquharson of Invercauld to
withdraw into the town. Forster's decision to abandon the bridge has
been much criticised but it was made on Borlum's advice. The river could
easily be forded at several places, especially at low tide, and, without
sufficient troops to defend these fords as well as the bridge, Borlum saw no
alternative to withdrawing all the Jacobite forces back into the town, where
they could better defend themselves.

General Wills reached the bridge with the main body of his forces around
1 p.m. on Saturday, 12 November. The Jacobites had spent the morning
erecting barricades across the main streets to defend the entrance to the
town, close to the market-place. Suspecting an ambush, Wills sent the
Cameronian foot regiment across the bridge, which then advanced unopposed up a deep lane towards the town. Wills left his local volunteers and
militia to guard the river south of Preston and ordered parties of dragoons to
ride through the fields to cut off any escape to the north, beyond the river.
Meanwhile, 250 dragoons left their horses behind to advance on foot against
the town from the east, while another detachment of dragoons attacked the
town on foot from the opposite direction from the Lancaster road.

Battle of Preston

Defeat in the battle for Preston was inevitable, although the Highlanders
defended the town vigorously. They were excellent marksmen, skilled in

ambush. They repulsed the first attack, made by 200 of Wills's men against their outer barricades, and killed 120 of his troops. They then fell back on Borlum's main line of defence, close to the Jacobite headquarters in the parish church, leaving the government forces to seize the houses they had abandoned. Next, the Jacobite barricade, defending the parish church from the north, resisted two fierce assaults in rapid succession, inflicting heavy government casualties. At the other end of town, the barricade manned by Colonel Lachlan Macintosh of Macintosh then withstood a sustained attack from the north-west. By nightfall, the Jacobites had held out against all attacks, losing very few men but inflicting considerable casualties.

Next morning, however, the balance shifted decisively when Carpenter arrived with massive reinforcements, including a large number of local volunteers. The Hanoverian army surrounding Preston were now so strong that a Jacobite escape was impossible. By midday, Forster saw no alternative to surrender, although the Highlanders wanted to fight their way out of the town. Without even consulting his officers, Forster sent a representative to discuss terms with Wills. Wills demanded the immediate surrender of the Jacobites as 'prisoners at discretion', stripped of all rights under the prevailing Rules of War.

When the Scots realised what Forster was planning, they sent their own messenger to Wills, only to receive the same terms, except that they were given until 7 a.m. next morning to reach a decision. Quarrels erupted between the English and Scots officers, and a shot fired by a Highland officer at Forster was only deflected by the quick reactions of an aide-de-camp. Meanwhile, Wills demanded the surrender of rebel hostages. Negotiations continued until the evening, when the Earl of Derwentwater and Colonel Lachlan MacIntosh of MacIntosh gave themselves up as hostages to the government.

Next morning, all the Jacobite forces in Preston surrendered as 'rebels caught in the act of rebellion'. More than 200 lords, officers and gentlemen and 1,250 men were taken prisoner. Over a hundred were sent south to London for trial at Westminster as the leading rebels. Six officers were immediately tried by court martial, since they still held commissions in the King's army. Captain Dalziel was acquitted because he had resigned his commission before joining the rebellion, while Lord Charles Murray obtained a reprieve through the influence of his family. The remaining four were shot by firing squad on 2 December 1715.

Trials, Executions and Escapes

Over six weeks later, seventy-four Jacobites still held in the gaols of Liverpool, Lancaster and Chester were tried, charged with high treason, and sixty-seven found guilty. Thirty-four were condemned to death by the peculiarly barbaric form of execution reserved under contemporary English law for traitors to the Crown. In the chilling words of Lord Cowper, the Lord Chancellor:

> You must be drawn [on a hurdle] to the place of execution; when you come there, you must be hanged by the neck, but not until you are dead, for you must be cut down alive; then your bowels must be taken out and burned before your faces; then your heads must be severed from your bodies, and your bodies divided into four quarters, and these must be at the King's disposal. And God Almighty be merciful to your souls.

Although the trials were held under a Grand Jury in Liverpool, the executions took place throughout Lancashire in such places as Preston, Wigan, Manchester, Garstang and Lancaster, as well as in Liverpool. This merciless savagery was clearly intended as an intimidating example to the local populace. But, on 9 February 1716, the trials were abruptly abandoned, a week after James Edward Stuart had left Scotland and the 1715 Rebellion was finally over. Well over 1,000 prisoners were still in custody, mostly to be deported to the colonial plantations in America. A considerable number had already died in prison.

Meanwhile, the Westminster trials had opened and the Commons voted to impeach such leading figures as the Earls of Derwentwater, Nithsdale, Wintoun and Carnwath; Viscount Kenmuir; and Lords Nairn and Wid-drington. Wintoun alone pleaded not guilty and his trial was delayed to give him time to prepare his defence. Although the other six were all sentenced on 9 February to be hung, drawn and quartered, only George Radcliffe, third Earl of Derwentwater, and William Gordon, sixth Viscount Kenmuir, were refused pardons by King George. They escaped the ghastly form of execution meted out to mere commoners but, on 24 February, were both beheaded at the Tower of London.

Of the other Jacobites tried and condemned to death in London, only four were actually executed. Most of the others were apparently never tried or else they succeeded in obtaining a stay of execution until King George signed an Act of Grace on 6 May 1717, whereby they were pardoned and released. Hardly any were acquitted. Among those who were was John Farquharson of Invercauld, who claimed that he had been forced against his will to join the rebellion by Mar, his feudal superior. Another five men turned King's evidence. By then, the executions of Kenmuir and especially that of Derwentwater (who was only twenty-six and married with a young son) had caused such a tide of revulsion against the brutality of the Hanoverian regime that further executions were abandoned.

Twenty prisoners did manage to escape. One of the first was William Maxwell, Earl of Nithsdale, who escaped from the Tower of London on the evening before he was due to be executed. His wife visited him in prison with two other ladies, one of whom, being conveniently pregnant, was 'not only of the same height, but nearly of the same size as my lord'. The other wore sufficient clothes under her outer garments to disguise Nithsdale as a woman. It was an old trick and it worked. After going into hiding for a few days, Nithsdale was smuggled into the Venetian ambassador's residence in London. He then left for Dover in the ambassador's coach, disguised in livery as one of his retinue, where he hired a small boat to take him to Calais. His wife joined him in exile soon afterwards.

Next was Thomas Forster, who escaped from Newgate prison. During an evening drinking with the prison governor, Forster excused himself to go to 'the necessary house' or latrine. After a few minutes, the governor became suspicious and decided to see why Forster was taking so long. All he found was Forster's nightgown, which he had worn over his outer clothes. Forster landed in France within twenty-four hours, after relays of horses had rushed him to the Essex coast.

A few weeks later, there was a mass breakout from Newgate on 4 May 1716, probably engineered by Borlum, who escaped along with another thirteen or fourteen prisoners. Apparently Borlum managed to overwhelm a gaoler and let himself and the others out, which sounds in character. Although eight of the prisoners were soon caught, Borlum managed to escape to France.

There were two other remarkable escapes. The Earl of Wintoun broke out of the Tower of London three months later, supposedly by sawing through the bars in his cell window with a watch spring. He too reached France. Then, on 13 December, Derwentwater's brother, Charles Radcliffe, walked out of Newgate prison, disguised as a visitor in a mourning suit and a brown tie-wig. He was eventually executed for his part in the '45 Rebellion.

Chapter Four

BATTLE OF SHERIFFMUIR

Engagement in the West Highlands

On 14 November 1715, the Jacobite forces at Preston surrendered, one day after the main body of Mar's army had lost the Battle of Sheriffmuir in Scotland. Any remaining hope that the Stuarts would be restored to the throne of Great Britain was effectively quashed, at least for the time being, by what should have been an avoidable defeat for Mar at Sheriffmuir.

While Forster and Borlum were marching their men south to defeat at Preston, Mar had spent weeks ineffectually at Perth, apparently waiting for the western clans to join him. Before the Jacobite standard had actually been raised, he had sent a message to Glengarry, Lochiel, Clanranald, Keppoch, Appin, Glencoe, MacDougall and Glenmoriston, appealing for their support, not just to restore James Edward Stuart to the throne, but also to break the 1707 Act of Union with England. Unfortunately for Mar's credibility, it had been only a year since he had persuaded many of them to sign a letter pledging loyalty to George I, soon after the king's accession. Although these clan chiefs had taken great offence when the king refused to accept their loyal address (and would later use this affront to justify their rebellion against the government), they were now slow to respond to Mar's call and, apparently, by early September, only Alasdair Dubh MacDonald of Glengarry had answered the summons. All the others had bided their time, wary of commitment. Coll MacDonald of Keppoch even wrote to excuse his inaction on the grounds that 'the country people being terrified by the garrison of Fort William, who threatens to destroy all the country how soon ever we leave it'. In fact, the fort never really posed a threat, needing repair and housing a mere 340 soldiers, apart from another eighty-five in the outposts at Invergarry, Duart and Eilean Donan. Its garrison rarely ventured out into the surrounding country and the outposts were soon taken.

When the western clans failed to appear, Mar dispatched General

Alexander Gordon of Auchintoul to mobilise them. It seems that Mar had already promised Glengarry a senior officer to give the Jacobite clans military leadership and training. Why Glengarry, a veteran of the Battle of Killiecrankie, should need this help is not obvious. A contemporary wrote of him: 'It's hard to say whether he has more of the bear, the lion, or the fox in him, for he is at least as rough and cunning as he is bold.' Possibly Mar only sent Gordon to chivvy the western clans.

General Gordon was a professional soldier in his fifties, who had served under Louis XIV in France, before becoming a Major-General in the Russian army of Peter the Great. He had returned home in 1711 after the death of his father, when he inherited the family estates at Auchintoul. Around the middle of September 1715, Gordon left for the west, meeting up a few days later with Glengarry's forces. John Grant of Glenmoriston was with Glengarry and, together, they had around 450 men under arms, enough to attack the government garrison at Fort William on their march south and to take a few prisoners. Marching south to the Braes of Glenorchy, they were joined along the way by the MacDonalds of Glencoe and, then, by Allan MacDonald, Captain of Clan Ranald, with 565 clansmen, responding to an appeal by Gordon.

Meanwhile, 300 MacGregors had joined the Jacobite camp under Gregor MacGregor of Glengyle, nephew of the notorious Rob Roy MacGregor. They had spent late September raiding the country around the southern end of Loch Lomond, launching hit-and-run attacks from their stronghold in the mountainous country east of Inversnaid, farther up the loch. On 29 September, seventy MacGregors had captured several boats on the loch and seized the island of Inchmurrin, which they used as a base to raid the western bank of Loch Lomond, before leaving to join Gordon and the rest of the Jacobite clans. However, Rob Roy MacGregor returned on 10 October to launch further raids against the western shore of Loch Lomond, especially targeting the lands of Sir Humphrey Colquhoun of Luss, a staunch Whig.

The government reacted to the MacGregor raids by mustering over 500 men, joined by 100 seamen from the men-of-war then lying in the Firth of Clyde. This expeditionary force towed a small armada of boats up the River Leven to the foot of Loch Lomond, using horses walking along its banks. The flotilla consisted of four flat-bottomed pinnaces and three long-boats from the men-of-war, armed with 'patararoes' or small cannon that fired stones, as well as four other boats, including one from Glasgow with two large screw-guns.

On 17 October, the men on foot embarked at Loch Lomond and sailed up the loch to Luss, with the horsemen riding along the western shore. Argyll's uncle, John Campbell of Mamore, together with Sir Humphrey

Colquhoun of Luss and his son-in-law, commanded this expedition, made up of:

> forty or fifty stately fellows in their short hose and belted plaids, armed each of them with a well-fixed gun on his shoulder, a strong handsome target, with a sharp pointed steel, of above half an ell in length, screwed into the navel of it on his left arm, a sturdy claymore by his side, and a pistol or two with a dirk and knife on his belt.

According to a contemporary account:

> the men on the shore marched with the greatest ardour and alacrity. The pinnaces on the water discharging their patararoes, and the men their small arms, made so dreadful a noise through the multiply'd rebounding echoes of the vast mountains on both sides [of] the loch, that perhaps there was never a more lively resemblance of thunder.

The main action took place on 18 October, when the naval force reached Inversnaid:

> In order to rouse these thieves from their dens, Captain Clark loosed one of his great guns, and drove a ball through the roof of a house on the face of the mountain, whereupon an old wife or two came crawling out and scrambled up the mountain, but otherwise there was no appearance of any body of men on the mountains, only a few, standing out of reach on the craggy rocks looking at them.
>
>   Whereupon . . . an hundred men in all, with the greatest intrepidity leapt on shore, got up to the top of the mountain, and drew up in order, and stood about an hour, their drums beating all the while, but no enemy appearing, they . . . found the boats drawn up a good way on the land, which they hurled down to the loch; such of them as were not damaged they carried off with them . . . to Dumbarton . . . and moored them under the cannons of the castle.

This flexing of government muscle effectively barred Loch Lomond to the Jacobite forces, whose camp had now moved to Strathfillan, sixteen miles north.

While this naval expedition was taking place, Gordon's Jacobite forces had left their camp at Strathfillan for an ineffectual attack on the Campbell stronghold of Inveraray. It was held for the government by 1,000 Campbells under the command of Argyll's younger brother Archibald Campbell, Earl of Islay (afterwards the third Duke of Argyll). His junior officers were highly critical of him: 'Islay acts all with a high hand, having a greatness about him more agreeable to a minister of state than an engaging officer.' This astute judgement was corroborated by his subsequent career as the arch-manipulator of Scottish politics until his death in 1761. Moreover, the Campbells were themselves deeply split, since the elderly John Campbell of Glenorchy, first Earl of Breadalbane, had thrown in his lot with the Jacobites, together with Campbell of Glendaruel and Campbell of Glenlyon, whose father had taken such a leading part in the Glencoe Massacre.

Gordon reached Inveraray on 19 October and established camp about a mile north-east, but refrained from attacking the town. In *The Jacobite Clans of the Great Glen*, Bruce Lenman comments that the great days of clan warfare, especially between the MacDonalds and the Campbells, had apparently gone, although clan loyalties still remained strong. The Jacobite chiefs did not ravage and plunder Inveraray as Alasdair MacColla had done in 1644 and, equally, Argyll made no attempt to wreak revenge after the 1715 Rebellion had collapsed. Instead, the argument had moved to a political plane. Scottish magnates now resorted to force only when trying to resolve otherwise intractable constitutional and dynastic problems. Yet, to judge from the outpourings of the Gaelic bards, anti-Campbell feeling was still harboured among the Jacobite clans until long after the 1745 Rebellion.

By 25 October, Gordon had abandoned his siege of Inveraray but did not join Mar's forces at Auchterarder until 10 November. Little is known of his movements over that fortnight; he may have returned to the camp at Strathfillan, to wait for the rest of the Jacobite clans. Certainly, the Hanoverian governor of Fort William reported on 28 October that John Cameron of Lochiel had ferried 300 of his men across Loch Linnhe near the Corran Narrows. The Camerons may have been among the last to appear, since it seems 350 men, under Sir John MacLean of Duart, and 240 men, under Robert Stewart of Appin, had already joined the Jacobite camp, together with 200 Campbells under Glenlyon and Glendaruel. By then, General Gordon had nearly 2,500 men. Only Coll MacDonald of Keppoch failed to arrive with his 250 men until after the Battle of Sheriffmuir.

Events in the North

Even before Mar had reached Braemar on 20 August, the government had mobilised its own supporters in the far north of Scotland. John Gordon, fifteenth Earl of Sutherland, was appointed Lord Lieutenant of Ross and Cromarty, together with Moray, Nairn, Caithness and Sutherland, while Brigadier Alexander Grant of Grant was made Lord Lieutenant of Banffshire and Inverness. However Sutherland did not leave London until

11 September, after warning the king of the danger to Inverness (which was indeed captured soon afterwards by the Jacobites). On 20 September, Sutherland reached Leith by ship, collected 300 stands of arms and sailed north for his seat at Dunrobin Castle, near Golspie. At Leith, he had arranged for another ship to follow him, loaded with more arms, and it was this ship that was captured by Mar's forces at Burntisland. Sutherland arrived at Dunrobin towards the end of September, after stopping to land Duncan Forbes of Culloden on the southern shores of the Moray Firth.

By then, William McKenzie, fifth Earl of Seaforth, had declared himself for James Edward Stuart and was mustering around 1,500 clansmen at Castle Brahan, south of Strathpeffer. There he was joined by another 500 men, chiefly MacKinnons, MacRaes and Chisholms of Strathglass, together with 700 clansmen from Skye under Sir Donald MacDonald, fourth Baronet of Sleat. At Dunrobin, Sutherland ordered the Whig clans loyal to King George to muster at Alness, a few miles north of the MacKenzie stronghold at Brahan Castle. A total of nearly 1,600 men arrived to support the government, made up of the following: the MacKays of Strathnaver under George, third Lord Reay; the Monros of Fowlis under Colonel Sir Robert Munro; and the Rosses of Balnagown. Sutherland joined them at Alness on 5 October but, four days later, withdrew his forces north of the Dornoch Firth when Seaforth advanced against him. However, this threat was rapidly removed when Seaforth received an order from Mar to join the Jacobite army at Perth.

By 15 October, Seaforth had reached Inverness on his way south to Perth. He was joined there by 400 Fraser clansmen, raised by Alexander MacKenzie of Fraserdale for the Jacobites in the absence of Simon Fraser, eleventh Lord Lovat, who had been held captive by the French authorities as a double agent ever since 1703. MacKenzie had taken control of the Lovat estates in the name of his wife Amelia, only daughter and heiress of Hugh Fraser, ninth Lord Lovat, while acting as the chief of the Frasers.

Seaforth left Inverness on 24 October with the bulk of his forces, leaving behind a small garrison to hold the town. Inverness later fell to the government when the Frasers changed sides after Simon Fraser broke out of prison in France and returned to the Highlands. A number of Fraser gentry had used their contacts with George I's court to sound out the benefits to Clan Fraser if it switched support to the government. Subsequently, several subscribed to a bail bond, which guaranteed Simon Fraser's good conduct on behalf of the government if he returned to Scotland, where he was still outlawed for abducting the Duke of Atholl's daughter and forcing her into marriage. His freedom safeguarded, Simon Fraser returned to his territories just in time to stop his clansmen marching south out of Inverness under MacKenzie to join the Jacobites. He ordered them back north and they probably deserted the Jacobite camp at Auchterarder on the night of 10 November.

Preparing for Battle

Mar evidently only felt strong enough to advance against Argyll at Stirling after the Highland clans under Seaforth and Gordon had joined his army at Perth. On 9 November, he called a council of war, which seems to have reached an agreement that the Jacobite army should try to cross the Forth well upstream of Stirling, while diversionary attacks would be launched closer to the town. This strategy was apparently influenced by a 'gentlemen's agreement' with Argyll to avoid damage to each other's estates east of Stirling, especially to Mar's prized gardens at Alloa. Any suggestion of crossing the headwaters of the River Forth was dismissed, since only Rob Roy MacGregor could guide them across the fords and he could not be trusted. Nevertheless, Mar's plans were aborted since Argyll had wind of them within a day from spies within the Jacobite camp. They were probably leaked by Rob Roy himself, who had his own ties with Argyll, and who was to sit out the Battle of Sheriffmuir.

Although Argyll's army was still outnumbered by Mar's forces, reinforcements of a further 900 men from Ireland had already reached Glasgow in late October. Eventually Argyll had amassed more than 3,000 troops to fight at Sheriffmuir and he was also able to leave behind another 1,000 men to defend Stirling and its approaches from the north across the River Forth. Apart from his battle-hardened officers and men, Argyll's only real advantage lay in his cavalry forces, more numerous and doubtless more effective than those of the Jacobites.

On the morning of 12 November, Argyll's forces rode out of Stirling, reaching Dunblane in the early afternoon. His plan of campaign was to occupy the high ground of Sheriffmuir above Dunblane, keeping the road from Perth to his left and so blocking Mar's advance five miles north of Stirling – well before the Jacobite army reached the River Forth and its marshy flood-plain. He moved out of Dunblane towards the higher ground at the southern end of Sheriffmuir, which rises in a series of low hills to around 1,000 feet at the foot of the Ochil Hills, north-east of Dunblane.

Argyll's army camped out for the night in the valley of the Wharry Burn, two miles south of this bleak and desolate moor land. Orders were given that the troops should remain in battle-readiness with their arms, lying out without tents on the bare ground despite the cold, while the junior officers should remain at their posts. Argyll himself spent the night in a sheep cot sitting on a bundle of straw.

However, Mar was still only advancing towards Dunblane from Auchterarder, fifteen miles north, having lost a day there reviewing his troops and so giving Argyll time to dictate the terms of the battle. By now, the Jacobite army was squabbling and becoming disorderly.

On the morning of 12 November, the Jacobite forces left Auchterarder, with General Gordon in command of the vanguard of 350 horse and nine foot battalions of Highlanders. His orders were to occupy Dunblane, while the rest of the army under Mar would follow, stopping for the night at the Roman camp of Ardoch, halfway between Auchterarder and Dunblane. Mar, therefore, followed the north bank of the Allan Water, rather than crossing Sheriffmuir by the drove road, still the shortest route between Auchterarder and Dunblane. Possibly Mar's odd choice of the longer route may be explained by a search for much-needed food and fodder.

The vanguard under Gordon was still halfway between Ardoch and the small hamlet of Kinbuck, three miles north of Dunblane, when news came that Argyll and his whole army were marching through Dunblane to confront the Jacobites. Drawing up his forces into battle array, Gordon sent patrols ahead to reconnoitre. Darkness started to fall around 4 p.m. and Gordon was forced to halt for the night at Kinbuck to avoid blundering into Argyll's forces, not knowing where they had camped out. The rest of the Jacobite army finally arrived around 9 p.m. and, while most of the officers spent the night under cover, the other ranks lay out in the open in freezing weather. Kinbuck lies in a hollow and 'never since the invention of powder were so many troops packed in one small place. It cannot be said that we had a front or a rear any more than has a barrel of herrings.' They would have been completely vulnerable if Argyll had discovered their position.

Before dawn on 13 November, the Jacobite army moved out towards higher ground a few hundred yards east. Ignoring the reports of Argyll's movements, Mar drew up his infantry regiments in two lines, facing south, to advance in battle order towards Dunblane. In the front line were the Highlanders under Gordon including the Stewarts of Appin, the Camerons of Lochiel, the MacDonalds of Glencoe, the MacLeans of Duart, the MacDonalds of Clan Ranald, the Campbells of Breadalbane, the Mac-Donalds of Glengarry and the MacDonalds of Sleat. Behind them, in the second line, were the Robertsons of Struan, the men of Atholl and the MacKenzies of Seaforth, together with the foot regiments raised by Lord Drummond, the Earl of Panmure and the Marquis of Huntly. Mar placed the bulk of his cavalry on the right wing, with a smaller detachment on the left wing.

Only after sunrise, at around 8 a.m., did Mar realise that a group of cavalry were facing him on the high ground of Sheriffmuir to the south. Argyll had come forward with his officers to reconnoitre at the south-western end of Sheriffmuir. However, Mar let another three hours elapse before eventually ordering his two lines to turn left, so forming two columns which started to climb towards the higher ground now separating the two armies, although the enemy army were not yet in sight. Indeed, Argyll and his officers had already been driven from their vantage point by a troop of Mar's dragoons.

The Highlanders under Gordon were now rushing so rapidly uphill that they became the vanguard. Reaching the broad summit of Sheriffmuir at its south-western end, they saw the enemy and fanned out towards the south to form Mar's ring wing. On their far right, the Highlanders were flanked by the bulk of the Jacobite cavalry, except that a squadron under the Earl Marischal somehow ended up in their centre. Worse confusion gripped what became the left wing of Mar's army under Major-General George Hamilton, which had lagged behind the Highlanders. Moving uphill, the cavalry originally on their left wing, for some reason, veered right, leaving the left wing of Mar's army unprotected from the cavalry on Argyll's right wing.

Almost too late, Argyll reacted by sounding the general call to arms. Cold and hungry after a night in the open and perhaps poorly trained, his men moved off sluggishly. Even so, the troops in front made good progress, along with much of Argyll's best cavalry, so making up his right wing. But the rearguard lagged behind, forming his army's left wing when it turned to face the enemy. Thus, each army found that its weaker wing was face-to-face with the stronger wing of the enemy.

Battle of Sheriffmuir

The infantrymen on Argyll's left wing were totally unprepared for their assault by the Highlanders facing them, who crested the slope, saw their enemy in front of them on the flatter ground and, within four minutes of Gordon's order to attack, were fighting them hand-to-hand after a classic 'Highland charge'. The charge had only faltered when Alan MacDonald, Captain of Clan Ranald, was shot from his horse and killed. However Glengarry spurred on his clansmen with the cry: 'Tomorrow for mourning, revenge for today.' The overwhelming strength and ferocity of the Highlanders quickly broke Argyll's left wing, driving his infantry back against the cavalry. They fled south from the battlefield in total disorder, pursued by more than half of Mar's army, across the Wharry Burn. Only General Whetham with 180 dragoons on the extreme left of Argyll's line escaped the rout, attacking the right flank of the Highlanders as they thundered past.

Despite this extraordinary attack by Mar's right wing, the Battle of Sheriffmuir was determined by events on his left wing. Reaching the broad

crest of Sheriffmuir behind Gordon's Highlanders, the mixed force under
Hamilton seems to have charged the enemy lines immediately but much
less effectively, since Argyll's right wing was ready for them under his own
command. Although Hamilton had more infantry, he also faced the bulk of
Argyll's cavalry. During nearly three hours of fighting, Hamilton's forces
were slowly driven back north towards the Allan Water, despite rallying
time and again to mount counter-attacks. The ranks of the Jacobite left
wing were finally broken by Argyll's cavalry and they were forced to flee
north across the Allan Water.

It was not until Argyll had finally pressed home his attack against Mar's
left wing that he heard that his own left wing had collapsed much earlier in
the battle. In the words of the quip: 'Argyll is a better Christian than he is a
General, since he does not let his right hand know what his left is doing.'
He then immediately recalled his troops from their pursuit of the Jacobite
forces under Hamilton, returning to the battlefield to face Mar's army with
the remnants of his own forces. By now, Argyll had barely 1,000 men,
while Mar was in command of more than 4,000. The Highlanders on Mar's
right wing were recalled from chasing the enemy and returned to the
battlefield to join a squadron of Jacobite horse, which, for four hours, had
been merely standing by, swords drawn, on the top of the ridge known as
the Hill of Kippendavie. However, the Highlanders then waited motion-
lessly until Argyll and his forces returned, approaching the Hill of
Kippendavie from the north-east.

Only at dusk, at around 4 p.m., did Mar at last rally his forces for a final
attack. Earlier in the afternoon, he had ridden up to the Hill of Kippendavie, 'stood a little time, [and] rode off, without pretending to give
orders', although his troops could have attacked the government forces
pushing back his left wing. Mar seemed transfixed with indecision, having
'no mind to risk himself', or so it was said later, unable to take effective
action by ordering his vastly superior army to attack the remains of Argyll's
troops.

As the light faded, Mar's forces advanced slowly to within 400–500
yards of the enemy, which had taken up a position at the foot of the Hill of
Kippendavie, behind some enclosures and mud walls. Mar seems to have
held his infantry back, wanting the Jacobite cavalry, who had been idle, to
prove themselves now by leading the attack. Half an hour elapsed before,
'night coming on, the Duke of Argyll seemed first to make a feint as if he
was moving towards us, and inclined after[wards] to Dunblane, and it
being almost dark, we soon lost sight of them'.

Mar had once again squandered his chance of victory, when a determined assault would have almost certainly succeeded – even at this late
stage of the battle. In his official dispatch to the government, General

Wightman admitted: 'If they had had either the courage or conduct they might have entirely destroyed my body of foot.' Mar's men were far fresher than Argyll's, who had fought hard all afternoon, and they outnumbered the enemy by four to one. Apparently a Highland officer cried out in frustration: 'Oh! For One Hour of Dundee.' But, unlike John Graham of Claverhouse, Viscount Dundee, Mar was neither vigorous nor decisive and handed victory to Argyll without the firing of a shot.

Sheriffmuir in Retrospect

Mar's failings as commander of the Jacobite army at Sheriffmuir were considerable. Despite having far more men, he had allowed Argyll to dictate the field of battle. Moreover, as James Hill emphasises in *Celtic Warfare, 1595–1763*, he had no understanding of the fighting capabilities of Highland clansmen, their methods of warfare or, indeed, their limitations. When Mar ordered his soldiers to advance uphill in two columns, which then had to reform into lines of battle, he had not appreciated that the Highland troops lacked the tight discipline needed for such a complicated manoeuvre. He, therefore, failed to take the heights of Sheriffmuir before Argyll, so that his clansmen were unable to descend upon the enemy with the full force of a Highland charge. It was only by sheer luck that Mar's right wing met Argyll's left wing before it had time to organise itself.

If Mar's army had advanced uphill in battle order, ready to attack at a moment's notice, it could well have won the battle with a simultaneous assault on both wings of the government's army, before Argyll could deploy his own right wing. Mar could then have put Argyll's entire army to flight. Argyll himself did not underestimate the Highlander's military capabilities, employing defensive tactics in meeting the full force of the Highland charge on his right wing, rather than attacking first.

The failure of Mar's army to achieve a decisive victory at Sheriffmuir, despite its massive numerical advantage, was the beginning of the end for the Jacobite Rebellion of 1715. As Peter Rae wrote in 1718:

By this battle, the heart of the rebellion was broken, the Earl of Mar was baulked of his design, his undertaking for a march to the south was laid aside and never attempted afterwards, and his numbers daily decreased, so that he could never gather such an army again.

Chapter Five

END OF THE 1715 REBELLION

After the Battle of Sheriffmuir, Argyll spent the night of 13 November at Dunblane, coming back next day to the battlefield to tend the wounded and to collect any arms Mar's forces had abandoned, before returning to Stirling. There, his army was greatly reinforced over the coming weeks, following the Jacobite defeat at the Battle of Preston. From 19 December onwards, government forces captured Burntisland and Dunfermline and soon occupied all of Fife. Meanwhile, Mar had retreated north to Perth, where he remained until 31 January 1716, his position becoming weaker by the day, as the Highland clans abandoned his camp. A comment in his journal suggests that Mar was not entirely realistic about the reason for these desertions: 'Amongst many good qualities, the Highlanders have one unlucky custom, not easy to be reformed; which is, that generally after an engagement, they return home.'

Those who deserted the Jacobite army immediately after Sheriffmuir included the MacKenzies under William MacKenzie, fifth Earl of Seaforth, whose lands were threatened by the Whig clans loyal to the government after the fall of Inverness. Seaforth was followed three weeks later by Alexander Gordon, fifth Marquis of Huntly. Together, they made half-hearted plans during December to recapture Inverness, which, however, were thwarted by the Earl of Sutherland who marched into Seaforth's lands with 1,800 men, to intimidate him into obedience. Seaforth now had only 1,100 clansmen under his command and he was forced to submit to the government by the end of December.

Meanwhile, most of the Athollmen in Mar's army also went home, as did the Robertsons of Struan, the Stewarts of Grandtully, the Campbells of Breadalbane and the Drummonds. Only Coll MacDonald of Keppoch appeared, belatedly, with 200 clansmen to augment the Jacobite army. Mar hoped in vain that the others would all return, especially after James Edward Stuart had finally landed in Scotland on 22 December 1715. But, by then, he had than 5,000 men fewer and was shortly down to 4,000, of whom not more than 2,500 were both armed and reliable.

James Edward Stuart in Scotland: Late Arrival and Early Departure

When Mar had raised the Jacobite standard at Braemar on 6 September 1715, James Edward Stuart was still exiled at Bar-le-Duc in the Duchy of Lorraine. He remained there for nearly two months, unable to influence events, while the government moved swiftly and effectively to put down the planned uprising in the West of England. Through subterfuge, James managed to leave Bar-le-Duc on 28 October, narrowly escaping assassination by two agents acting for the Earl of Stair who in his role as British ambassador in Paris had kept a close watch on the Prince. Disguised as an *abbé*, James reached Saint-Malo with the help of an innkeeper's wife at Nonancourt, near Dreux. Suspecting Stair's agents of plotting a murder, she persuaded the local magistrates to arrest them, after locking them in a room.

James arrived at Saint-Malo in early November, planning to sail across the English Channel to land near Plymouth for a march upon London, but he was met with the report that the West of England was now held securely by the government. Only at this point did James realise that he would have to land to Scotland, as his half-brother, the Duke of Berwick, had always recommended. Berwick wrote in the summer of 1715: 'Now or never he must make the attempt, otherwise he may make himself a Cardinal – he will never be a King.' Ironically, this remark held some degree of prophecy as James's younger son, Henry, did indeed, become a cardinal of the Catholic Church, after the failure of the 1745 Rebellion under James's elder son, Charles Edward Stuart.

James initially planned to sail from Saint-Malo by way of Ireland to land at Dunstaffnage Castle, north of Oban on the west coast of Scotland, but, before he could leave, he learnt that Dunstaffnage had fallen to the government. He was, therefore, forced to travel from Saint-Malo on another dangerous journey across France to reach Dunkirk, from where he could sail across the North Sea to the east coast of Scotland. Delayed by contrary winds until mid-December, he then embarked on what was to be a repeat of his 1708 winter voyage, at risk both of capture and from storms. James may not have attracted the same admiration as his son thirty years later, but, as Sir Charles Petrie comments in *The Jacobite Movement*:

> It was hardly the act of a coward to set sail in the middle of winter across a sea infested with enemy frigates for the sake of sharing the dangers of a dwindling band of adherents, whom, as he well knew, nothing save the direct interposition of the Almighty could save from destruction.

On 22 December 1715, James finally landed at Peterhead in his 'own ancient kingdom' of Scotland with only six companions. He then travelled south in disguise, reaching Feteresso Castle near Stonehaven on Christmas Eve, then the principal seat of George Keith, tenth Earl Marischal. There he was joined on Boxing Day by Mar and several other Jacobite leaders, including the Earl Marischal. However, James caught a feverish cold with fits of shivering and was not fit to travel until 2 January. After making a formal entry into Dundee on 6 January, he finally arrived at Perth on 9 January 1716 to review what remained of the Jacobite army.

James was in Perth for only three weeks. Contrary to popular legend, he was never crowned at Scone, judging the moment inopportune. An air of despondency settled upon the Jacobite camp soon after his arrival, as his followers realised the strength of the forces being marshalled against them at Stirling. Before James's arrival, Mar had written to him:

> Unless your Majesty have troops with you, which I'm afraid you have not, I see not how we can oppose them even for this winter, when they have got the Dutch troops to England, and will pour in more troops from thence upon us every day.

The Jacobite forces in Perth were bitterly disappointed that James had brought no reinforcements from France. After arriving in Scotland, James wrote immediately to the Duke of Orleans (then acting as Regent to Louis XV), appealing for troops, but there seemed no hope that he would help, given the closeness of Anglo-French relations after the Treaty of Utrecht.

Unfortunately, James's personality also did not inspire confidence in his followers. One contemporary account, possibly written by Daniel Defoe in his role as a government agent, described him as:

> tall and thin . . . [and] sanguine in his constitution . . . [He] has a vivacity in his eye that would perhaps have been more visible if he had not been under dejected circumstances and surrounded by discouragement . . . His speech was grave, and not very clearly expressing his thoughts, nor overmuch to the purpose . . . His behaviour and temper always seemed composed . . . I must not conceal that when we saw the person who we called our King, we found ourselves not at all animated by his presence, and if he was disappointed in us, we were tenfold more so in him . . . we saw nothing in him that looked like spirit.

Meanwhile, Argyll had made his final preparations to march north against Perth. He was encouraged to act by General William Cadogan, sent north by the government in London when Argyll appeared ready to offer terms to the rebels after Sheriffmuir. The Hanoverian forces had now more than 9,000 men in seven regiments of cavalry and twenty battalions of infantry, after reinforcement by 6,000 Dutch auxiliaries. At the end of January, additional munitions arrived from Berwick, Edinburgh and England. By then, Argyll was ready to march out of Stirling, although the weather was bitterly cold with heavy snowfalls.

On 21 January, Argyll had dispatched 200 dragoons to reconnoitre the state of the roads leading to Perth. Three days later, he left Stirling in person for another reconnaissance, along with many of his officers and a large party of dragoons. They advanced as far north-east as Auchterarder, greatly alarming the Jacobites at Perth, who responded by creating a belt of 'scorched earth' between Dunblane and Perth. The burning of the Perthshire villages became notorious. It should, however, be seen in the context of mutual reprisals – the Hanoverian forces under Argyll also had been ordered to plunder Jacobite estates in the Lowlands before Sheriff-muir and, afterwards, raided other estates in the Perthshire Highlands.

James himself was reluctant to sign the order for

> destroying all the corn and forage which may support them [Argyll's forces] on their march, and burning all the houses and villages which may be necessary for quartering the enemy, which nevertheless it is our meaning should only be done in case of absolute necessity.

Mar wrote to Gordon: 'The burning goes mightily against the King's mind, but there is no help for it.'

Ranald MacDonald, now chief of Clan Ranald after the death of his brother at Sheriffmuir, was detailed to carry out the burnings, although he too had qualms. He left Perth on the evening of 24 January with 600 clansmen, mostly Camerons and MacDonalds. On 25 January, they arrived long before daybreak in Auchterarder, which they put to the flames, moving on to burn Blackford and Crieff the same day. The weather was atrocious, with heavy falls of snow, and many of the inhabitants were stripped of their clothes as they struggled through the snowdrifts and were then left out in the open. Lord George Murray joined whole-heartedly in the action on 28 January, when he burnt Dunning:

> while men, women and children were exposed to the injury of the weather and the rigour of that severe and stormy season, it being in the midst of a terrible storm of frost and snow . . . and some of them died in a few hours thereafter, particularly one man and two women, who had formerly been weak and tender, and thereby the less able to

bear up under such a terrible [ordeal], and to endure the sharp and cold air.

The burning of the villages in Perthshire gave the government a propaganda coup, which it exploited to the full. The Jacobite cause was irreparably damaged and James regretted the action for the rest of his life. Indeed, the memory of it preyed more on his mind than the failure of the 1715 Rebellion itself. Before he left Scotland, he gave instructions that the inhabitants of the burnt-out villages were to receive any money left over from paying off the Jacobite army. However, it was left to the government to pay compensation, which it eventually did in 1781, sixty-five years later, distributing the sum of £3,474 to the descendants of those survivors that could then be traced.

On 29 January, Argyll's army eventually marched out of Stirling towards Perth, making slow progress as the snow had first to be cleared from the roads. The Jacobites had already heard, from their spies in Stirling, that Argyll was ready to depart and their camp promptly split into two factions. The Highland clansmen and their chiefs were said to be delighted at the news and were eager to move into action. But, cautious as ever, Mar and his senior officers had already agreed in secret that the army should withdraw from Perth if Argyll advanced from Stirling.

Mar now called a council of war, which started on the evening of 29 January and lasted all the next day, without reaching agreement. After it had broken up, Mar hinted at a meeting with his closest advisers that there was a plot to seize the Prince and surrender him to Argyll. This story, whether true or not, horrified those present, who then united behind Mar in his decision to retreat. The speech given by James himself to his troops before they marched out of Perth, showed that he also evidently sided with Mar:

I am in despair at finding myself compelled to withdraw from Perth without a fight; but to offer battle would be to expose brave men for no reason, since the enemy is twice as strong as we are, and I wish to preserve them for a more fitting occasion.

Accordingly, the Jacobite army started to withdraw from Perth on 31 January, leaving the city to be occupied by government forces just a day later.

The Jacobite forces now retreated towards Aberdeen by way of Dundee, Montrose and Stonehaven, closely pursued by Argyll's army, just a day or two behind them. Only at Aberdeen did they realise that James Edward Stuart had already left Scotland for France with Mar. They had embarked on the night of 4 February at Montrose, where two small vessels were waiting, having sailed from Dundee. Since the vessels had left Dundee before the Jacobite army had actually begun to withdraw north from Perth, there appears to have been a pre-arranged plan, although Mar claimed later that it was providential.

In order to distract their attention from James's movements, the troops had been actually ordered to parade after dark on the evening of 4 February, while his baggage had already been sent ahead to Aberdeen. While his army was marching out of Montrose, James Edward Stuart's horses were being made ready at his lodgings. But, instead of following his men, James slipped down to the harbour and boarded the *Marie-Thérèse*, along with a few senior officers, including Mar himself. A number of Jacobite commanders were missing from the party including Berwick's son (afterwards the Duke of Liria), William Murray, Marquis of Tullibardine, George Keith, tenth Earl Marischal, and several others. It had proved impossible to alert them all in time, although it seems George Keith deliberately stayed behind to command the Jacobite rearguard as it retreated towards Aberdeen without its other commanders.

The Jacobite forces were now under the command of General Alexander Gordon of Auchintoul. They marched from Aberdeen through Old Meldrum and Inverurie towards Strathbogie, where Alexander Gordon, fifth Marquis of Huntly, refused them any help. Indeed, he ordered all his cannon to be buried to prevent them being used for a projected attack upon Inverness. Soon afterwards, Huntly surrendered to the Earl of Sutherland and Gordon Castle was garrisoned by forces loyal to the government. Meanwhile, the remnants of the Jacobite army had reached Ruthven in Badenoch, after marching through Keith, Glen Rinnes and Strathdon into Strathspey. Gordon wrote from there to Argyll, seeking a general indemnity, but his letter was never answered. On 16 February 1716, the clansmen dispersed to their own territories at the end of hardly the most glorious chapter in Highland history. Their leaders would mostly escape abroad to exile.

Clanranald returned to the safety of South Uist, apparently with George Keith and his younger brother, while Gordon took refuge on Skye with Sir Donald MacDonald, fourth Baronet of Sleat. Another party of 160 officers rode north from Ruthven, after hearing that two French frigates were patrolling the Pentland Firth. From Burghead on the southern shores of the Moray Firth, they first sailed to Orkney and then to Gothenburg, where most of them took service in the Swedish army under Charles XII.

Even at this late stage, the Highland chieftains apparently still hoped to renew the struggle. On 31 March 1716, Clanranald reported that Seaforth had joined Glengarry, Lochiel and Keppoch in raising fresh forces with

Gordon on the mainland, although he had earlier surrendered to the government. These hopes were illusory and many of the Highland chieftains of the Jacobite clans sailed soon afterwards from the Western Isles to join James Edward Stuart in exile on the Continent.

James, however, was not welcomed by the French government, given their friendly relations with Britain following the Treaty of Utrecht and the Anglo-French alliance of 17 November 1716. By the last week of March 1716, James was forced to retreat to the papal enclave of Avignon, where many of the Jacobite exiles joined his court. Within a year, he had left Avignon for Urbino in Italy before moving to Rome in 1719 at the insistence of the British government, which wished to emphasise his close attachment to the Catholic Church for propaganda purposes. James Edward Stuart remained in Rome for the next fifty years until his death on 1 January 1766.

Legal Reprisals and Military Occupation

Despite his success in putting down the 1715 Rebellion, Argyll soon lost the command of the victorious Hanoverian army in Scotland to his deputy, General William Cadogan. Argyll had wanted lenience towards the rebels, whereas Cadogan preferred a more ruthless policy, although he never put it into effect. Moreover, Argyll had alienated the government of George I, criticising its measures taken to suppress the 1715 Rebellion and cultivating the friendship of the Prince of Wales who, he thought, should act as sole regent whenever the king was absent in Hanover. Before leaving his post, Argyll placed garrisons, not only in Edinburgh, Stirling, Glasgow and Aberdeen, but also elsewhere around the country, guarding the fringes of the Highlands from Dumbarton in the west to Inverness in the north. At Fort William, the garrison town had been reinforced by an additional 500 government troops, who seized Lochiel's house at Achnacarry. Glengarry's house at Invergarry was also occupied, after he had submitted at Inverness with Coll Macdonald of Keppoch. After accepting the submissions of a number of the other Jacobite chiefs who had not fled abroad into exile, Cadogan returned south to the comforts of London in late April, after two months in the Highlands.

Many of the leading figures in the 1715 Rebellion were subsequently convicted of high treason, under what was known as an Act of Attainder, as they had not surrendered themselves by 30 June 1716. In the most summary form of justice imaginable, those named in the Act could be executed immediately if declared guilty of treason. Very few rebels surrendered to the government, as nearly all had already fled abroad to join James Edward Stuart. Apart from Mar himself, these exiles included

Lord William Murray, Marquis of Tullibardine, who had already been convicted of treason at the outbreak of the rebellion, as well as many of the nobility and other gentry who had attended the great deer hunt of 26 August 1715. Their estates were all forfeited to the Crown, as well as their titles. Thanks to a legal nicety, Major-General Alexander Gordon of Auchintoul and John Farquharson of Inverey both escaped forfeiture, as their Christian names were wrongly cited in the Act.

Nevertheless, Scottish prisoners escaped the savage reprisals meted out in Lancashire after the Jacobite defeat at Preston. Many were simply released in June 1716, when the Act of Habeas Corpus came back into force after being suspended for a year. They were mostly men seen as unimportant or thought likely to support the government in pacifying the country if freed. Many had submitted well before the fighting had ended. Their release left around eighty others still held prisoner. As Scottish juries were thought unlikely to convict their fellow Scots, Cadogan persuaded the authorities in London that they should be brought to trial in Carlisle, south of the Border.

This flagrant violation of the Act of Union caused widespread and bitter opposition, especially from Scottish judges, but was carried out regardless. Early in September 1716, seventy-four Scottish prisoners were marched south to Carlisle. Seven others were certified as too ill to travel, while three peers of the realm remained behind in Edinburgh Castle. Alexander Gordon, Marquis of Huntly, was ordered to march south with the other commoners. But, after he had protested vigorously, he was recalled to Edinburgh and, indeed, was later pardoned by George I.

Of the prisoners who reached Carlisle to be tried under English law, thirty-four were released due to lack of evidence, while another thirty-two were brought to trial. But of the twenty-four found guilty, not all were condemned to death sentence. It may be that no sentence was passed on them, since they were not executed. A possible exception was a former regular soldier who had abetted the Jacobite attempt upon Edinburgh Castle but, otherwise, all Jacobite prisoners convicted of treason at Carlisle were released under the Act of Grace in 1717.

This leniency was almost inevitable, given the widespread support for the Jacobite cause among the higher levels of society throughout much of Scotland and, especially, in the north-east and the Highlands. As Duncan Forbes of Culloden put it in August 1716, there were 'not two hundred gentlemen in the whole Kingdom who are not very nearly related to someone or other of the rebels'. An anonymous pamphlet of the same year, possibly written by him, pleaded for clemency for the 300–400 men of social standing who had escaped into the hills at the end of the uprising. They represented a potential threat to the Protestant succession, especially if they went into exile. Around 500 Jacobites were said to be already in Avignon, mostly Scots. If they converted to Catholicism, their family contacts and influence in Scotland would make them dangerous enemies of the government, whereas a pardon would allow them to be safely absorbed back into Scots society.

Nevertheless, the government did purge the Justices of the Peace, accusing many of Jacobite leanings. Even before the 1715 Rebellion, 261 Justices had been dismissed, nearly one-fifth of the total. Afterwards, despite the new appointments already made, the Justices became suspect again and a further purge dispensed with a third of those north of the River Tay. However, many of those left were clearly still considered Jacobites at heart, since there was yet another purge after the 1745 Rebellion. The fact that such action was thought necessary is clear evidence of the widespread support for the Jacobite cause by the landed society of Scotland.

The only other serious attempt to pacify the Highlands was the building of well-fortified barracks. The process of strengthening Fort William had begun in 1698, been resumed after the failed French invasion in 1708 and, by 1715, had involved the construction in stone of the governor's residence, guardhouse, officers' quarters, a barracks block for over 400 men, a powder magazine and store houses. After 1715, new barracks were also constructed at Inversnaid (near the head of Loch Arklet), Ruthven (in Badenoch), Bernera (at Glenelg, guarding the short sea-crossing to Skye) and Kilcumein (at the head of Loch Ness). Work started in 1718 but took years to complete. The barracks were all built to a common plan, adapted to local circumstances. Each consisted of two blocks of three-storeyed barracks, separated by a parade ground. The outer defences each side of the parade ground were completed by two high walls, pierced with vaulted musket loops and topped by a parapet and walkway. Two towers at opposite corners of the buildings were constructed to allow covering fire along the outer walls. The towers contained the guardrooms, the bake-house and the brewhouse, as well as quarters for the officers on the upper floor. Kilcumein was the largest, capable of housing six companies of 360 men, while Bernera could take four companies and Ruthven and Inver-snaid two each. Kilcumein and Inversnaid were soon built, but Ruthven, and especially Bernera, took years to complete. Indeed, work was not actually started at Bernera until May 1720, although it was close to Glenshiel, where the 1719 Rebellion had ended.

Suppression of the Episcopalian Church

In the Scottish Church and the universities, Jacobite sympathisers were also penalised. In May 1716, George I wrote to the Lord of Justiciary, complaining that prayers were not said for himself and his family in some Episcopalian meeting houses in Edinburgh and elsewhere in Scotland. All clergymen were then ordered to produce their Letters of Orders and to register them with the authorities under the 1712 Act of Toleration, after taking the Oaths of Allegiance and Abjuration. Twenty-one offenders were fined in the Edinburgh district for not praying for the king, although they were then allowed to minister to their congregations after registering their Letters of Orders.

Similar measures were taken against the Episcopalian clergy in the diocese of Aberdeen, who were especially active in the Stuart cause. Many still had their parish churches, owing their survival to the protection of the local Episcopalian magnates. Even so, thirty-six clergymen were now expelled from their livings to make way for Presbyterian ministers. Nearly all those Episcopalian meeting houses which had not already been destroyed by government forces were closed. The two colleges of Aberdeen University were purged of any remaining Episcopalians, bringing them into line with the other Scottish universities. George Keith, tenth Earl Marischal, who had held the patronage of Marischal College as a descendant of its founder in 1593, forfeited this privilege along with all his other offices. Only Thomas Blackwell, its Professor of Divinity, had remained loyal to the government in 1715, and he was rewarded by being appointed Principal of the College in 1717. All the other professors were dismissed.

By expelling these academics, the government may have actually nurtured the growth of Jacobite sentiment in the north-east. Many opened schools throughout the region, disseminating their own brand of Episcopalianism. According to the two principals of the Aberdeen colleges, writing in 1749 after the 1745 Rebellion:

They poisoned the greatest part of the young gentry of those parts with principles that have since thoroughly appeared – For as the young gentlemen came to their estates, non-juring meeting-houses were instantly erected on their lands; and they were themselves almost to a man the officers in the rebel army in 1745.

Whatever the consequences of this religious intolerance, another Act of Parliament followed in 1719, forbidding any clergyman to minister to a congregation of nine or more persons (apart from the members of a household) without praying for King George and his family, and without first taking the Oath of Abjuration, as required by the 1712 Act of Toleration. Those who refused to comply were liable to six months' imprisonment. However, this Act was rarely enforced after the threat of invasion had receded in the aftermath of the 1719 Uprising and many clergymen remained as non-jurors. Nevertheless, congregations often preferred to appoint ministers who 'qualified' under the Act as this allowed them to use the liturgy of the Church of England. A rift, therefore, opened between the clergy and the bishops, who still refused to recognise any clergyman who had taken the Oath of Allegiance to George I.

Chapter Six

JACOBITISM IN ECLIPSE

As the Jacobite Rebellion of 1715 was largely a story of inaction, dithering and ineptitude, it is hardly surprising that writers other than historians have neglected it in favour of the 1745 Rebellion, attracted by the more romantic exploits of the Old Pretender's son, Charles Edward Stuart. By any stretch of the imagination, Mar was not a charismatic figure. As Sir Walter Scott observed in *Tales of a Grandfather*:

> With a far less force than Mar had at his disposal, Montrose gained eight victories and overran Scotland; with fewer numbers of High-landers, Dundee gained the Battle of Killiecrankie; and with about half the numbers [of] the troops [that Mar] assembled at Perth, Charles Edward in 1745 marched as far as Derby, and gained two victories over regular troops. But in 1715, by one of those mis-fortunes which dogged the House of Stewart since the days of Robert II, they wanted a man of military talent just at the time they possessed an unusual quantity of military means.

Even with a more dynamic leader, it is doubtful that the 1715 Rebellion could have overthrown George I without the promised French help which did not materialise. The 1715 Rebellion might well have ended differently had Louis XIV not died before he could honour his word to provide the Jacobites with men, money and arms.

Nevertheless, George I remained deeply unpopular in Britain, where he was seen as a foreigner barely able to speak the language, committed above all else to the interests of Hanover. Despite its failure, Mar's challenge to the king with such impressive military strength convinced the Whig government in London that it must maintain peace with France. British diplomacy after 1715 was, therefore, directed at securing an alliance with France, which lasted until 1744. James Edward Stuart would need the support of the other European powers opposed to this alliance (which later included the Netherlands and the Holy Roman Empire), if he were ever to reach the British throne.

European Politics and the Jacobite Cause

After the disaster of 1715, the Jacobite cause was in fact completely dependent on foreign military and financial assistance and could, therefore, only thrive when Britain (or rather Hanover) had enemies who might support the restoration of the Stuart dynasty. But, to these nations, Jacobitism was only a means to an end, never an end in itself, and they would only exploit it against Britain when they had little or nothing to lose.

Initially, Sweden seemed the country most likely to help the Old Pretender, since it was challenging George I for naval supremacy in the Baltic and still claimed its former territories of Bremen and Verden, now in the hands of George I as Elector of Hanover. Ever optimistic, the Jacobites had been conspiring with envoys from Charles XII, the Swedish king, but he was killed in December 1718 while invading Norway. Otherwise an army of 10,000 Swedes might have swept from Norway into Scotland or northern England. Britain had been rife with rumours of an impending invasion.

The Jacobites came closer to successful collaboration against the Hanoverian regime with Spain. Under the Treaty of Utrecht in 1713, Spain had finally lost the remnants of the Spanish Netherlands, along with Sardinia and Sicily, as well as various territories on the Italian mainland. Influenced by Cardinal Alberoni, his first minister, Philip V of Spain was determined to win back the former Spanish possessions in Italy. His forces successfully invaded Sardinia in 1717 and then Sicily in 1718. However, the fleet guarding the Sicilian expedition was destroyed by the British navy, under Admiral Byng, off Cape Passaro near Messina. Spain promptly declared war on Britain, while, soon afterwards, France declared war on Spain, after the French had discovered a plot to overthrow their Regent in favour of Philip V of Spain. Meanwhile, Alberoni was planning an invasion of Britain with James Butler, second Duke of Ormond, with the aim of placing James Edward Stuart on the British throne.

What Alberoni envisaged was a two-pronged attack on Britain, with the main thrust directed at the West of England and only a small-scale diversionary sortie against the Scottish Highlands. He made the unrealistic assumption that there would be sufficient Jacobite support in England for the country to rise in arms against George I – no doubt encouraged by the wishful thinking and exaggerations of the Jacobites in exile and their sympathisers in England, who always interpreted any popular discontent in Britain in their favour. But, even amongst the Tories, Jacobite support in England rarely amounted to much more than drinking toasts to 'the king over the water'. There were no disturbances, even after the death of George I in 1727 and the accession of George II.

In the event, Jacobite support in England was never put to the test by a Spanish invasion. A sizeable fleet, consisting of five men-of-war and more than twenty transports, did assemble at Cadiz. Carrying 5,000 well-armed men, with enough arms for another 30,000, it sailed for Corunna on 7 March 1719. However, on 29 March, a violent storm off Cape Finisterre scattered the fleet before it reached Corunna. Only ten ships managed to limp into harbour, their masts broken and their sails in tatters. The planned invasion was abandoned.

Meanwhile, James Edward Stuart had left Rome to join the expedition. Like all his attempts to travel to the kingdom he claimed as his own, this journey was characterised by drama, hazard and sickness. Amid wild rumours of James's destination, the authorities arrested what they thought was his party as it left Papal territory, only to find that James was being impersonated by one of his entourage. James himself had slipped away to a small fishing port thirty miles south. Sailing from there, racked with fever, he narrowly escaped capture by the British navy as he crossed the stormy seas to Las Rosas in Catalonia. When he finally arrived in Corunna, the invasion plans had already been abandoned and, with his expectations crushed once again, he returned to Rome. It was there, on 22 August 1719, that James Edward Stuart married Clementina Sobieski, granddaughter of King John of Poland.

1719 Uprising in Scotland

After the storm off Cape Finisterre, the planned attack on the Scottish Highlands was the only element of the invasion strategy still intact. Apart from the main fleet at Cadiz, a smaller force had gathered at San Sebastian in the Basque country, commanded by George Keith, tenth Earl Marischal. He had two Spanish frigates at his disposal, carrying around 500 Spanish troops, as well as 2,000 muskets, some ammunition and money. The expedition had sailed on 8 March, long before disaster had hit the main fleet. Avoiding the British men-of-war patrolling the western approaches to the English Channel, the little flotilla eventually reached the Isle of Lewis in the Outer Hebrides, dropping anchor on its western coast before sailing round to Stornoway.

Meanwhile, the Marischal's younger brother, James Keith, had left San Sebastian for France, where he gathered together a small group of Jacobite exiles in Paris. They included William Murray, Marquis of Tullibardine, and his younger brother, Lord George Murray, as well as George

MacKenzie, Earl of Seaforth, and Colin Campbell of Glendaruel. On 19 March, they set off from Le Havre in a small boat, intending to sail east into the North Sea and then north around the Orkneys, before making for the Outer Hebrides. But strong easterly winds forced them to head west around Ireland to Stornoway, which they reached on 24 March. A few days later, the two Spanish frigates, with the Earl Marischal and his forces on board, also arrived.

After a quarrel over leadership of the expedition between Tullibardine and the Earl Marischal, Tullibardine took command, but the Earl Marischal refused to relinquish control of the Spanish frigates entrusted to him by Alberoni. Worse arguments followed about tactics but it was eventually agreed to land immediately on the mainland and then advance rapidly against Inverness, which was believed to be garrisoned by only 300 troops loyal to the government. On 4 April 1719, the ships sailed from Stornoway for Loch Alsh, were forced by contrary winds to put into Gairloch and set out again, only to be driven back to Lewis. It was not until 13 April that they finally entered Loch Alsh, dropping anchor off the MacKenzie castle of Eilean Donan. All of the arms and ammunition were ferried ashore, to be stored in the castle, which now became the Jacobite headquarters. Next day, Campbell of Glendaruel sounded out the Jacobite chiefs, who all refused to make a move until they knew that Ormonde had landed in strength.

The next few weeks were frittered away in more arguments amongst the leaders of the expedition. Matters deteriorated when John Cameron, Younger of Lochiel, and Ranald MacDonald of Clan Ranald arrived from the Continent with the news that Ormonde's fleet had not even left Corunna. Tullibardine was all for sailing back to Spain but the Earl Marischal forced the issue, marooning the Jacobite forces on the mainland by ordering the Spanish frigates to put to sea. They then had a narrow escape from five British navy ships blockading the mouth of Loch Alsh.

Under an artillery bombardment from the British warships, the forty-five Spaniards guarding Eilean Donan Castle offered little resistance and, on 10 May, it was soon captured. Having seized its large stock of gunpowder and musket bullets, the government forces blew up the castle and destroyed its buildings, along with a magazine at the head of the loch.

By now, the government had sent Major General Joseph Wightman north with more troops to reinforce the garrison at Inverness. On 5 June, he marched out of the town with nearly 1,000 troops, mostly Dutch, and was joined by over a hundred Highlanders, recruited from the Whig clans loyal to the government. Tullibardine also tried to raise more Jacobite clansmen but only Seaforth provided a sizeable detachment, consisting of 500 MacKenzies. Smaller numbers were raised by Lord George Murray,

John Cameron, Younger of Lochiel, and also by Rob Roy MacGregor, and a few others arrived later. All together, the Jacobite clans contributed at most 1,000 men and they were apparently less than enthusiastic.

At Loch Ness, the Hanoverian forces rested for a day, before marching west along Glenmoriston towards Kintail on 7 June. As a stand now had to be made, Tullibardine took up a defensive position near the head of Glenshiel. W. R. Dickson, writing much later as the historian of the 1719 uprising, described it as being:

> where the present road crosses the River Shiel by a stone bridge, some five miles above Invershiel [and the sea]. Here a shoulder of the mountain juts into the glen on its northern side, and the glen contracts into a narrow gorge, down which the Shiel, at this point a roaring torrent, runs in a deep rocky channel, between steep declivities covered in heather, bracken, and scattered birches. Above the pass the glen opens out into a little strath . . . between the river and the hill, from which it was entirely commanded.

The Jacobite forces took up their positions on the evening of 9 June, throwing up trenches, and barricading the road.

By 2 p.m. on 10 June (which happened to be James Edward Stuart's birthday), Wightman's forces came into sight of the Jacobites who were entrenched in a position of considerable strength. James Keith later wrote: 'Our right was covered by a rivulet that was difficult to pass, and our left by a ravine, and in the front the ground was so rugged and steep that it was almost impossible to come at us.' Under the command of Tullibardine and Glendaruel, the Spanish infantry occupied the trenches north of the river, along with the Camerons of Lochiel, the MacDonalds of Glengarry and 200 of Seaforth's MacKenzies. The rest of Seaforth's clansmen, under the Earl Marischal, defended the extreme left of the Jacobite line. Another 150 men under Lord George Murray occupied the slopes lying to the south of the River Shiel. Wightman's men were similarly disposed, with the bulk of the infantry on the right wing, while the left wing consisted of a single regiment, flanked by eighty Munro clansmen. The dragoons kept to the road, where the mortars were also positioned.

By the time the engagement began, it was late in the afternoon. Lord George Murray's men were initially attacked by Wightman with a barrage of mortar fire and then they were assaulted by Hanoverian infantry. They withdrew beyond the high banks of the stream. Next, the Jacobite forces north of the road were targeted. Again, Wightman's mortars opened up from the road before his infantry advanced against Seaforth's position on the extreme left of the Jacobite line, in such a powerful assault that Seaforth called on Rob Roy MacGregor for reinforcements. But it was too late. Seaforth himself had been wounded and his men scattered. Then the MacGregors and then the MacDonalds of Glengarry also retreated, abandoning the Spanish troops to fend for themselves.

Only the Spanish came out of this battle with any military credit. Despite coming under a devastating mortar barrage, their commander still wanted to attack the enemy. But, by then, the Jacobite officers had given up.

Next day, the Spaniards surrendered to Wightman. Treated as prisoners of war, they were eventually taken to Edinburgh, where they joined their countrymen captured at Eilean Donan Castle and, finally, they were all sent back to Spain. As for the Scots, the rank and file clansmen mostly headed home quietly, while their officers took to the hills, eventually slipping away to the Continent. James Keith and his brother, the Earl Marischal, took a boat from Peterhead to the Continent. James Keith became a Field Marshal under Frederick the Great of Prussia and died in his service in 1758, while his brother served as Prussian ambassador, first to France and then Spain, visiting Scotland briefly in the 1760s, after receiving a pardon from George III. Only Tullibardine returned to Scotland to fight for the Jacobite cause, raising the Stuart standard at Glenfinnan in 1745 in the presence of the Old Pretender's son, Charles Edward Stuart.

General Wade's 'Royal Protection': Soldiers, Barracks and Military Roads

The year after the failed 1719 uprising, Spain was forced to abandon its war with Britain and France, and Alberoni fell from power. Britain subsequently enjoyed nearly two decades of peace under the ministry of Sir Robert Walpole as diplomatic relations flourished with the other European powers. Even so, the Hanoverian regime remained vulnerable to foreign intervention, while the Jacobite clans still posed a danger at home. The government was sufficiently alarmed by a report by Simon Fraser, Lord Lovat, about the lawless state of the Highlands to dispatch General George Wade north in July 1724. He had a commission 'to go into the Highlands of Scotland, and narrowly to inspect the present situation of the Highlanders, their customs, their manners, and the state of the country'.

General Wade is best known for the many miles of military roads that he and his successors built throughout much of the Highlands during the eighteenth century. He was a professional soldier of Anglo-Irish ancestry, who became the MP for Bath in 1722. An expert in counter-insurgency, Wade was charged with maintaining the internal security of the country and his status was such that a verse in his honour was even added to the National Anthem around this time: 'May he sedition hush, And like a torrent rush, Rebellious Scots to crush.' However, as *Brewer's Dictionary of Phrase and Fable* comments, the words 'send her victorious' have a distinctly Jacobite ring, while the verse containing the line was apparently engraved on a glass tankard belonging to a family of staunch Jacobites.

Reporting back to the government, Wade estimated the total fighting strength of the Highland clans as 22,000 men, of which only 10,000 were likely to remain loyal to the government in a crisis, while the other 12,000 were 'ready, whenever encouraged by their superiors or chiefs of clans, to create new troubles and rise in arms in favour of the Pretender'. Like Lord Lovat, Wade deplored the state of endemic lawlessness in the Highlands and advocated the same solution – namely, the restoration of the Independent Companies. These had been disbanded in 1717 after proving incapable of stemming the 1715 Rebellion. The government responded by appointing Wade as commander-in-chief of the Hanoverian forces in North Britain, accepting his proposal that:

> companies of such Highlanders as are well-affected to his Majesty's Government be established, under proper regulations and commanded by officers speaking the language of the country . . . [and] that the said companies be employed in disarming the Highlanders, preventing depredations, bringing criminals to justice, and hinder[ing] rebels and attainted persons from inhabiting that part of the Kingdom.

Six companies were established with a total of 300 men, divided between three full-strength companies of sixty to seventy men and three half-strength companies. William Grant of Ballindalloch, Sir Duncan Campbell of Lochnell and Simon Fraser, Lord Lovat, had command as the captains of the full-strength companies, while Colin Campbell of Skipness, John Campbell of Carrick and George Munro of Culcairn were the lieutenants of those of half-strength. In 1727, their total complement was raised to 525 men. They were eventually amalgamated in 1739 to form the regiment of the regular army known as the Black Watch.

The duties of these Independent Companies included the further disarming of the Highland clans, since Wade reported that the 1716 Act had largely been evaded. In 1725 another Act was passed, requiring the clans to surrender their arms but, although Wade was satisfied with the final tally of 2,685 weapons, it left a great many arms still in the possession of the clans. Spanish arms had flooded into the Highlands at the time of the 1719 Rebellion and had been kept hidden from the military authorities.

The fact that searches for any illegal arms needed a warrant from a Justice of the Peace did not help, since they were often reluctant to offend their neighbours.

Moreover, it was the Whig clans who mostly surrendered weapons, leaving them seriously ill-equipped to rally to the Hanoverian cause in 1745. The Disarming Act of 1725, therefore, had exactly the opposite effect to the one intended, leaving clans loyal to the government without arms, whereas Jacobite sympathisers still had hidden stashes of weapons. Of the Jacobite clans, only the MacKenzies handed in large quantities of arms on the express orders of Seaforth, evidently as part of his bargain with the Hanoverian regime, whereby he received his estates back. Wade, however, believed that no more uprisings were likely in the Highlands, apparently taken in by the fulsome expressions of loyalty to the government that he now received from the Jacobite chiefs, who claimed to deeply regret their past support for James Edward Stuart.

Wade now began strengthening the existing forts in the Highlands, while planning to link them together by a network of military roads. At Castle Hill in Inverness, the tower-house was repaired and extended to provide substantial quarters for a garrison of 400 men, with a parade ground and three-storey barracks. The governor's residence completed the scheme, along with a powder magazine and a chapel. The whole complex became known as George's Fort, presumably after Wade himself, although he named it Fort George in honour of his sovereign. The name was later transferred to the military fortress built at Ardersier after the 1745 Rebellion.

The fort at Kilcumein at the head of Loch Ness was completely rebuilt on a separate site, closer to the loch. It was named Fort Augustus after George II's younger son, William Augustus, third Duke of Cumberland. Work started in 1728 but was not completed until 1742. A central parade ground was flanked on four sides by substantial ranges of buildings, all three storeys high, providing a prison, a room for courts martial, the governor's residence and staff quarters, as well as barrack blocks capable of housing 300 men. Massive stone-faced bastions at the four corners of the parade ground formed the defences of the fort. Diamond-shaped in plan, these bastions each had a central tower and walls capped by a parapet and walkway, leading to sentinel boxes. They were linked together by curtain walls around the parade ground, formed in part by the back walls of the various buildings. Beyond the walls were further defences, consisting of a ditch and a covered way, while a gently sloping *glacis* provided an open field of fire to twelve six-pounder cannons. A thirty-ton armed sloop, capable of carrying 80 men patrolled Loch Ness. A small harbour was built for it, close to the walls of Fort Augustus.

In the years after 1727, Wade constructed a network of military roads linking these forts, in the greatest road-building programme in the British Isles since the Roman occupation. At Aberfeldy, Wade's bridge across the River Tay (built to a design by William Adam) bears this sonorous exhortation:

Admire this military way which extends for 250 miles beyond the Roman frontiers, striding across deserts and marshes, cutting through rocks and mountains, and crossing the impatient Tay. George Wade, prefect of the forces in Scotland, completed this arduous work in 1733, by his cleverness and the immense labours of his soldiers. See what the royal protection of George II is worth!

Wade adopted many Roman techniques, constructing his roads with troops drawn from the standing army. They first dug out the foundations to form a trench, two feet deep, levering out the larger stones with crowbars and smashing smaller ones with sledgehammers. According to Edmund Burt, in the construction of the road along the south-eastern shore of Loch Ness, any solid rock was blasted away by 'miners hung by ropes from the precipice over the water'. Where the road crossed bog, a timber raft was laid instead. Once the foundations were complete, gravel was laid and levelled out with shovels to form a surface for wheeled traffic, including trains of artillery. The roads were quite narrow – no more than sixteen feet wide, often less in difficult terrain. Where rivers were too deep to be forded, bridges were built, usually of undressed stone.

Around 240 miles of these roads and forty bridges were constructed by Wade. One road went along the entire length of the Great Glen, linking Fort George at Inverness to Fort Augustus and Fort William to the south-west. Another ran north to Inverness from the military strongholds of Perth and Stirling in the Lowlands. The branch from Perth followed the line of the present-day A9 for much of the way, passing through Dunkeld, Pitlochry and Blair Atholl, before crossing the Drumochter Pass to the barracks at Ruthven. From there, the road followed the Spey valley almost to Carrbridge, before crossing the hills to Inverness by way of the summit at Slochd Mor. The branch from Stirling passed through Crieff and the Sma' Glen to Aberfeldy, where the best-known of Wade's bridges still spans the River Tay, carrying the present-day B846. It then crossed the hills to the north, passing through Tummel Bridge to Dalnacardoch on the present-day A9, where it joined the other branch from Perth.

Perhaps Wade's most spectacular feat was the road over the Corrieyairack Pass, linking these two lines of military communication. Built in 1731, this road ran north from Dalwhinnie to the headwaters of the River Spey, where it was joined by a spur from Ruthven Barracks. It then crossed the mountains to the north by the Corrieyairack Pass at a height of 2,500 feet in a series of formidable zigzags, before descending the other side almost as steeply to join the road along the Great Glen at Fort Augustus. Wade's contribution to Highland communications was honoured in the contemporary couplet:

If you had seen these roads before they were made,
You would lift up your hands, and bless General Wade.

After Wade was recalled to London in 1740, another 1,200 miles of military road were built by his assistant, Major William Caulfield, mostly in the years following the 1745 Rebellion. Wade's military roads had been intended for the rapid deployment of regular troops at times of emergency but, ironically, the only army that ever marched to victory along them was the Jacobite army under Charles Edward Stuart, which moved south across the Corrieyairack Pass to take Edinburgh in the summer of 1745. Barely six months later, that army returned along the same road, crossing the Drummochter Pass to occupy Inverness in the few weeks that remained before the Battle of Culloden on 16 April 1746.

War of the Austrian Succession

Up to 1740, the Jacobite cause had languished, starved of European support by Walpole's success in maintaining British neutrality in Europe for two decades. However, in 1739, Walpole's hold on power began to slip as he was forced against his better judgement to declare war on Spain in the so-called War of Jenkins's Ear. He eventually resigned in early 1742, after losing a vote of confidence in the House of Commons to an alliance of Jacobite MPs and dissident Whigs, made on the instructions of James Edward Stuart.

The ministry that replaced Walpole was composed largely of dissident Whigs. The office of Secretary of State for Scotland was restored under John Hay, fourth Marquis of Tweeddale, an appointment which proved a disaster for the government as Tweeddale was weak and indecisive. He allowed a vacuum of political power to develop in the Highlands, which meant the Jacobite Rebellion of 1745 could not be promptly contained when it erupted.

Meanwhile, the outbreak of war with Spain had revived Jacobite hopes in England and, particularly, in Scotland. Once again, it seemed possible that European powers hostile to Hanover might support James Edward Stuart's cause. Moreover, in 1740, Britain was drawn into a much wider

European conflict, following the death of Charles VI of Austria. Although Maria Theresa succeeded her father on the Habsburg throne, her position was threatened by Frederick the Great of Prussia, who seized the Austrian territories of Silesia in the same year. It marked the start of what became known as the War of the Austrian Succession.

In fact, the war, embroiling nearly all the European powers, was aimed with wresting the Habsburg lands from Maria Theresa of Austria, who was particularly threatened by a powerful alliance between France, Bavaria, Spain and Prussia. She turned for help to Britain and the Dutch Netherlands, who had guaranteed her position under the Treaty of Vienna in 1731. In June 1743, George II, at the head of an army of British, Hanoverian and Hessian troops, was nearly trapped at Dettingen, trying to drive a wedge between the French and Bavarian forces. However, he led a vigorous infantry counter-attack to win an outstanding victory over the French. The battle itself was the last time a reigning British monarch personally commanded an army in the field.

French Plans to Invade Britain
and Restore the Stuarts to the Throne

Once the Allied victory at Dettingen had forced France back behind its own borders, the French could no longer menace Hanover as a means of exerting pressure on Britain and, indeed, were now threatened by Austria. France now decided to play the Jacobite card, especially as the British government had encouraged Charles Albert of Bavaria to expect territorial gains in Alsace and Lorraine. Encouraged by English Jacobites, who visited the French court at Versailles that same year, Louis XV now decided to try to restore the Stuart dynasty under James Edward Stuart.

By the end of November 1743, Louis XV had agreed a plan for the invasion of Britain, although the two countries were still not formally at war with one another. He appointed the formidable Marshal de Saxe as the Protestant commander-in-chief of an expeditionary force of 10,000 men, which assembled at Gravelines near Dunkirk. However, the French rejected the proposal that three battalions of the Irish Brigade, under that veteran of the 1719 Rebellion, George Keith, tenth Earl Marischal, should simultaneously land in Scotland, deciding to concentrate all their effort on capturing London.

Apparently, Louis XV had summoned Charles Edward Stuart from exile in Rome and, almost inevitably, his presence in France aroused suspicion. Known to history as 'Bonnie Prince Charlie' or the Young Pretender, the elder son of James Edward Stuart was just twenty-four years old. A young man of great energy and personal courage, he possessed all the qualities so lacking in his father, who was known as 'Old Mister Melancholy'. Spirited, attractive and with impeccable manners, Charles charmed all he met.

On 29 January 1744, the Young Pretender arrived in Paris, having left Rome in great secrecy and adopted various disguises. But the British government soon had wind of trouble. British agent 101 (who was François de Bussy, a senior official in the Foreign Ministry in Paris) revealed the French invasion plans in return for £2,000, although his report was not deciphered until 14 February. By then, it was known that a French fleet of twenty-two ships had already left Brest making for the English Channel in late January. British troops were recalled urgently from Ireland and Flanders, while Admiral Sir John Norris was ordered to Portsmouth to take command of the British fleet, which sailed two days before the arrival of the French fleet off the Isle of Wight. Meanwhile, five French men-of-war had arrived in Dunkirk to escort the invasion force to the mouth of the Thames. However, French troops only embarked at Dunkirk on 22 February, after Charles Edward Stuart had arrived at Gravelines as Prince Regent to his father, the Old Pretender.

By then, the British fleet had taken up a position off the coast of Kent to resist the invasion. On 24 February, the two fleets came in sight of one another, drawn up in line of battle off Dungeness. But, as so often in the past, disaster overtook the Stuart cause. A high storm hit the French fleet in the Channel, causing them to slip cables in the night and forcing them to run before the weather back to safety at Brest. In the same storm, the French fleet of transports from Dunkirk was scattered and twelve ships foundered, of which seven were lost with all hands. Providence had once again intervened on behalf of the Protestant succession and the Hanoverian dynasty. Meanwhile, Norris clung grimly to his position off Dungeness against the teeth of the storm, although eighteen of his ships were damaged and one man-of-war went down with all its crew after it was accidentally rammed. A few days later, another storm inflicted further damage upon the remnants of the French fleet at Dunkirk and Marshal de Saxe wrote to Charles Edward Stuart, informing him the expedition was over.

In October 1744, in response to a British demand for Charles's expulsion from French territory, France formally declared war on Britain. The French then attacked the allied forces defending the Austrian Netherlands (as Flanders had been known since the Treaty of Utrecht in 1713).

Precursors to the Forty-Five

On 30 April 1745, the French campaign in the Austrian Netherlands reached a climax when the French army, under Marshal de Saxe, won a decisive victory at Fontenoy over an allied army of British, Hanoverian,

Dutch and Austrian troops. The allied commander was William Augustus, Duke of Cumberland, second son of George II. Fontenoy was a very important boost to the Jacobite revival, raising morale and increasing determination to repeat this victory in Britain. Cumberland's defeat also meant that British troops had to be deployed in Europe, rather than staying to defend the government at home. The effectiveness of a Highland charge against English infantry had also been demonstrated, at Killiecrankie. Shortly after the French victory at Fontenoy, the towns of Tournai, Ghent, Bruges and Ostend all capitulated.

On 25 July 1745, barely a week after Ostend had surrendered to the French, Charles Edward Stuart landed at Lochailort, twenty-five miles west of Fort William, and, on 19 August, he would raise the Jacobite standard at Glenfinnan. However, the government in London were so preoccupied with the fear that France might follow up its recent run of successes with another invasion attempt, that it did nor react with alarm to the news from Scotland. Reports were reaching London that the French fleet was being prepared at Brest and a Spanish force of around 6,000 was thought to be gathering at Ferrol in north-west Spain, along with a squadron of warships. Meanwhile, the English Jacobites were unusually active during August, promising to rise in rebellion if France would send them 10,000 men and 30,000 stands of arms, to be landed near Maldon in Essex.

George II met the threat of a French invasion by drawing on the 6,000 Dutch troops promised to Britain, if needed, for its defence, while two regiments of infantry were recalled from Dublin to garrison Chester. By the end of August, he had hurried back to London, congratulating himself on his prompt action 'when there was any apprehension of danger affecting this country'. But, by then, Charles Edward Stuart was already marching south towards Perth after giving General Sir John Cope and his army the slip in the Highlands.

Nevertheless, by 4 September, the king was anxiously ordering the immediate withdrawal from Flanders of the ten best battalions, under the command of Sir John Ligonier. They reached Gravesend on 23 September, two days after the Jacobite victory at Prestonpans, reinforcing the Dutch troops that had already landed. Their withdrawal so weakened the allied army in Flanders that Marshal de Saxe completed the French conquest of the Austrian Netherlands within a year. After taking Brussels and Antwerp in February 1746, he defeated Britain and its allies near Liège on 11 October 1746. In 1747, he invaded the Netherlands before peace was finally achieved the following year.

It can be argued that the 1745 Rebellion represented the most serious crisis that an eighteenth-century British government had to face. The '45 forced the withdrawal of the British army from Flanders, seriously

threatening British strategic interests and, in particular, the position of
George II as Elector of Hanover. Moreover, the conflict between Britain
and France spread beyond Europe, triggering colonial struggles over
British overseas possessions in North America and India. This is the
broader context to government suppression of the Jacobites after Culloden,
however much its brutality may be deplored.

Chapter Seven

CHARLES EDWARD STUART
ARRIVES IN SCOTLAND

'A Part Worthy of My Birth'

Charles almost certainly did not collude with the French authorities when he set sail for Scotland in 1745, without the approval of his father or of Louis XV and against the advice of his supporters. No doubt, he wanted to force France to support his lone attempt to overthrow George II. Indeed, he wrote to Louis XV shortly before leaving, saying:

> After vainly trying all means of reaching Your Majesty, in the hope of obtaining from your generosity the necessary help to enable me to play a part worthy of my birth, I have made up my mind to make myself known by my actions, and undertake alone a project which some small aid would make certain of success. I venture to hope that Your Majesty will not refuse me such aid. I should never have come to France if the expedition planned more than a year ago [under Marshal de Saxe] had not led me to recognise Your Majesty's good intentions on my behalf, and I trust that the unforeseen accidents, which rendered that expedition impractical for the time being, have in no way changed these intentions of yours . . . Your Majesty's most affectionate nephew, Charles.

The letter failed to mention that he was acting in the name of his father and, in fact, James Edward Stuart was shocked and horrified at the news of his son's adventure. Clearly James knew nothing about it before he too received a belated letter, written before Charles left Nantes.

Revival of Jacobitism in Scotland

The years before 1745 had seen a gradual revival of Jacobitism in Scotland, which had long remained dormant. Discontent against the government had erupted in the Porteous Riots of 1736, when an English officer was lynched in Edinburgh after ordering his troops to open fire on a mob, causing several deaths. But it was only in the late 1730s, as diplomatic relations between Britain and Spain slowly deteriorated into outright war, that the possibility of another Jacobite insurrection was taken seriously.

The first overtures had been made by John Gordon of Glenbucket, who, as a veteran of the 1715 Rebellion, had subsequently come to terms with the Hanoverian regime. However, early in 1738, he sold his estate in Strathdon and visited Paris and Rome on behalf of MacDonald of Glengarry and Gordon of Auchintoul. Claiming to speak for the Highland chiefs, he raised the hopes of the exiled Jacobites that the time was ripe for another uprising, if only James Edward Stuart would come to Scotland to lead it in person.

Glenbucket's initiative had come to nothing but it probably spurred Donald Cameron of Lochiel into action. 'Young Lochiel' (as he was known to distinguish him from his father, still living in exile after the failure of the 1715 Rebellion) had succeeded his grandfather as the chief of Clan Cameron in 1719. In 1739, he was persuaded by Simon Fraser, Lord Lovat, to join what became known as the 'Concert of Gentlemen', a group dedicated to the Jacobite cause. Although Lovat still declared himself a Jacobite at heart, he had pursued power and self-interest after 1715 by posing as an ardent government supporter, achieving reinstatement as Lord Lovat in 1730 and finally receiving a charter to his estates in 1738. By then, however, he had fallen out of favour with the Hanoverian regime in Scotland, which stripped him of his Independent Company in 1739.

Lovat had then brought together several other Jacobite sympathisers, who formed themselves into an Association, dedicated to promoting the cause of James Edward Stuart in Scotland. Its members included: Young Lochiel and his father-in-law, Sir John Campbell of Auchinbreck; James Drummond, third Duke of Perth, and his uncle, Lord John Drummond; and Lord Linton and his brother James Stewart.

As the 'Concert of Gentlemen', they had signed a petition in 1741, promising to raise a force of 20,000 men from the Highland clans if France provided 7,000 or 8,000 troops from the Irish Brigade to fight for James Edward Stuart. The petition was taken to Paris and, although it had no immediate effect, the 'Concert of Gentlemen' was sufficiently encouraged by the French response to contact their English counterparts in London. They declared themselves willing to act if French men and arms were forthcoming.

By 1743, the hopes of the 'Concert of Gentlemen' reached a peak, with Lochiel even arguing that Scotland could go it alone. It would need only '20,000 stand of arms, his Majesty [James Edward Stuart] or the Prince

[Charles Edward Stuart] with a good general . . . to strike a bold stroke for the King'. While the French plans for invading England were being put into place in late 1743, there were rumours that George Keith, tenth Earl Marischal, would set sail for Scotland with 3,000 men of the Irish Brigade. Fifteen hundred men were to land at Inverness and would be joined there by Lovat and his Fraser clansmen, while the rest were destined for the western Highlands, where they would raise the MacDonalds, the Mac-Leods and the MacLeans. However, nothing came of it, since Louis XV evidently decided to concentrate the French attack on southern England.

Nevertheless, Lochiel had hurried north from Edinburgh 'to put things on the best footing he could'. His fellow conspirators were just as active. James Drummond persuaded Lord George Murray, younger brother to the Duke of Atholl, to commit his support for the Jacobite cause. When the French abandoned their planned invasion of England early in 1744, the conspirators in Scotland still remained optimistic that something might be salvaged from the wreckage of their scheme. They instructed John Murray of Broughton to write to James Edward Stuart in Rome, assuring him that their plans for an uprising in Scotland were still in place.

Broughton then went to Paris to find out if France would back this uprising. However, in October 1744, he returned with distinctly alarming news – Charles Edward Stuart had told him that he was prepared to land in Scotland the following summer 'with but a single footman'. The Prince did still have hopes of French support, petitioning Louis XV for 3,000 troops for his expedition. The rejection of this demand was enough to harden Charles's resolve to go it alone, as it was virtually his only remaining choice. Lochiel called the Prince's plans 'a rash and desperate undertaking'.

'A Rash and Desperate Undertaking'

The failed French invasion of England the previous year had left Charles in a quandary. He had returned to Paris to receive a modest pension from the French government but was strictly required to live incognito, while Louis XV and his ministers resolutely refused him an audience. France now appeared to have no interest in supporting the Jacobite cause, after French victories over Britain and its allies in the Austrian Netherlands. Furthermore, although the Whig ministry was not popular in England, the country was evidently not seething with anti-Hanoverian discontent, as France had been led to believe.

Charles Edward Stuart needed to break a deadlock. He knew that France would only offer him military support if a rebellion was already underway and looked like succeeding; however, success was only likely with an irrevocable French commitment to supply men and arms. More-over, the English Jacobites would clearly not rise in arms unless French troops had already invaded the country. Scotland was, therefore, the only place where an uprising could be started without French help, given the reservoir of Jacobite support among the Highland clans. Once a Jacobite uprising seemed on course to oust the Hanoverians, France would then have every incentive to supply men and arms to restore the Stuart dynasty. This now became Charles's strategy.

The Prince may have been encouraged by reports from Edinburgh over the winter. John Murray of Broughton had joined with David Lord Elcho, heir to the Earl of Wemyss, in founding the 'Loyal Club', whose members gave a solemn oath that they would rally to the Prince's cause when he arrived in Scotland. Others, such as the Duke of Hamilton and even the Member of Parliament for Inverness-shire, Norman MacLeod of MacLeod, as well as Dugald Stewart of Appin, Alasdair Ruadh MacDonald, Master of Glengarry, and MacDougall of Dunollie, were drawn into the Jacobite camp. These men still expected the Prince to arrive in Scotland at the head of French troops.

Late in 1744, Charles O'Brien, Lord Clare, had introduced the Prince to Antoine Walsh, as well as several other privateers with Jacobite sympathies. Walsh was a key figure behind the '45 Rebellion. His father Philip was an Irishman who, in 1690, had captained the ship carrying James VII back to France after his defeat at the Battle of the Boyne. Philip had subsequently thrived as a slave trader and shipbuilder for the French navy. Born in 1703 at Saint-Malo, Antoine had carried on the family tradition of slave trading, which went hand in hand with a lucrative career in privateering. By the 1740s, he was among the wealthiest of all the French privateers and an ardent supporter of the Jacobite cause.

By April 1745, Antoine Walsh had agreed to provide Charles Edward Stuart with a passage to Scotland. The Prince wrote back with his heartfelt thanks, saying, 'what you have engaged to do is the most important service anyone could ever do me'. He obtained money for arms and supplies by pawning his jewels in Rome and by borrowing the sum of 180,000 livres from the staunchly Jacobite Parisian bankers, Walters and Son, (who would eventually be reimbursed by Charles's father). By June 1745, a warehouse at Nantes held 20 small field guns, 11,000 muskets, 2,000 broadswords and a good supply of gunpowder.

Despite this massive stockpiling of arms and ammunition, the French authorities apparently had no inkling of the Prince's plans. However, it is difficult to believe that they were taken wholly by surprise when he left for Scotland. Antoine Walsh and his fellow privateers apparently had tricked the French Minister of Marine into letting them charter the *Elisabeth* from the French navy, supposedly to carry messages to France from the Jacobites in Scotland.

In Scotland, the Prince's supporters were becoming alarmed, having heard nothing definite from him. Lochiel offered to visit Charles in France to dissuade him from setting out without French troops. After a long delay, the Prince's secretary wrote back, fobbing him off with the false promise that once the Prince 'knows the intentions of the [French] court . . . he [Lochiel] may be sure of hearing further from him'. John Murray of Broughton also wrote to Charles but had only heard indirectly by May 1745 that the Prince was 'determined to come by the west coast to the Isle of Uist or Mull and hoped to be there in June'. The Jacobite chiefs promptly sent Alexander Ruadh MacDonald with a message for the Prince, begging him not to come without French men and arms. However, it was too late, as Charles's expedition had already left by the time MacDonald reached France.

A few days later, Sir Hector MacLean of Duart arrived at Leith to let Murray know 'the Prince's intended voyage and the signals he was to make' on his arrival. Although Duart was rapidly arrested, the news spread like wildfire among the Prince's supporters in Scotland. Murray rode west into Lanarkshire to alert the Duke of Hamilton and then travelled incognito into the Highlands to visit Lochiel. Lochiel, who had already heard, sent his brother to warn Norman MacLeod of MacLeod. Neither Murray nor Lochiel knew that MacLeod of MacLeod had already written to Duncan Forbes of Culloden, the government's chief agent in the Highlands, saying, 'I cannot help informing you of a extraordinary rumour spread all hereabouts . . . which is that the Pretender's eldest son was to land somewhere in the Highlands in order to raise the Highlanders for a rebellion . . . I shall spare no pains to be better informed and if it's worth while, run you an express'.

The Prince Lands in Scotland

On 23 July 1745, Charles Edward Stuart set foot for the first time on the shores of Scotland. He landed in driving rain on the small island of Eriskay between Barra and South Uist in the Outer Hebrides, after sailing from France with a handful of companions, on board the *Du Teillay*. The ship was a handsome French privateer of sixteen guns, used for trading with the West Indies by its owner and captain, Antoine Walsh. It had a cargo of 1,500 muskets and 1,800 broadswords, along with ammunition and a war chest of 4,000 *Louis d'Or*. After leaving Nantes nearly a month earlier, the *Du Teillay* had sailed north to Belle Ile for a rendezvous with the *Elisabeth*, a man-of-war of sixty-four guns chartered from the French navy. The

Elisabeth carried more arms and ammunition, including 2,000 muskets and 600 broadswords, as well as a hundred well-seasoned troops, known as the Compagnie Volontoire de la Marine de France. Almost certainly, they came from Clare's Regiment of the Irish Brigade.

On 9 July, four days after leaving Belle Île, the ships were sighted by HMS *Lion*, a British man-of-war patrolling the western approaches to the English Channel a hundred miles off the Lizard. For four hours the *Elisabeth* engaged the *Lion*, allowing the *Du Teillay* to escape, and both ships were crippled. The *Lion* was dismasted and took heavy losses, with 45 dead and 107 wounded, and damage to the *Elisabeth* was just as bad. She was unable to continue the voyage and instead had to make her way back to Brest with her valuable cargo of men and arms. Fast and well-armed, the *Du Teillay* escaped unscathed and, having evaded the British navy again on 11 July, reached Eriskay twelve days later.

Charles's companions on his journey from France have been heavily criticised for their influence on him during the '45 Rebellion. They were romantically dubbed the 'Seven Men of Moidart' after the area of mainland where the party landed from Eriskay on 25 July (although there may actually have been eight or nine of them). They included: William Murray, Marquis of Tullibardine, veteran of the Jacobite Rebellions in 1715 and 1719, and now more than sixty years old; Sir John MacDonald, a cavalry officer of French nationality in the Spanish army; Sir John Strickland, an Englishman, exiled in Rome after the 1715 Rebellion; Colonel John O'Sullivan, an Irishman who had served with distinction in the French army (the Prince's quartermaster general); Sir Thomas Sheridan, another Irishman and a veteran of the Battle of the Boyne who was formerly the Prince's tutor in Rome; Reverend George Kelly, secretary to the Prince, who had escaped from the Tower of London into exile in 1736; Duncan Buchanan, a minor Jacobite agent in Paris; and Aeneas MacDonald, brother of Donald MacDonald of Kinlochmoidart and banker to the Jacobite exiles in Paris. Only Aeneas MacDonald had any connection with Moidart.

Often disparaged as unlikely leaders of an insurrection in the wilds of the Scottish Highlands, they had probably just accompanied the Prince as loyal members of his household, together with a score of officers from the Irish Brigade. Even so, they made up an influential coterie of Irish expatriates, who often clashed with the Scots officers in command of his army. Their presence contributed to the failure of the 1745 Rebellion, since the two factions were always quarrelling over strategy.

Charles Edward Stuart only landed on Eriskay because M. Darbé, master of the *Du Teillay*, sighted what looked like a British man-of-war, cruising the waters off the Outer Hebrides. The Prince found himself in

Clanranald country and was visited the next morning by Clanranald's brother, Alexander MacDonald of Boisdale. Instead of the welcome the Prince expected, he brought a distinctly discouraging message from Alexander MacDonald, seventh Baronet of Sleat, and Norman MacLeod of MacLeod, both of whom were especially vulnerable to attack by the British navy. The message was that 'if he came without troops, that there was nothing to be expected from the country, that not a soul would join with them, and that he should go back and wait for a more favourable occasion.' The Prince's party was devastated, especially as Boisdale also refused to join any uprising, saying he would advise his brother to do likewise, and strongly suggesting that the Prince should go home. Charles, however, replied with bravado: 'I am come home, sir, and I will entertain no notion at all of returning . . . I am persuaded my faithful Highlanders will stand by me.'

This painful discouragement appears to have only increased the Prince's determination, and he sailed at once across the Minch to the mainland. Aware of a British man-of-war on the horizon, the *Du Teillay* set sail around midnight on 24 July for the Sound of Arisaig, north of Moidart. The ship anchored at the head of Loch an Uamh (the Loch of the Caves), while Aeneas MacDonald went off in the ship's boat to sound out his brother Donald MacDonald of Kinlochmoidart. The two men returned next morning with several MacDonalds, including young Ranald MacDonald, Master of Clanranald, who also pressed the Prince to return to France to wait for a better opportunity.

Call to Arms

Taking no notice of these negative reactions, the Prince now dispatched Kinlochmoidart with letters to James Drummond, Duke of Perth, John Murray of Broughton and Donald Cameron of Lochiel, asking them 'to advertise all his friends to be in readiness to join him'. Instead of coming in person, Lochiel sent his younger brother Dr Archibald Cameron. Young Clanranald had also been sent to Skye to summon Sir Alexander MacDonald of Sleat and Norman MacLeod of MacLeod. Both, however, still refused to join the Prince, treating his plans as quixotic. In fact, MacLeod of MacLeod rapidly warned Duncan Forbes of Culloden (the government's chief agent in the Highlands) that the Prince had definitely landed, asking Forbes not to name him or Sir Alexander MacDonald as the source of his information.

Lochiel waited until 30 July to answer the Prince's call in person, arriving in a high-prowed galley with Alexander MacDonald of Keppoch. By then, the *Du Teillay* had moved anchorage to the mouth of Loch Ailort, where she lay off the small hamlet of Forsy on the northern shores of Moidart. Her cargo of arms and ammunition had been ferried ashore and carried along the rough tracks through Glen Uig to Kinlochmoidart.

The accepted description of Lochiel's meeting with the Prince was given in 1802 by John Home in his *History of the Rebellion in Scotland in 1745*, following an 1769 account by Thomas Pennant. According to Home, Lochiel advised delay, at the very least, but

> Charles, whose mind was wound up to the utmost pitch of impatience, paid no regard to this proposal, but answered, that he was determined to put all to the hazard. In a few days, (said he), with the few friends that I have, I will erect the royal standard, and proclaim to the people of Britain that Charles Stuart is come over to claim the crown of his ancestors, to win it, or to perish in the attempt: Lochiel, who, my father had often told me, was our firmest friend, may stay at home, and learn from the newspapers the fate of his Prince. No, said Lochiel, I'll share the fate of my prince; and so shall every man over whom nature or fortune hath given me any power.

The likely source of this account was Lochiel's younger brother, John Cameron of Fassifern, whom Thomas Pennant and John Home had both met. He had warned Lochiel not to meet the Prince, worried that he would be swayed by Charles's magnetic charm. Recently, another more authoritative account has come to light in a manuscript entitled *Mémoire d'un Ecossais*, written by Lochiel himself in 1747 and quoted in full by J. S. Gibson in *Lochiel of the '45: the Jacobite Chief and the Prince*. According to this memoir,

> Three weeks passed in argument . . . but at last Mr Cameron of Lochiel, alive above all else to the danger to which the Prince's person was exposed, came out in his support along with the majority of his people whom he made take up arms. The example of the Camerons . . . brought in some neighbouring clans, and the Prince found himself at the head of 2,500 men, reasonably well-armed.

Contrary to popular legend, Lochiel appears not to have fallen immediately under the Prince's spell, since the next three weeks were spent in indecisive arguments about what to do. Charles obviously became exasperated, since he wrote on 6 August to all the Jacobite chiefs, summoning them to muster with their clansmen at Glenfinnan on 19 August 1745. Two days later, before the Prince had any firm promise of support from the clans, the *Du Teillay* sailed for France with Antoine Walsh. The ship's log records that 'we left him [Charles Edward Stuart] with two of the gentlemen who had come over with him, two chiefs of the district, and with no more than a dozen men–these being all his companions'. The die was cast.

The ship's departure had cut off all possibility of retreat for the Prince, who stayed at Borrodale for the next few days, guarded by Clanranald's men, before moving to Kinlochmoidart. Soon all the capitals of Europe would hear the startling news of his dramatic landing in Moidart from Antoine Walsh, who reached the Netherlands on 23 August, after sailing around the north of Scotland. He promptly hired a carriage to take him to Versailles, where he pressed Louis XV to help the Young Pretender with men and arms.

By effectively stranding himself, Charles had forced Lochiel's hand, ten days before he was finally persuaded to join the uprising. No doubt, Lochiel felt that he had no honourable choice but to support the Prince, whatever his misgivings. Even so, Lochiel's decision was probably influenced by a warrant issued in June to arrest him, together with James Drummond. Both had been incriminated by papers that Sir John MacLean of Duart had been carrying when seized in Edinburgh. Duncan Forbes of Culloden regretted the action taken against Lochiel, on the grounds that it could have tipped him into outright rebellion. Nevertheless, Lochiel did insist on security from the Prince for the full value of his estate if the rebellion aborted. It was a promise the Prince would honour after the failure of the '45, when he procured the command of a French regiment for Lochiel, giving him, in exile, a greater income than all the rent from his estates in Scotland.

Reaction of the Government

Although the Prince's supporters in the Highlands were shocked by his sudden arrival, Charles had achieved the crucial element of surprise, not to say incredulity, for the outbreak of the uprising. The government in London was only alerted to possible danger at the very end of July 1745, when Tweeddale, Secretary of State for Scotland, wrote that 'the French Court was mediating an invasion of His Majesty's dominions; [and] the Pretender's son had sailed from Nantes in a French man-of-war, and was actually landed in Scotland, which last part I can hardly believe to be true.' A proclamation was issued in London on 1 August, offering a reward of £30,000 'to any person who shall seize and secure the eldest son of the Pretender, in case he shall land, or attempt to land, in any of his Majesty's dominions'.

The Young Pretender's landing was soon confirmed. Archibald Campbell, third Duke of Argyll, was among the first to hear the 'very extraordinary news . . . that a vessel is landed in Arisaig with 200–300 men . . . among whom are the Pretender's eldest son, General Keith and old Lochiel'. Argyll wrote at once to the Duke of Newcastle in London, who received the news on 13 August. He was immediately convinced that:

> the description of the vessel; the number of men and arms said to be on board; and the circumstances reported, that they sailed in company with a man-of-war which had engaged an English vessel . . . answer so exactly the accounts we have received of the frigate that was in company with the *Elisabeth* that there hardly can be any doubt but that it is the same; and that the Pretender's son is now actually landed in some part of Scotland.

Newcastle was, however, more concerned that the French might actually be planning to invade the south of England.

Although, a fortnight later, Tweeddale was still incredulous, Lieutenant-General Sir John Cope was ordered, as the commander-in-chief of the Hanoverian forces in Scotland, 'to assemble as great a number of troops as he could get together and march directly to the place where the enemy were to rendezvous; and to endeavour to attack and suppress them at once'. Cope had just under 4,000 men in Scotland, consisting of two regiments of Irish dragoons, three and a half regiments of infantry and nine 'additional' companies of raw recruits. The dragoons were commanded by Colonels Gardiner and Hamilton but they were undisciplined and poorly trained, and their horses had never been exposed to gunfire. The infantry regiments were mostly under strength and only one had seen action. Moreover, although Edinburgh Castle held plenty of field guns and ammunition, there was not a single artillery officer in all of Scotland. Furthermore, Cope did not have enough money for food for his army. Not until 17 August did the government in London give him authority to raise a loan from the merchants of Edinburgh. Two days later, he marched north into the Highlands to confront the Jacobite threat.

Chapter Eight

MARCH SOUTH TO EDINBURGH

The Standard is Raised

On 19 August 1745, the Jacobite standard was raised at Glenfinnan, after Charles Edward Stuart had sailed up Loch Shiel from Kinlochmoidart. The rendezvous itself was set for 1 p.m. but only 150 clansmen, under Alan MacDonald of Morar, appeared on time. After the Prince and his followers had waited anxiously for two hours, Lochiel and Alexander MacDonald of Keppoch at last arrived with around 700 Camerons and 300 MacDonalds. Sir John Macdonald later described their relief: 'Never have I seen anything so quaintly pleasing as the march of this troop of Highlanders as they descended a steep mountain by a zig-zag path.' The Highland army, now around 1,200 strong, was rapidly drawn up in ranks and Tullibardine had the honour of unfurling the Stuart Standard and of proclaiming James Edward Stuart king.

The ceremony at Glenfinnan was witnessed by Captain Swettenham, a government military engineer, and by a number of his men, who had all been taken prisoner by the Jacobites in the first engagement of the 1745 Rebellion. Earlier in August, Jacobite spies had reported that three companies of government troops were to march from Inverness to Fort William and another three companies from Ruthven of Badenoch would escort provisions to Fort Augustus. Lochgarry was immediately sent to watch the Corrieyairack Pass, while Keppoch and his clansmen were to attack the government troops advancing along the Great Glen from Inverness, where two companies of newly-raised troops under Captains Swettenham and Scott were marching along the military road towards Fort William. The government troops had almost reached Wade's High Bridge across the River Spean when they were ambushed by a group of MacDonalds guarding its far side and several of them were killed or wounded, including Scott himself. He was then forced to surrender along with eighty-two of his men, including Swettenham, later a witness to the ceremony at Glenfinnan.

Afterwards, Swettenham was released on parole after promising he would not serve against the Jacobites for a year and a day. He honoured his promise, and, according to John O'Sullivan, proved useful to the Jacobites:

> This officer behaved very gallantly, he frightened the governors of the garrisons he passed by, and even Cope. For he told them all, that the Prince had 6,000 men, and that neither arms or money was wanting to them; he gave everywhere the most favourable account that could be given of the Prince's activity and person. It is said the Elector [George II] sent for him when he arrived in London, and asked him what kind of a man the Prince was, [and] he answered that he was as fine a figure, as a clever a Prince as a man could set his eyes on, upon which George turned his back, and left him there.

The Corrieyairack Pass

After the Jacobite Standard was raised, Charles stayed at Glenfinnan for two days, while Young Clanranald brought in more men. Then the Jacobite army marched off to Kinlochiel, where the Prince was first told about the £30,000 reward for his capture. Charles retaliated with a proclamation, offering the insulting sum of £30 for George II, although he later had to increase it to match the £30,000 on his own head – he had also managed to offend the Highlanders who failed to see why they should be expected to risk their lives for a pittance. On 23 August, the Prince marched to Fassifern, where he was received graciously by Lochiel's sister-in-law, although her husband, John Cameron, had sought sanctuary in Fort William. He would take no part in the uprising.

Next day, a British warship was reported to be lying off Fort William, so the Prince and his army crossed the hills to Moy on the Great Glen. After a day's rest, they marched twenty-five miles along Wade's military road to Glengarry's house at Invergarry, arriving after dark on 26 August. By then he knew Cope was advancing towards Dalwhinnie from the Lowlands. The Prince needed to secure the military road over the Corrieyairack Pass immediately, in what proved to be a critical day.

At Invergarry, the Prince received a message of loyalty from Simon Fraser, Lord Lovat, who also pressed him to march north through the Fraser country of Stratherrick to seize Inverness. According to Lovat, all the northern clans would then rise on his behalf. Devious as ever, Lovat also wrote to Duncan Forbes of Culloden, whom he praised for his 'constant, uncommon, and fiery zeal for this Government', while shame-lessly criticising 'my dear cousin Lochiel who, contrary to his promises, engaged in this mad enterprise'. Lovat assured Forbes that his clansmen would defend the Hanoverian regime, if given arms. However, the Prince disregarded Lovat's suggestion and decided to challenge Cope by marching south across the Corrieyairack Pass instead. If Cope could be swept aside, the way would be open for a rapid advance upon the Lowlands through Badenoch and Atholl.

A sense of urgency now took hold of the Jacobite camp. Long before daybreak on 27 August, an advance party set out on a forced march to forestall Cope by seizing the Corrieyairack Pass. Meanwhile, the rest of the Prince's army marched to Aberchalder, close to Fort Augustus. On the admission of its governor, writing on 13 August, the garrison contained not 'one man who knows how to point a gun or even saw a shell fired out of a mortar'. By now, 400 MacDonalds of Glengarry had joined the Prince under Donald MacDonald of Lochgarry. They brought with them a contingent from their close allies, the Grants of Glenmoriston. The Prince now had around 1,600 men.

On 28 August, the Prince's army made a forced march across the Corrieyairack Pass, ironically exploiting the road designed by Wade as part of a network to control further Jacobite insurrections after 1719. Late in the evening, he reached Garvamore and was most disappointed to learn that Cope was actually heading away from him at breakneck speed towards Inverness. Cope had left Stirling on 20 August with all his available forces, first marching to Crieff to meet John Campbell, Lord Glenorchy, and James Murray, second Duke of Atholl. Cope had expected them to raise a considerable number of men for the government and was shocked to find that all they could come up with were a dozen MacGregors, who promptly deserted. Cope had brought north 1,500 stands of arms for the men he had hoped to recruit en route and was now forced to send half back to Stirling under armed escort.

Having originally wanted to send only a token force of 300 men north to reinforce the garrisons along the Great Glen, Cope himself was inclined to return to Stirling. But he received repeated orders from London to advance in strength against the Jacobite threat and had to comply. He made slow progress through Aberfeldy, Tummel Bridge and Dalnacardoch, only crossing the Drumochter Pass to reach Dalwhinnie on 26 August. The country was hostile and his army was subjected to random acts of sabotage, while he was unable to requisition the transport needed to haul his artillery pieces and stores.

Cope's intention had been to continue from Dalwhinnie over the Corrieyairack Pass to Fort Augustus. However, one of his officers advised him that:

the south side of the Corrieyairack Pass is of so sharp an ascent, that
the road traverses the whole breadth of the hill seventeen times before
it arrives at the top . . . each traverse in ascending is commanded by
that above it; so that even an unarmed rabble, who were poised on the
higher ground, might, without exposing themselves, extremely harass
the troops in their march. Whence, the attempting to force the
seventeen traverses, every one of them capable of being thus
defended, was an undertaking which it would have been madness
to engage in.

Cope decided not to take the risk.

In *Cope's March North, 1745*, Rupert Jarvis has emphasised that Cope
was now faced with a difficult choice. He could remain at Dalwhinnie to
confront the Prince's army, but he was running low on stores and there
were many other passes heading south through the mountains which the
Prince's army could take. Alternatively, Cope could withdraw south to
Stirling, to try to stop the Jacobites from crossing the River Forth. But the
country now behind him had been distinctly hostile, while the Jacobite
forces might well cut off his retreat by advancing south faster than his own
army. He, therefore, decided to march along the other branch of Wade's
Road from Dalwhinnie, making for Inverness by way of Strathspey.

By the evening of 27 August, Cope was at Ruthven Barracks in
Badenoch. There, a spy in the Jacobite camp gave him the disquieting
news that the Prince intended 'to meet our army next morning, if we came
by Corrieyairack; if not, to meet us at Slochd Mor', where Wade's road
passed through a deep ravine as it crossed the hills towards Inverness from
Strathspey. Faced with this threat, Cope left the following morning,
marching in the 'greatest hurry and disorder' along Strathspey. After
camping overnight near Carrbridge, he crossed safely over Slochd Mor to
reach Inverness on the evening of 29 August after yet another forced
march. Cope had extricated his army with 'prudence and expediency' from
a difficult position, covering forty-four miles in two days after 'making his
front his rear', as O'Sullivan succinctly put it.

Charles Advances South to Perth

The Prince was now more determined than ever to march south from
Garvamore, since there was 'nothing to oppose him from thence to
Edinburgh' and he was no longer looking for an early confrontation with
Cope's army. However, an early victory over government forces would
certainly have helped recruit men to the Jacobite army. Instead, there was a
hiatus of more than three weeks before Charles defeated Cope and then it

was in the Lowlands at Prestonpans. Delaying a potential military success in the Highlands probably set the Prince's cause back, since it took most of October 1745 until all of the strongly pro-Jacobite clans had joined his army in Edinburgh.

The decision taken, the Prince marched his army south to Dalwhinnie on 29 August. This was Charles's first day of hot and sunny weather in Scotland and tradition has it that he spent the night in the open, sleeping out in the heather. He frequently marched on foot at the head of his army, often setting so fast a pace that the rank and file complained to their officers. Charles himself was very buoyant: 'I keep my health better in the wild mountains here than I used to the *Campagnie Felice* [gentle country] and sleep sounder lying on the ground than I used to in the palace at Rome.' Next day, he and his army crossed the Drumochter Pass into Atholl, staying overnight at Dalnacardoch, before moving on to Blair Castle the following day. According to John Murray of Broughton, the Prince

> on the road was extremely pleased with the sight of the people of the country; men, women and children who came running from their houses, kissing and caressing their master [Tullibardine] whom they had not seen for thirty years before, an instance of the strongest affection, and which could not fail to move every generous mind with a mixture of grief and joy.

On 1 September, the Prince reviewed his army at Blair Castle. Growing daily in strength, its ranks were now swollen by 300 Stewarts of Appin under Charles Stewart of Ardshiel ('a very worthy sensible man, but of prodigious bulk') and by 120 MacDonalds under Alasdair MacIain of Glencoe, grandson of the chief murdered by government forces in the Glencoe Massacre of 1692. A shortage of arms, however, forced Lochiel to send 150 of his own men home. Lord William Nairne also joined the Prince at Blair Castle. He was a cousin of Lord George Murray, younger brother of Tullibardine. Like his two cousins, Lord Nairne was a veteran of the 1715 uprising, during which he had been captured at Preston. Another recruit welcomed for his military experience was Colonel John Roy Stewart, a cavalry officer holding a commission in the British army. He later commanded the Jacobite regiment raised at Edinburgh.

The following day, the army resumed its march south, crossing the battlefield at Killiecrankie (where, in 1689, 'Bonnie Dundee' had won a famous victory for the Prince's grandfather) and then negotiating the Pass of Killiecrankie. That night, Charles stayed at the House of Lude, where he cut a fine figure, dancing a minuet after dinner. He spent the following night at Dunkeld House and then, on the evening of 4 September, he made a triumphal entry on horseback into Perth, to proclaim his father King James VIII.

Lord George Murray and Charles Edward Stuart:
Personalities at War

Charles spent nearly a week at Perth, where he was joined by a number of leading Jacobites. The most important figures included Lord George Murray, younger brother to the Duke of Atholl, and James Drummond, whom the Jacobites recognised as the Duke of Perth. Few men could have been so different in character, but the Prince gave them joint responsibility as lieutenant-generals of the Jacobite army, while he himself held supreme command. William Drummond, Lord Strathallan, was made brigadier-general, while John O'Sullivan was confirmed as quartermaster with the rank of major-general. Other leading figures, such as John Gordon of Glenbucket, Lord David Ogilvie, and Lord William Nairne, acted as regimental commanders.

The appearance of Lord George Murray in the Jacobite camp caused a sensation throughout Scotland. Since 1725, when he had been pardoned for his part in the Rebellions of 1715 and 1719, Murray's Jacobite sympathies had lain dormant for twenty years. Once an ardent opponent of the Act of Union in 1707, he had later come to terms with the Hanoverian regime but did not take the oath of allegiance to George II until 1739. Moreover, he had just been appointed Sheriff Depute of the Regality of Atholl, while his eldest son, John, was an officer in Loudon's Regiment.

In a letter to his children, Lord George Murray explained why he joined the 1745 Rebellion:

> Ever since I could form a judgement of things, I have been fully convinced that the setting aside of the Royal line [of the Stuarts] was an act of the greatest injustice . . . I am as much against Popery and arbitrary power as any person in the land, whatever was the danger at Revolution times – and things are now so altered that I think it impossible for the Roman Catholic religion being established in Britain – and that for our liberties they are, in my opinion, at an end without another Revolution. Can anybody be persuaded that we are free when corruption and bribery are come to such a pitch that not only the Members of Parliament but even the electors are bribed? Has not this evil increased every seven years these thirty years passed? It is come to such a pitch that the Ministers of the Reigning Family have openly declared that every man has his price. Has not the

practice of these Ministers shown that by bribery alone they would rule? God forbid that mankind should be so degenerate as these men make them – though their success has indeed been greater than could have been conceived!

Have not infinite treasure been expended by Britain these thirty years in wars all entered into for and upon account of the Electors of Hanover? The whole debts of the nation might have been extinguished by this time had it not been for these wars. None since the Peace of Utrecht [1713] has been for the interest of Britain – but merely for that of Hanover. Upon the whole I am satisfied there is a much greater need of a Revolution now to secure our liberties and save Britain than there was at the last – even if the King's right were not in question.

These forthright views, expressed with such vehemence, were probably shared by many of his fellow-Jacobites in Scotland.

Despite his earlier commitment to Jacobitism, Murray was always seen as suspect by the Prince's household, who denigrated him behind his back and would later blame him for the failure of the Forty-Five. He did not even have a good relationship with the Prince himself, and it was to deteriorate alarmingly during the campaign, as cam be seen from correspondence between Murray and Charles in January 1746, soon after the Jacobite army had returned to Scotland from Derby.

In his letter, Murray asked that a council of war should be called from time to time, which all commanders would attend to reach majority agreement in the Prince's presence on all military operations. But this desire for consultation was anathema to the Prince who was convinced of his own absolute authority to act as he saw fit. Charles replied in a tone of injured pride and furious incomprehension:

When I came into Scotland I knew well enough what I was to expect from my enemies, but I little foresaw what I meet with from my friends. I came vested with all the authority the King [James Edward Stuart] could give men, one chief part of which is the command of his armies, and now I am required to give this up to fifteen or sixteen persons . . . By the majority of these [persons] all things are to be determined, and nothing left to me but the honour of being present at their debates . . . I am often hit in the teeth that this is an army of volunteers, and consequently very different from one composed of mercenaries. What one would naturally expect from an army whose chief officers consist of gentlemen of rank and fortune, and who came into it merely upon motives of duty and fortune, is more zeal, more resolution and more good manners than those that fight merely for pay; but it can be no army at all where there is no general, or which is the same thing no obedience or deference paid to him. Everyone knew before he engaged in the cause, what he was to expect in case it miscarried, and should have stayed at home if he could not have faced death in any shape; but can I myself hope for better usage? At least I am the only person upon whose head a price has already been set, and therefore I cannot indeed threaten at every other word to throw down my arms and make my peace with the Government. I think I show every day that I do not pretend to act without taking advice, and yours [Murray's] oftener than anybody's else, which I shall still continue to do . . . My authority may be taken from me by violence, but I shall never resign it like an idiot.

Frank McLynn, in *Charles Edward Stuart: A Tragedy in Many Acts*, describes Murray as 'a cold, aloof, blunt-spoken aristocrat, who always told the truth as he saw it, regardless of the unpopularity of his advice.' Unused to such straight talking, Charles took offence, especially when Murray proved immune to the Prince's much-vaunted charm. Mutual antipathy surfaced at their very first meeting, when the Prince insisted that 'it is the obedience of my subjects I desire, not their advice.' Another account of Murray's qualities was given by James Johnstone in his *Memoirs*, having acted as aide-de-camp to both Murray and to the Prince:

Lord George Murray, who had the charge of all the details of our army, and who had sole direction of it, possesses a natural genius for military operations; and was indeed a man of surprising talents, which, had they been cultivated by the study of military tactics, would unquestionably have rendered him one of the greatest generals of our age. He was tall and robust, and brave in the highest degree; conducting the Highlanders in the most heroic manner, and always the first to rush sword in hand in the midst of the enemy. He used to say, when he advanced to the charge, 'I do not ask you, my lords, to go before, but merely to follow me', [which was] a very energetic harangue, admirably calculated to excite the ardour of the High-landers; but which would sometimes have had a better effect in the mouth of the Prince. He slept little, was continually occupied with all manner of details, and was altogether most indefatigable, for he alone had the planning and directing of all our operations; in a word, he was the only person capable of conducting our army.

Lord George was vigilant, active, and diligent; his plans were always judiciously formed, and he carried them promptly and vigorously into execution. However, with an infinity of good qualities, he was not without his defects: proud, haughty, blunt, and imperious, he wished to have the exclusive disposal of everything; and, feeling his superiority, he would listen to no advice. There were few persons, it is true, in our army, sufficiently versed in military affairs, to be capable of advising him as to the conducing of his operations.

James Johnstone (known as the Chevalier de Johnstone to the French-speaking followers of the Prince), went even further, declaring that:

had Prince Charles slept during the whole of the expedition, and allowed Lord George to act for him, according to his own judgement, there is every reason for supposing he would have found the crown of Great Britain on his head, when he awoke.

Yet it might be argued that Charles was far more astute in his intuitive grasp of military strategy, while Murray was supreme as a tactician in the field. These differences could simply reflect youthful impetuosity compared to the mature caution of the older man. The difficulties they led to, however, lay in the future.

Edinburgh is Taken

When Cope reached Inverness after his breakneck march from Ruthven, he sent to Edinburgh for ships to take his army south to the Firth of Forth. On 10 September, a fleet of transports and a man-of-war duly sailed from Leith and headed for Aberdeen. Meanwhile, in Perth, the Prince was holding a council-of-war which decided to advance rapidly against Edinburgh, rather than to attempt to intercept Cope's army before it could embark at Aberdeen. The Scottish capital might even fall to the Jacobites before the Hanoverian forces had time to return south. The Prince, therefore, marched out of Perth on 11 September with his army, long before all the expected reinforcements had arrived.

However, more men joined the Prince's army on its way south to Edinburgh, including 150 men raised by James Drummond, together with 60 MacDonalds of Glencoe and over 250 MacGregors under Gregor John MacGregor of Glengyle. The MacGregors had already seized the Hanoverian barracks at Inversnaid, capturing eighty-nine men. Glengyle was now left behind with a detachment of his own men to hold Doune Castle and to keep a constant watch on the garrison in Stirling Castle in case it attacked the rear of the Prince's army.

Two days after leaving Perth, the Jacobite army crossed the River Forth at the Ford of Frew, six miles upstream from Stirling as the crow flies. The crossing went unchallenged by Gardiner's dragoons, who were supposed to be guarding the Forth at Stirling but promptly pulled back as the Prince's army approached. Charles passed the night of 13 September at Leckie House, while his army camped nearby at Touch, beneath the northern slopes of the Campsie Fells. The next day, the army moved on towards Stirling Castle.

Although Stirling Castle was still garrisoned by government troops, the Prince conspicuously marched his army past it with colours flying and pipes playing. Several cannon shots were fired at them as they passed. From Stirling, the army continued through St Ninians and Bannockburn to Falkirk, where the Prince spent the night of 14 September with the Earl of Kilmarnock at Callendar House, while his army camped nearby in the grounds of Callendar Park.

That night, Lord George Murray left Falkirk for Linlithgow, with 800 men under Lochiel, Keppoch, Glengarry and Ardshiel, planning to surprise Gardiner's Dragoons in their camp, only to find it deserted. Early on the morning of 16 September, the Prince took Linlithgow, before advancing towards Edinburgh. Gardiner's Dragoons had already fallen back from Linlithgow to the outskirts of Edinburgh, where they were joined by Hamilton's Dragoons, briefly exchanging fire with the Jacobite vanguard near Corstorphine, just a mile west of Edinburgh Castle. Both regiments promptly abandoned the city at full gallop through Leith and Musselburgh to Haddington.

From Corstorphine, the Prince sent a summons to the magistrates of Edinburgh, calling upon the city to surrender. But, while the city magistrates were agonising over their reply to the Prince's ultimatum, they learnt that the ships carrying Cope and his army from Aberdeen had been sighted off the Firth of Forth. Playing for time, the Edinburgh magistrates sent first one delegation and then another, after nightfall, to discuss terms for the city's surrender. The return of the second delegation's carriage to its stables in the Canongate outside the city walls may have been the opportunity taken by the Prince to enter and seize the city without firing a single shot.

Once darkness had fallen, Charles had ordered the Camerons under Lochiel, along with some MacDonald detachments, to watch the city gate at the Netherbow. The Highlanders avoided the guns of Edinburgh Castle by keeping well to its south and then approached the Netherbow at the foot of the High Street in complete silence. Lochiel initially sent a clansman disguised as an officer's servant to ask for the gate to be opened so that he might retrieve belongings left behind by his master, but the city guard threatened to open fire if he did not withdraw.

Before dawn, as Lochiel was preparing to leave, the gate suddenly opened to let a carriage through. Snatching the opportunity, Lochiel and his men rushed in, dispersing the guard, and 900 Highlanders poured through behind them to take possession of the Edinburgh streets and secure the other city gates. Any remaining government troops retreated to the security of the Castle, commanded by the 85-year-old General Joshua Guest. When the people of Edinburgh woke on the morning of 17 September, they found their city in the hands of 'Bonnie Prince Charlie'.

All was now ready for the triumphal entry of Charles Edward Stuart into Edinburgh, capital of the kingdom once ruled by his Stewart ancestors. Riding at the head of his army, he circled around Arthur's Seat to the south-east, to avoid the guns of Edinburgh Castle, and entered Holyrood Park. There he reviewed his troops briefly, before continuing to Holyrood House with James Drummond, Duke of Perth, and David Wemyss, Lord Elcho, who had joined the Prince the previous night. Charles cut a dashing figure in Highland dress, with a tartan short-coat without a plaid, trousers of red velvet and a blue bonnet trimmed with gold lace and topped by a white satin cockade. Meanwhile, amid scenes of wild jubilation, Lochiel, Keppoch and O'Sullivan had proclaimed his father, James Edward Stuart, King James VIII of Scotland at the Mercat Cross, outside the Kirk of St Giles on the High Street. It was barely a month since the Jacobite Standard had been raised at Glenfinnan.

Chapter Nine

'MASTERS OF SCOTLAND'

Battle of Prestonpans

On 17 September, the very day that Charles Edward Stuart was entering Edinburgh in triumph, Cope began to disembark his army at Dunbar, hardly twenty-five miles away. Had Cope arrived forty-eight hours earlier, history would have taken a different course, as Charles would have been forced to besiege a city already garrisoned by a substantial army. However, it took Cope a full day to land all his artillery, troops and supplies, before moving towards Edinburgh on 19 September to confront the Prince's army. Cope had 2,500 troops at the most (including the dragoons who had abandoned Edinburgh so precipitately a few days earlier). His army spent the night camped out at Haddington, before heading for Musselburgh.

Cope had only reached the village of Preston, just west of Seton House, when he heard that the Prince's army was advancing against him from Edinburgh. He decided to halt, drawing up his troops in battle order to await events. According to some accounts, his army initially faced west, expecting the Jacobites to attack from the direction of Edinburgh. But, when the Prince's army came into view over the higher ground to the south, Cope's lines had to perform a complicated manoeuvre to turn to face south with their backs to the Firth of Forth. Even so, their position seemed impregnable, given the wide area of flat ground they were occupying. As Cope later wrote: 'There is not in the whole of the ground between Edinburgh and Dunbar a better spot for both foot and horse to act upon.' He faced the Prince across a broad stretch of flat and marshy ground, crossed by ditches and walls. As John O'Sullivan said, 'this was not a proper situation for Highlanders for they must have nothing before them that can hinder them to run upon the enemy'. Moreover, Cope's left flank was protected by 'two large ponds and a morass' and his right flank by the high walls of the gardens around Preston House.

In the days after Charles's triumphal entry into Edinburgh, reinforcements had reached his army, including 250 men from Atholl under John

Murray, Lord Nairne, among them Menzies and Robertsons. Lachlan MacLachlan of MacLachlan also arrived with 150 clansmen from Cowal, having evaded the Hanoverian forces of the Duke of Argyll, and they were followed by 100 Grants of Glenmoriston. However, the Prince's army badly needed equipment as well as men, so 1,000 tents, 2,000 targes, 6,000 pairs of shoes and 6,000 canteens for cooking were ordered from the merchants of Edinburgh under pain of military execution. Arms were another priority and 1,200 weapons were found in a thorough search of the city, along with some ammunition.

After two nights in the King's Park, the army itself moved camp on 19 September to the village of Duddingston, just south of Arthur's Seat, leaving a detachment behind to guard Holyrood House. That evening, the Prince was told that Cope's army was at Haddington and he immediately hurried from Holyrood House to Duddingston, where he found his commanders squabbling over who should have the position of greatest honour on the army's right wing. The MacDonalds claimed it as theirs by right because they had occupied it ever since the Battle of Bannockburn. However, after drawing lots, the MacDonalds of Glengarry, Clanranald and Keppoch found themselves placed on the left wing, with the Camerons and the Stewarts of Appin to the right. The argument was only settled when Lochiel agreed to relinquish the right wing position to the MacDonalds if there was no action next day.

According to John O'Sullivan,

His Royal Highness lost no time, got the pipes to play immediately, and set his little army in order of battle. You cannot imagine what courage the Prince's activity, in setting every regiment in order, the joy that he had painted in his face, and his talking some words of Erse [Gaelic] to his men inspired them all. When all was in order the Prince . . . called for all the Chiefs and spoke to them thus: 'You are all agreed upon your ranks, and the order and conduct you are to observe this day, you cannot be ignorant that our good success depends very much on it . . . Remember that . . . you fight for a good cause, while our enemies' consciences will reproach them, to fight against their King [James Edward Stuart] and country . . . So God protect us.' Upon which he drew his sword, 'Now, Gents,' says he, 'the sword is drawn, it will not be my fault, if I set it in the scabbard, before you be a free and happy people. I desire you may retire to your posts, inform your men of what I have said and march.' When the clansmen heard what the Prince had said, all the bonnets were in the air, and such a cry, that it would be wherewithal to frighten any enemy; His Royal Highness made a signal with his hat, and marched.

With his cavalry in the vanguard, the Prince marched at the head of his army through Musselburgh towards Tranent. Just before Tranent, they saw the enemy, occupying the lower ground along the coast to the north. As the Chevalier de Johnstone later wrote:

> We spent the afternoon in reconnoitring his position; and the more we examined it, the more our uneasiness and chagrin increased, as we saw no possibility of attacking it, without exposing ourselves to be cut to pieces in the most disgraceful manner.

Faced with this impasse, further quarrels broke out among the Jacobite commanders and especially between Lord George Murray and John O'Sullivan. Anxious that Cope's army might move off towards Edinburgh to avoid engagement, the Prince gave an order to O'Sullivan that the Atholl Brigade should guard the road to Musselburgh, west of Preston House. Lord George Murray was furious when he discovered what had happened to his men and they were recalled. Even so, the abortive manoeuvre had the effect of unsettling Cope, who apparently now thought himself threatened by a two-pronged attack from the south and the west. Yet, when the attack materialised early next morning, it came from the direction that Cope least expected – the east.

Charles and his commanders had the advantage of local knowledge, provided by a Mr Robert Anderson of Whitburgh in East Lothian, who told them of a concealed narrow track crossing the marshy ground immediately east of Cope's position. A rapid reconnaissance verified this and established that Cope had not even thought of placing any sentries on that side. At 4 a.m. on 21 September, the Jacobite army was ordered to move off in silence, while it was still dark. The MacDonalds of Clanranald, Keppoch, Glengarry and Glencoe pulled ahead under the command of the Duke of Perth. They would become the right wing of the Prince's army when it turned to face the enemy. They were followed by the Duke of Perth's Regiment, the MacGregors, the Stewarts of Appin and the Camerons of Lochiel, who made up its left wing under Lord George Murray. The cavalry was left behind in case the neighing and snorting of the horses alerted the enemy.

Not until daybreak did Cope's sentries warn him that the Prince's army were now only 800 yards away on his left flank, where he least expected them, looking 'like a black hedge moving towards us'. By outflanking the enemy with such a daring manoeuvre under cover of darkness, Murray had achieved the crucial element of tactical surprise. Cope immediately ordered his army to wheel around to meet this new direction of attack, but his men were inexperienced and the manoeuvre was disorganised. Even so, he managed to place his 2,000 infantrymen in the centre of his line, flanked on either side by dragoons. The few field guns he possessed were now on his right wing, guarded by a detachment of infantry. His army was almost completely unprotected.

Thick mist still obscured the movements of the Prince's army as it assembled in lines of battle with some difficulty, so that the left wing started to advance slightly in front of the right. The Highlanders emerged from the mist only 200 yards from Cope's lines, forming themselves into the tightly packed wedges that gave the Highland charge its devastating impact. With a single, terrifying war cry, they broke swiftly into a run and hurled themselves at the Hanoverian lines, although they wavered under sustained fire from the dragoons advancing against them. Even so, the Highlanders returned the fire with a single volley and then threw down their muskets to run at the dragoons, slashing with their swords at the muzzles of the enemy's horses, which bolted. This ferocity drove back the dragoons, who soon fled the field at full gallop, leaving Cope's infantry to its fate. Colonel James Gardiner was almost alone in staying to fight, dying on the battle-field. General Wightman believed that 'he prayed for it, and got his desire; for the state of his health was bad, and his heart broken by the behaviour of the Irish dogs whom he commanded'.

At the far left of the Jacobite line, the Camerons of Lochiel, under Murray, were the first to engage the Hanoverian infantry in hand-to-hand fighting with sword and targe, and, without the dragoons' support, it buckled almost immediately. By then, the Camerons had overwhelmed the artillery on Cope's right wing, stopping the guns after they had only fired a few salvos. However, the Highlanders did not have the expertise to use the field guns effectively.

Elsewhere, a dangerous gap had opened up in the centre of the Jacobite lines, which might have allowed Cope's infantrymen to set up a devastating crossfire. Just as the Camerons had veered left in charging the enemy lines to prevent Gardiner's Dragoons from outflanking them, so the Mac-Donalds, under the Duke of Perth, on the other wing swerved in the opposite direction, concentrating their attack against Hamilton's Dragoons to their right. However, the gap was plugged almost immediately by the Jacobite troops in the second line. Cope's infantry were badly trained to meet such a charge and unnerved by the 'fierce, barbarous and imposing aspect' of the Highlanders, they discharged their muskets too soon. They had no time to reload before the Highlanders were at them and their bayonets were not fixed for hand-to-hand fighting.

The battle was now a rout, as Cope's infantrymen broke under the onslaught of the Highlanders. The casualty figures are revealing – just over twenty Jacobites were killed and only fifty were wounded, while 300–400

of Cope's army died (including five or six officers) and another 500 were
wounded. Fifteen hundred of Cope's men were taken prisoner, trapped
trying to escape through a narrow gap south of Preston House. The
battlefield itself 'presented a spectacle of horror, being covered with heads,
legs and arms and mutilated bodies; for the killed all fell by the sword'.
Even the army surgeons said 'they never saw such terrible gashes as the
Highlanders made with their broadswords'. The carnage was made worse
because the Jacobite officers found it difficult to stop the slaughter. When
Charles Edward Stuart arrived on the battlefield to find Cope's army in
headlong flight, he pleaded with his troops to 'make prisoners, spare them,
they are my father's subjects'.

Such indiscriminate killing allowed the Prince's enemies to exploit the
savage aspect of Highland warfare as a propaganda victory. According to a
Whig historian, writing at the time, many of Cope's army

> were killed in cold blood . . . the foot seeing themselves naked and
> defenceless, and the enemy rushing impetuously upon them sword in
> hand, they threw down their arms and surrendered prisoners. But the
> merciless enemy would grant no quarters, until they were compelled
> by their superior officers. The unheard of manner in which the dead
> were mangled and the wounded disfigured was the great evidence of
> the truth of this.

However, the nature of the Highland charge as a military tactic made such
casualties almost inevitable, since it could only succeed by taking on a
momentum of its own. The belief that the Highlanders gave no quarter to
the Hanoverian troops at Prestonpans made it much easier to justify the
ghastly butchery that followed Culloden.

Cope himself fell back to the west, where he found the remnants of
Gardiner's and Hamilton's Dragoons. He then rode south through Lauder
and Coldstream, reaching Berwick the next day, where he apparently
brought news of his own defeat in person. He left behind an army utterly
destroyed, even if those prisoners eventually released on parole by the
Jacobites did not honour their promise not to fight again.

The government in London already knew that the Young Pretender had
seized Edinburgh and now it heard of the defeat at Prestonpans. Argyll's
secretary wrote to Major-General John Campbell of Mamore, expressing
the initial government alarm:

> We have not got the particulars but that it was all over in five minutes,
> a panic having seized both foot and dragoons who ran off . . . We do
> not know as yet whether the enemy are to return to Edinburgh or

march south . . . God knows what they may turn to; a handful of the scum of the Highlands are the masters of Scotland without burning a pound weight of powder.

George II had already returned from Hanover and he rapidly recalled all the remaining battalions of infantry from the continent, as well as nine squadrons of cavalry. The rest of the cavalry followed later in November.

Return to Edinburgh:
a Hero's Welcome but a Divided Council of War

Charles Edward Stuart spent the night after his victory at Prestonpans at Pinkie House, writing to his father, before returning to jubilation in Edinburgh the following day. News of his victory had an electrifying effect on public feeling in Scotland, as Duncan Forbes of Culloden later described:

All Jacobites, how prudent so ever, became mad; all doubtful people became Jacobites; and all bankrupts became heroes, and talked of nothing but hereditary rights and victory. And what was more grievous to men of gallantry – and if you will believe me, much more mischievous to the public – all the fine ladies, if you will, except one or two, became passionately fond of the Young Adventurer, and used all their arts and industry for him in the most intemperate manner.

According to one account, even the most staunch of Whig ladies were susceptible to his charms since, when the Prince reviewed his troops at Duddingston:

the ladies made a circle round the tent and after we had gazed our fill at him, he came out of the tent with a grace and majesty that is inexpressible. He saluted the circle with an air of grandeur and affability capable of charming the most obstinate Whig . . . Indeed in all his appearances he seems to be cut out for enchanting his beholders and carrying people to consent to their own slavery in spite of themselves.

Hard decisions now had to be made. The Prince's instinct was to follow up his victory at Prestonpans by pursuing the remnants of Cope's army to Berwick. But his generals argued that his own army was still too small and ill equipped to fight effectively, while the troops needed rest after their long march south and the battle. Moreover, Berwick's fortifications would be difficult to overcome. Against his own better judgement, Charles was persuaded to march his army back to Edinburgh. He then blockaded the Castle to try to starve out its garrison under General Preston, who reacted by threatening to bombard the city and opened fire more than once with his cannon, killing several citizens in the streets and damaging many houses. Eventually, the Prince agreed a truce, allowing provisions into the Castle if the shelling ceased.

The Prince now set up a permanent council to meet each day at Holyrood but its makeup reflected the divisions within the Prince's camp. One faction was made up of his closest supporters, including Sir Thomas Sheridan, John O'Sullivan and John Murray of Broughton, who followed his views with question. Also present were the Duke of Perth, Lord William Nairne, Lord Pitsligo and the Earl of Kilmarnock, who all deferred to him publicly whatever their private misgivings. The other was headed by Lord George Murray, usually supported by Lochiel, Clanranald, Keppoch, Glencoe, Ardshiel and Lochgarry, acting as the regimental commanders of the Highland clans, as well as Lord Elcho, Lord David Ogilvie, Lord Lewis Gordon and John Gordon of Glenbucket.

Hoping that Jacobite sympathisers in England would rise in his support once they heard of his victory at Prestonpans, Charles sent off an agent to call them to arms, but the man was captured at Newcastle on 27 September. Amazingly, the Prince made no further effort to rally his supporters in England. Soon after hearing that Charles had landed in Moidart, the English Jacobite leaders had petitioned Versailles for troops to be landed near London to support the rebellion – only with several thousand French troops would they join the Prince 'if his Highness could force his way to them'. Meanwhile, they were busy raising money for arms on the pretext of defending George II.

Reaction in France and the Treaty of Fontainebleau

On 26 September, the Prince had sent George Kelly to Paris with glowing dispatches of Jacobite progress in Scotland and asking for French troops and arms. Kelly, however, was detained in Holland, so that he arrived in Paris long after the news of Prestonpans had reached Louis XV through English smugglers. It placed the French king in a quandary and his ministers, too, were divided. Some advised him that the Jacobite uprising should be exploited as a useful diversion, freeing him to pursue the conquest of the Netherlands even more vigorously; whereas other ministers wanted troops sent to Scotland. A Scottish expedition would mean using the French fleet at Brest but it was also needed in Nova Scotia, where the British had attacked the French stronghold of Louisbourg.

Faced with this conflicting advice, Louis XV stalled. He decided to send Alexandre de Boyer, Marquis d'Eguilles, as his personal envoy to Edinburgh on a fact-finding mission, taking personal greetings to Charles Edward Stuart and the gift of 4,000 guineas.

Nevertheless, once the Irish expatriate officers in the French Army heard of the Prince's progress, they began to look for passages to Scotland. Around 26 September, *L'Espérance* sailed from Dunkirk, followed over the next few weeks by another three ships, *Le Hareng Couronné*, *Le Neptune* and *La Sainte Geneviève*. All Dunkirk privateers, they carried six Swedish field guns and 1,280 muskets, as well as small arms and ammunition for another 1,200 men. Their passengers included the Marquis d'Eguilles and Lochiel's elderly father, John Cameron, as well as a number of Irish officers and their men.

All four ships managed to dodge a British squadron on patrol off Dunkirk, landing in Scotland at Montrose and Stonehaven. The precious supplies were then transported south to Edinburgh in around 500 carts, escorted by the Duke of Atholl's men and the MacPhersons. The Jacobites were buoyed up by the arrival of the Marquis d'Eguilles at Montrose on 6 October, apparently confirming the Prince's argument that France would help once his own forces had proved themselves.

In fact, before the Marquis d'Eguilles had been able to report back to him, Louis XV had actually signed a treaty at Fontainebleau on 13 October, committing himself to a formal alliance with James Edward Stuart against their common enemy, the Elector of Hanover. Under the terms of this treaty, France no longer recognised George II as the King of Great Britain, accepting, instead, the claim of James Edward Stuart to the throne of Scotland and promising also to recognise him as the King of England, if this was the wish of the nation and a free parliament. In addition, France would provide Charles with troops from the Irish Brigade under Lord John Drummond. The bulk of these Franco-Irish troops consisted of the Royal Scots, Drummond's own regiment in the Irish Brigade, supplemented by detachments of fifty men from the other Irish regiments, known as the Irish Piquets. They also included some gunners, as well as a cavalry troop known as FitzJames's Horse. These reinforcements eventually arrived in Scotland during the third week of November, landing at Montrose, Stonehaven and Peterhead, too late to join the Prince on his ill-fated invasion of England. Moreover, although Drummond set sail with around 1,200 men, two transports were captured by the British navy, so that only around 800 troops reached Scotland. This was not the army of several thousand that the Jacobites had expected.

Louis XV was sufficiently encouraged by the news from Scotland to begin laying contingency plans for an all-out invasion of the south of

England. This would involve an invasion force of around 10,000, made up of six battalions of French infantry, as well as the remaining six battalions of the Irish Brigade, a hundred gunners with 200 cannon and three corps of military engineers. The force was to assemble at the harbours of Calais, Boulogne and Ambleteuse (rather than Dunkirk or Ostend) and cross the English Channel in fishing boats and other small vessels capable of sailing close inshore to land troops. They would sail on a single tide, preferably under a strong north-easterly or south-easterly wind to foil the British navy, and start by capturing the ports of Folkestone, Romney and Hyde, lying directly across the English Channel. Once these towns were taken, the French and Irish troops would then march upon London. While preparations went ahead for this landing on the south coast, other forces were to muster further east at Dunkirk and Ostend, to dupe the British authorities into thinking the invasion was directed against Essex.

The Prince's Army Grows

In Scotland, Charles Edward Stuart was raising more troops as a matter of urgency. Two days after Prestonpans, he sent a messenger north once again to MacDonald of Sleat and MacLeod of MacLeod, asking for support. MacDonald of Sleat wavered but was persuaded by Duncan Forbes of Culloden to remain loyal to the government. (He would eventually raise two Independent Companies for government service, although, apparently, they had not even left Skye when the Young Pretender was defeated at Culloden.)

Of the MacLeods, only Malcolm MacLeod of Raasay and his cousin, Donald MacLeod of Berneray, rallied to the Jacobite cause but could only raise forty men and they stayed behind to occupy Perth when the Prince marched south into England. Norman MacLeod of MacLeod, chief of Dunvegan, reneged his earlier promise to support the Prince, raising several Independent Companies for the government during November 1745. Of the other Skye chieftains, John Dubh MacKinnon of MacKinnon alone responded to the Prince's appeal, having little to lose, since he had forfeited all his estates after the 1715 Rebellion. MacKinnon could only get 120 men together, bringing them to Edinburgh by mid-October at which time they were attached to Keppoch's Regiment.

This poor showing from the Skye chiefs was particularly damaging to the Jacobite cause. It meant that Charles could not follow up the victory at Prestonpans by marching south against Newcastle as he wanted to do. Instead, he spent five precious weeks in Edinburgh, waiting for reinforcements and this gave the government time to recall all its troops from Flanders.

Very few reinforcements joined the Prince's army before 3 October, when 300 men, under Lord David Ogilvie, arrived from Angus to form the nucleus of the Forfarshire Regiment. Also arriving at this time was James Graham of Duntrune, Viscount Dundee, who became an officer in Elcho's troop of lifeguards. Given the urgent need for money, Lord Ogilvie was sent to collect excise in Angus. Two more recruits were Francis Farquharson of Monaltrie and his brother, James Farquharson of Balmoral, nephews of John Farquharson of Invercauld, who had played a prominent role in the 1715 Rebellion. They took command of two battalions of their clansmen. Then 400 men arrived under Sir John Gordon of Glenbucket, mostly Grants and Gordons from the upland districts of Strathavon, Glenbucket, Strathbogie and the Cabrach, and they were joined by another 480 from the Gordon country of Strathbogie and the Enzie. Two days later, more men swelled the ranks of the Camerons of Lochiel and the MacDonalds of Keppoch.

The only cavalry at the Battle of Prestonpans had been fifty horsemen under William Drummond, Viscount Strathallan, and they had taken no part in the action. After the battle, a troop of 70–80 light cavalry, known as the Hussars, had been raised in Edinburgh, under John Murray of Broughton. However, on 9 October, Lord Pitsligo arrived in the city. Almost 70 years old and a fervent Episcopalian, he had recruited a number of gentlemen and their servants from Aberdeen and Banffshire to form a troop of 132 cavalry and he also brought a party of 248 infantry from Aberdeen, who joined the Duke of Perth's Regiment. More recruits began to appear, including Kilmarnock's son, Charles Boyd, with some gentlemen, and 300 troops from Balquhidder.

On 15 October, Lord Lewis Gordon, third son of the Duke of Gordon, arrived, to be appointed to the Prince's Council, and was sent north as Lord Lieutenant of Aberdeenshire and Banffshire to raise feudal levies throughout the north-east of Scotland and to collect taxes and excise. Eventually, he commanded around 800 men, who mostly remained behind in Scotland when Charles marched south into England. Recruiting went on all winter and, by late November 1745, the Jacobite army in the north-east had apparently reached a strength of nearly 5,000 men.

On 18 October, the Earl of Kilmarnock finally broke with his family's Whig loyalties and joined his son with the Prince. Two elite troops of lifeguards were also founded, consisting of 70 horse under Lord Elcho with a further 30–40 horse under Arthur Elphinstone. Their officers and men were nearly all Lowlanders, chiefly from the cities of Edinburgh, Dundee and Aberdeen. A week later, a hundred MacGregors arrived from Balquhidder, followed by Ewan MacPherson of Cluny and his clansmen. Marching through Badenoch at the end of August, the Prince had had

Cluny seized and taken as a prisoner to Perth. Cluny, the eldest son of Lachlan MacPherson, already held a government commission to raise a company of his clansmen. However, he had changed sides at Perth, having received the Prince's security for the value of his estates, and he was sent north to raise his clan for the Jacobites. He finally reappeared with 400 clansmen at the end of October.

On 30 October, the last reinforcements reached Edinburgh prior to the Prince setting out on the march into England. The 600 men raised by Tullibardine from his estates in Atholl joined the Atholl Brigade and Colonel James Grante, a French artillery officer, arrived with twelve French gunners, having reached Montrose a fortnight earlier with the Marquis d'Eguilles and bringing six Swedish field guns from France. Together with the seven light field guns captured at Prestonpans, the artillery was attached to the Duke of Perth's Regiment for the march south into England. Another six field guns of heavier calibre were added later, having been brought by Lord John Drummond from France in November.

This, then, was the army that marched south into England, early in November 1745. Contrary to popular legend, it was not exclusively composed of Highland clansmen, although the men did wear Highland dress (perhaps because plaids saved on tailoring costs). Nearly every eye-witness account speaks of Highlanders in Highland dress. Bonnie Prince Charlie himself rode into Edinburgh, wearing a blue bonnet to identify himself with his clansmen. But, as Lord George Murray wrote, on leaving Carlisle: 'I was this day in my philabeg [kilt] . . . without britches . . . Nothing encouraged the men more than seeing their officers dressed like themselves.' Even the men of the Manchester Regiment, recruited in England, 'wore the white cockade, and a "plaid sash" or "plaid waist-coat" '.

Unsurprisingly, the myth soon arose that the 1745 Rebellion was an exclusively Highland affair, an idea vigorously promoted by contemporary Whig propaganda, referring, for example, to the Jacobite army as 'a ragged hungry rabble of Yahoos of Scotch Highlanders'. Such denigration reached its extreme in the words of 'Scoto-Britannus' in the *Caledonian Mercury,* who wrote that the Young Pretender had stolen like a thief into the far recesses of the Highlands, 'there to hatch his dark treason amid dens of barbarous and lawless ruffians . . . men without property or even any settled habitation; a hungry rapacious and uncivilised crew . . . of ungrateful ruffians, savages, and traitors'.

In fact, the Jacobite cause enjoyed much the same basis of support in 1745 as it had done in 1715. Although the Jacobite army at Prestonpans consisted predominantly of clansmen from the western Highlands, its ranks after the battle were swollen by an influx of recruits from the Lowland districts of Perthshire, Angus and the Mearns, Aberdeenshire and Banff-shire. Many of these recruits were raised after Charles had left Edinburgh to march south into England, so that historians of the 1745 Rebellion have tended to overlook them. Given such widespread recruitment north of the River Tay, Gaelic-speaking Highlanders probably did not amount to half of the Jacobite army, although they were the backbone of its fighting strength.

Apart from the Highland clans, it was, therefore, the Episcopalian heartlands of Scotland north of the Tay that lent the greatest support to the 1745 Rebellion, just as it had done in 1715. Hardly any recruits came from the Scottish Lowlands south of the River Forth, where the Presbyterian Church was now well established. However, north of the River Tay, the Episcopalian Church survived, despite its repression since 1715, and it was still a source of strength to the Jacobite cause. Cumberland later recognised this when he wrote to the Duke of Newcastle, soon after arriving in Aberdeen in February 1746:

> The only people to be trusted are the Church of Scotland . . . and here in the North they own that almost all the people are Jacobites and led away by the Episcopals . . . In the South [of Scotland] the common people are as well-affected as in any part of England.

His aide-de-campe also described the non-juring meeting houses as 'deservedly styled the seminaries of Jacobitism', while the Lord Justice-Clerk declared them to be 'the nurseries for . . . spreading disaffection'. Cumberland ordered all Episcopalian meeting houses and chapels to be destroyed as he marched north to Culloden and, after 1746, the Church itself was virtually proscribed by government degree. But, although the Church had, by then, been reduced to four bishops and forty-two clergy, individual congregations might still consist of nearly 1,000 members. As Murray Pittock has commented, the Episcopalian 'clergy were leaders, and the [Prince's] army . . . was recruited from their congregations'.

Although the MacDonalds of Clanranald, Glengarry and Keppoch, who had rallied in strength to the Jacobite cause when the Prince first landed, were all Roman Catholic, the Highland clans who later joined the Prince's army were mostly Episcopalian. One interesting example was that of the Camerons of Lochiel, with chaplains to the clan regiment representing all three denominations. Lochiel's brother Alexander was a Jesuit priest of the Catholic Church, the Reverend Duncan Cameron of Fortingall was an Episcopalian clergyman and the Reverend John Cameron of Fort William was a Presbyterian minister of the Church of Scotland. Although few other clans were so varied in their faith, nearly all the Highland clans of mixed Presbyterian and Episcopalian make-up were Jacobite supporters to some

degree, although often with divided loyalties. Only the staunchly Presbyterian Highland clans stayed loyal to the Hanoverian regime, just as they
had done in the 1715 Rebellion, and they were mostly Campbells or their
allies, apart from northerners such as the Munros and the MacKays.

Several previously undecided clans rallied to Charles Edward Stuart
after he had marched south from Edinburgh in early November 1745.
George MacKenzie, third Earl of Cromartie, had let it be known he
intended raising a regiment, although it was not clear at first which side he
would support. He had assured Duncan Forbes of Culloden of his loyalty
to the government but subsequently turned down the command of an
Independent Company. Cromartie now visited Simon Fraser, Lord Lovat,
at Beaufort Castle on 6 November, where, it seems, the two men agreed to
support the Jacobites. Although Lovat still hesitated, Cromartie raised
around eighty MacKenzies and others from farther north.

Another divided clan were the MacIntoshes, whose chief Aeneas
MacIntosh of MacIntosh, held a captain's commission in the Black Watch.
He was, however, married to 'Colonel Anne' of Jacobite legend. When her
husband refused to declare as a Jacobite, Anne promptly raised 300 of his
clansmen, and placed them under the command of Alexander MacGillivray
of Dunmaglass. She was also instrumental in raising another 600 men from
Deeside under John Gordon of Avochie, who joined the Jacobite forces
around Inverness in February 1746.

The MacLeans were also split, since Lochbuie remained aloof from the
conflict, while Coll spoke out against the uprising, without joining the
government side. The MacLeans of Duart were the clan's main Jacobite
supporters. However, as Sir Hector MacLean of Duart was held prisoner
throughout the Rebellion, they were led by Charles MacLean of Drimnin.
According to the late Fitzroy MacLean, Charles had 500 MacLeans under
his command, although records suggest that only 182 clansmen were
present at the Battle of Culloden. What part they had played in the earlier
campaigns is not clear.

The Government Response to the Jacobite Threat

On 9 August, after hearing news of the Pretender's arrival in Scotland,
Duncan Forbes of Culloden, chief government agent in the Highlands, had
hurried out of Edinburgh 'in his boots to go northwards'. Once there, he
hoped to rally the pro-Hanoverian clans while exerting all his influence to
dissuade the others from joining the Prince. A few days later, he arrived at
his country residence of Culloden House, near Inverness, and persuaded
the leading government supporters in the north to raise a number of
Independent Companies for its defence.

However, there were legal difficulties, as Forbes knew in his capacity as Lord President of the Court of Session. Writing on 8 August 1745, he had admitted that, although 'the Government has many more friends in the Highlands than it had in 1715, yet I do not know that there is at present any lawful authority that can call them forth to action'. This view was echoed by Andrew Fletcher, Lord Milton, Lord Justice Clerk of Scotland, that there was a 'want of proper authority from the government, to take off the prohibition to arm the country, contained in the Disarming Act'. In fact, legal opinion ruled that, in order to call out the local militia, the authority of a lord-lieutenant or else that of the Privy Council would be needed. Both had been abolished. The government was falling foul of its own previous measures to pacify the Highlands.

The Hanoverian regime was learning that it could ill afford to offend the legal establishment in Scotland, which guarded its privileges more jealously than ever after the indignities of the years following the 1707 Act of Union. Nevertheless, the government did manage to recruit a local militia from such Lowland towns as Edinburgh, Stirling, Glasgow, Paisley and Beith. According to the *Scots Magazine*, 3,000 men were raised in Glasgow and the surrounding districts, after Tweeddale had signed a warrant to allow the local magistrates to arm the townspeople. They had 1,000 stands of arms but did not resist the Prince's army when it occupied Glasgow towards the end of December 1745.

On 13 September, a month after arriving in the north, Duncan Forbes finally received twenty blank commissions from the Government

to be distributed among the well affected clans, as [your Lordship] shall think proper. Such a number of Highlanders, being formed into regular companies will . . . not only hinder more men to be raised for the Pretender's service, but a part of them may go and live at discretion in the countries which the rebels have left.

They were to join the Highland regiment already being raised by Loudon. It seems the legal difficulties were simply ignored.

Even so, Duncan Forbes was given little support in raising these Independent Companies, as he confided to Tweeddale's secretary:

I found myself almost alone, without arms, and without money or credit, provided with no means to prevent extreme folly, except pen and ink, a tongue, and some reputation; and if you will except MacLeod, whom I sent for from the Isle of Skye, supported by nobody of common sense or courage. Had arms and money come when they were first called for, before the unexpected successes blew

up this folly to madness, I could have answered it with my head that
no man from the North should have joined the original flock of rebels
that passed the Forth.

Over the next month, Forbes made little progress in raising troops to
support the government. However, on 14 October, Loudon arrived at
Inverness by sea after fleeing from the Battle of Prestonpans, bringing arms
and money. He took command of the 150 Highlanders from his own
regiment, making up the garrison at Fort George. The following night,
Forbes's own residence, Culloden House, was suddenly attacked by 200
clansmen under James Fraser of Foyers, who had received a commission
from the Prince to seize the Lord President and take him as a prisoner to
Edinburgh. The attack was beaten off.

From then on, government recruiting gathered momentum and the
newly formed Independent Companies began to march into Inverness. On
23 October, the first to appear were the Munros, to be followed by a
company raised by the Earl of Sutherland and then by the Grants and the
MacKays. A week later, the sloop *Saltash* brought in £4,000 and 1,500
stands of arms. Meanwhile, Sutherland was actively recruiting more men
for a second Company, which arrived in Inverness on 8 November, after
which MacLeod of MacLeod brought in 400 clansmen with more
reinforcements towards the end of the month. They made the strength
of the Independent Companies up to around 800 men, including 100 from
Inverness itself. Finally on 9 December, 200 MacKenzies, under the former
Earl of Seaforth, appeared, leaving only the MacDonalds of Sleat, who did
not rally to the government until after the Battle of Culloden.

In the western Highlands, Archibald Campbell, third Duke of Argyll,
received a belated royal warrant on 22 October, authorising him, as Lord
Lieutenant of Argyll, to call out the local militia. This happened over a
month after the rout of the Hanoverian forces at Prestonpans and only ten
days before the Jacobite army marched south from Edinburgh towards the
Border with England. Any legal objections were simply bypassed in
Argyll's case since he was seen as having a hereditary right to this position.
Argyll had left Scotland for London a month earlier, at news of the Prince's
landing, but he could not impress the gravity of the situation upon
Tweeddale, who, although Secretary of State for Scotland, did not think
it warranted raising the local militia from among his own tenants. In fact,
Tweeddale refused to listen to his arch-rival, Argyll, until George II
intervened. The government were, therefore, fortunate that John Campbell, Earl of Loudon, had already been granted a commission in May 1745,
to raise three Independent Companies from the Campbell territories in
Argyll and the western Highlands. However, recruiting had been very slow

since men would only enlist on condition that 'they shall be free in 3 months and consequently cannot be sent out of the country'. This was because they were worried that they would be sent to serve abroad to Flanders like the Black Watch. By mid-October enough men to make up the three companies had very reluctantly been recruited but they had no arms for another six weeks, until, at the very end of November, 500 muskets with sufficient ammunition and 500 broadswords eventually reached Inveraray.

Meanwhile, Major-General John Campbell of Mamore had returned from active service in Flanders, where he had distinguished himself at Dettingen and Fontenoy. He was ordered:

> to go to the West Highlands by way of Liverpool, and raise eight Independent Companies of 100 men each with proper officers; and likewise to arm sixteen such companies more without the charge of commissioned officers who are to serve without pay, to be raised from the Duke of Argyll's and the Earl of Breadalbane's countries for His Majesty's service.

On 6 December, six weeks later, Campbell of Mamore finally left Spithead on the *Greyhound*, accompanied by two naval tenders. Stormy weather delayed his arrival at Inveraray until 21 December, where he found around 1,000 armed men.

By then, the Prince's army was already withdrawing north from Derby after its lightening strike into England and was threatening Stirling. Campbell of Mamore was, therefore, asked to send all available troops to its defence, but the six companies he dispatched had only reached Dumbarton by 27 December, three days after the Prince's army had started to enter Glasgow. Meanwhile, another 600 men had been recruited in Inveraray and it was expected that 2,000 men would be under arms by the New Year. By 10 January, there were apparently 700 government troops at Dumbarton, to be augmented by another four companies of the Argyll militia that day. The government forces at Dumbarton followed ten days behind the Jacobite army on its way out of Glasgow to Stirling and they would finally join up with the main Hanoverian army in Scotland on the morning of 17 January, the day of the Battle of Falkirk.

The government forces at Inverness were now strong enough to act. Despite a severe frost, Loudon set out from Inverness on 3 December with 600 men to relieve Fort Augustus, then under siege by the Frasers, under Lovat's eldest son Simon. However, Loudon's forces met no opposition, returning to Inverness after replenishing the garrison with food and supplies. Loudon now decided 'to obtain the best satisfaction that he could for the peaceable behaviour of the Frasers'. Accordingly, on 10 December, he left Inverness for Lovat's country with 800 men and took Lovat into custody, holding him under house arrest in Inverness until his clansmen had surrendered all their arms. But Lovat managed to escape, despite his great age and ill-health. As Duncan Forbes commented ruefully:

> My Lord Lovat, who has for many years been complaining of colds and fevers . . . has mended, as I am told, much in his health since he made a moonlight flitting into the mountains. I wish his march may be found to have been as prudent as it has proved medicinal.

Lovat now committed himself to the Jacobite cause, although he did not command the Fraser clansmen who fought for the Prince at Culloden.

Meanwhile, MacLeod of MacLeod had orders from Loudon to march his forces into the north-east of Scotland, where Lord Lewis Gordon was said to be 'raising men and levying money by force and threats' for the Jacobite cause. MacLeod left Inverness on 10 December with 700 men and, passing through Elgin, secured the boats on the River Spey before the Jacobites could seize them. He was then supposed to continue towards Aberdeen, disarming the country as he went. But, on the night of 23 December while camped near Inverurie, he was surprised and defeated by a superior force commanded by Gordon, including Lord John Drummond's men of the Royal Scots, recently landed from France. It was more of a moonlight skirmish than a full-scale battle but, nevertheless, around seventy of MacLeod's men were killed, wounded or captured and the rest fled, probably only lukewarm in their support of the government. This engagement left the Jacobites in full possession of all the country from Aberdeen to the River Spey. MacLeod fell back to Elgin but many of his men deserted, leaving his force reduced to two companies.

Chapter Ten

NEMESIS AT DERBY

The Young Pretender Marches into England

In early November 1745, after five weeks of waiting in Edinburgh for reinforcements, Charles Edward Stuart finally marched across the Border into England at the head of his army, in the confident belief that large numbers of his English sympathisers would enthusiastically emerge to welcome and support him. In John O'Sullivan's version of events, it was the Marquis d'Eguille's arrival from France in mid-October that

> set everybody in high spirits, and I believe determined more and more the Prince's resolution of going to England. The Prince's intention was always to go into England by Berwick and Newcastle, but the account he had, of the Dutch being landed at Berwick, and the 4,500 prisoners, that the French gave liberty to come over . . . made him change his sentiments or resolution, so it was determined to take the road to Carlisle.

In fact, Charles's council only made the decision after a long and heated debate about strategy, and then only by a single vote.

Once again, crucial disagreements on strategy split the Prince's council. On the one side was Charles himself, who had landed in Moidart in the determination to reclaim the throne of the three kingdoms of England, Scotland and Ireland for his father, James Edward Stuart, or die in the attempt. According to the Chevalier de Johnstone, the Prince 'had his mind occupied only by England, and appeared little flattered by the possession of the kingdom to which, nevertheless, the race of the Stuarts owed their birth and loyalty'. He was supported by the Irish exiles who had come with him from France, as well as by several of the Lowland peers, whose absolute loyalty to the Prince forbade them to question his judgement. They wanted an invasion of England as soon as enough reinforcements had arrived. The opposing faction, led by Lord George Murray, backed by most of his senior officers, rejected this policy, wanting to wait until it was clear that France would support them with men and arms.

Aware of advancing government forces, Murray actually recommended a tactical withdrawal into the Highlands, a terrain more suitable for the irregular guerrilla warfare waged by the Highland clans, evidently aiming to gain enough time for French reinforcements to reach Scotland. However, the Prince would not hear of retreat, insisting that the Jacobite forces, and especially the Highland clansmen, needed another victory to keep up their spirits; with Scotland now in their hands, the only possible next move was to cross the Border and confront the growing strength of the Hanoverian forces.

At Doncaster, Field Marshall Wade was already mustering a substantial force of cavalry and infantry on the orders of George II and, on 19 October, it assembled to march north to Newcastle. Faced with this build-up in enemy strength, Charles argued for an immediate advance against Newcastle, which might have been the best option unless withdrawal into the Highlands was taken as a serious alternative; if Wade's army could be defeated before it actually reached Scotland, the way would be open for a Jacobite march upon London. Victory in the north of England would not only confirm the Prince's control over Scotland, but might also encourage the French to launch a large-scale invasion across the English Channel against London, in a strategy which would threaten the capital from two directions, as the Prince's army marched south. In fact, Louis XV did dispatch 1,200 troops to Scotland under Lord John Drummond that month, while at the same time laying contingency plans for a French invasion across the Channel on a much larger scale.

However, this approach had its obvious disadvantages. Charles seemed to believe that his mere presence on English soil would be enough for the country to rise in arms with him. Admittedly, the Jacobite party in England had agreed to do so eighteen months earlier, when the French invasion was being planned under Marshal de Saxe, but their promise was never put to the test. Equally, Charles seemed blind to the likelihood that the French, under Louis XV, would pursue their own strategic interests at the expense of the Stuart cause and, in particular, there was no certainty that they would jeopardise their recent victories in Flanders by invading England. Apparently, the Prince simply assumed that France would persist in the very policy it had abandoned in early 1744, when storms had destroyed the French fleet at Dunkirk. This gamble evidently did not appeal to Murray and his regimental officers from the Highland clans. As Murray wrote, after the failure of the '45: 'certainly 4,500 Scots had never thought of putting a king upon an English throne by themselves.'

These arguments were raging in the council of war of 30 October, after the last reinforcements expected in Edinburgh had arrived. The following morning, a compromise was eventually reached – rather than advancing against Newcastle, the army would cross the Border just north of Carlisle. By avoiding confrontation with Wade's army at Newcastle, the Prince may have hoped to gain enough time to test out French intentions. Moreover, support for the Jacobite cause was greatest in the north-west of England, especially in Lancashire, where there were many Catholic families. By making for Carlisle, it would soon be clear whether or not the English Jacobites were prepared to risk their lives and fortunes for the Stuart cause. Yet, as Lord Elcho wrote, Charles

knew nothing about the country nor had not the smallest idea of the force that was against him, nor where they were situated. His Irish favourites . . . had always represented the whole nation as his friends, had diminished much of the force that was against him, and he himself believed firmly that the soldiers of the regulars would never fight against him, as he was their true Prince.

The Jacobite army now marched out of Edinburgh towards Carlisle, dividing to take two different routes to deceive the enemy. One column, made up of the Lowland regiments and the artillery, marched south-west through Peebles and Moffat. The other, which consisted of the Highland clans with the Prince and Murray at their head, marched by a less direct route through Lauder and Kelso farther to the east, deliberately giving the impression that they were heading for Newcastle and going so far as to send a troop of cavalry as a feint across the Tweed towards Wooler in Northumberland. However, Wade made no attempt to intervene or to leave Newcastle.

The Prince's column continued south-west through Jedburgh, over the hills by Bonchester Bridge and then down Liddlesdale, crossing the Border on 8 November. Next day, the two columns met up a few miles north of Carlisle, only to find that a large quantity of tents, stores and ammunition had somehow been lost at Moffat. Worse, perhaps as many as 1,000 men had deserted on the way south, while very few recruits had joined up. Crossing the Eden to spend the night in the villages west of Carlisle, Charles Edward Stuart had probably around 5,000 foot soldiers and 500 cavalry at his command.

The following day, the Prince called upon Carlisle to surrender 'to avoid the effusion of English blood' but, receiving no reply, he ordered a siege of the town. Carlisle surrendered within a week, after an abortive attempt to relieve it by Wade, who had marched out of Newcastle on 16 November towards Brampton, where Charles had already mustered the bulk of his army. In fact, due to bad weather, Wade's army got no farther than Hexham, where he was told that Carlisle had already fallen. Wade returned to Newcastle, while the Prince entered Carlisle in triumph, mounted on a white charger.

After the capture of Carlisle, another council of war was held and, again, Murray argued for a return to Scotland. The question was only settled when the Marquis d'Eguilles finally revealed his instructions from Louis XV, over a month after his arrival in Scotland. They made it clear that the French king wanted confirmation of English, as well as Scottish, support for the Jacobite cause. There was no alternative but to march south into Lancashire which was the Jacobite heartland in England outside the city of London.

Murray now had sole command of the Prince's army as it moved south out of Carlisle on 21 November, since the Duke of Perth had resigned as joint commander-in-chief. The Duke, a Catholic, had supervised the siege of Carlisle and negotiated its terms of surrender. Murray objected vehemently since, in the words of Lord Elcho, 'it would have been more proper for Lord George as a Protestant to have signed the capitulation in which there was question of securing the people in the enjoyment of their religion'. Murray promptly resigned his commission to the Prince, who reluctantly accepted it. However, the Highlanders refused to be led by anyone else and the difficulty was only overcome when the Duke of Perth resigned instead.

The Prince's progress south of Carlisle was spectacular. Leaving on 21 November, the army moved on via Penrith to cross the Shap Fells, reaching Kendal two days later. There it halted for a day, to allow all persons of rank to attend Sunday service, both Protestants and Catholics, before resuming its gruelling march south through Lancaster to Preston, where it arrived on 26 November. There the Prince was greeted 'by a great concourse of people and welcomed with the loudest shouts and acclamation of joy'. After a day's rest and another fruitless council of war, called at Murray's insistence, the Jacobite forces moved on through Wigan and the Prince made a triumphal entry into Manchester on 29 November.

Manchester was another Jacobite stronghold and a regiment was raised in its name on St Andrew's Day, 30 November 1745. Colonel Francis Townley, who had joined the Prince at Preston, was given command of its 300 men, mostly recruited during the march south from Carlisle. One volunteer, John Daniel, wrote:

The first time I saw this loyal army was betwixt Lancaster and Garstang: the brave Prince marching on foot at their head like a Cyrus or a Trojan hero, drawing admiration and love from all those who beheld him, raising their long-dejected hearts and solacing their minds with the happy prospect of another Golden Age. Struck with this charming sight, and seeming invitation *leave your nets and follow me*, I felt a paternal ardour pervade my veins.

Daniel's emotional description, while somewhat excessive, does reflect two elements of Charles Edward Stuart's appeal: the first is that some of his supporters may have seen him as an apparent saviour whose right to rule was divinely ordained, so requiring them to follow him as disciples; and the second being the courage and charm of his impetuous youthfulness which also made him seem vulnerable and this generated a fatherly protectiveness towards him.

Despite such passionate declarations of loyalty, only a few hundred recruits had actually rallied to the Stuart standard in England, instead of the many thousands confidently expected by the Prince. Yet another council of war was called and, again, withdrawal to Scotland was argued. The Prince still got his way, for he now had news of an actual French plan to invade the south coast of England, with 9 December given as the proposed date for sailing. This information had come from his brother Henry, Duke of York, sent by James to Paris on hearing of Charles's victory at Prestonpans. Murray reluctantly agreed to march the length of Derbyshire, but only to give the English Jacobites enough time to rally to the Prince. If they did not appear, he would again propose withdrawing north to Scotland.

On 1 December, the bulk of the Prince's army marched out of Manchester, crossing the River Mersey at Stockport on the road to Macclesfield, while Lord Elcho's Lifeguards and the Manchester Regiment crossed farther downstream to probe the country south-west into Cheshire as far as Wilmslow. Smaller parties rode out as far as Knutsford, Northwich, Middlewich and Nantwich.

By now, George II's younger son, William Augustus, Duke of Cumberland, had succeeded General Sir John Ligonier as commander of the Hanoverian forces that were still mustering in the Midlands. Cumberland apparently thought that the Jacobites might now make for North Wales (where a leading Jacobite, Sir Watkin Williams Wynn, had extensive estates) and had, therefore, already taken the precaution of having the bridges over the River Mersey destroyed at Warrington. Cumberland moved his headquarters from Lichfield to Stafford on 1 December, so that he could strike north-west or north-east, depending on whether the Prince's army marched towards North Wales or towards Derby.

Early on 2 December, Murray was told of the disposition of Cumber-

land's forces and suggested a diversionary gambit in strength by striking
south-west from Macclesfield towards Congleton, while the Prince remained behind in Macclesfield with the rest of his army. The tactic
succeeded brilliantly, especially as the earlier detour through Manchester
made Cumberland believe that the Jacobites were now definitely marching
towards North Wales. Murray's forces entered Congleton in the afternoon,
where he announced the imminent arrival of the Prince and demanded
billets for the troops still on their way. Murray already knew, from a
Hanoverian agent captured at Congleton, that the bulk of Cumberland's
army was then at Stafford, apart from his cavalry and two foot regiments,
forming a vanguard at Newcastle-under-Lyme.

Once Cumberland heard that the Jacobites were at Congleton, he
immediately ordered all his army to muster at Stone, concerned that his
advance battalions of artillery already there might be cut off. He then spent
the next morning drawing up all his troops on a wide tract of ground just
outside the village, where he waited for a battle that never came. Only by
the afternoon of 3 December, when the Jacobite army still had not
appeared, did Cumberland realise he had been fooled.

Although Murray had outflanked Cumberland at Stone, leaving the way
open for a march upon London, he did not fully exploit this advantage.
The Duke of Richmond, the commander of Cumberland's cavalry,
admitted this, writing to Newcastle:

> if the rebels had attacked us at Stone on Monday night [2 December],
> as we thought they would, we had been undone, and Ligonier said so
> himself. And it must be so, if they ever attack us at night, if we are not
> encamped; and at Stone it was impossible for want of straw. It is
> necessary to hurry on our troops else they will be in London before
> us, and yet these dreadfully fatiguing marches, will make them
> incapable of fighting.

Doubtless Murray did not have sufficient strength at Congleton to give
battle to the whole of Cumberland's army of 8,250 infantry and 2,200
horse. Nevertheless, he consistently failed to confront the Hanoverian
forces unless he had no alternative, whether or not he had the tactical
advantage over them.

Long before dawn on 3 December, Charles Edward Stuart marched out
of Macclesfield along the hilly road to Leek with the bulk of his army,
joining Murray's forces on the morning of 4 December at Ashbourne, well
on the way to Derby. Charles and his men had left Leek just after midnight,
marching by the light of a full moon. The reunited army started to enter
Derby early in the afternoon and the Prince finally rode into the city at

6 p.m. It was barely a fortnight since the Jacobites had marched out of Carlisle and just five weeks since they had left Edinburgh.

Decision at Derby: 'We Shall Never Come this Way Again'.

The Prince was buoyantly self-confident, expecting to continue his lightening descent on London after a brief halt at Derby. The day after the army's arrival, advance parties were sent to reconnoitre the roads to Leicester and even further south towards Northampton. The bridge over the River Trent at Swarkestone had already been seized just south of Derby. Morale was high among the rank and file, whose 'heroic ardour', to quote the Chevalier de Johnstone, '[was] animated on that occasion, to the highest pitch of enthusiasm, and breathing nothing but a desire for . . . combat'. They crowded into the cutlers' shops, 'quarrelling about who should be the first to sharpen and give a proper edge to their swords'. But the mood of the Prince's commanders had turned sour, as he discovered next morning, when his council met to discuss strategy.

Murray spoke first, already convinced that the military situation demanded a tactical retreat, because they were apparently outnumbered four to one by highly disciplined and experienced soldiers, converging from their left, their right and from across their path to London. They were, he said:

> An army not five thousand men, brave men indeed, but not disciplined, surrounded with a number of the best disciplined troops in Europe and four times their number. One army within twenty miles on their right hand [the Duke of Cumberland's] of at least 9,000 men; another on their left [General Wade's] as numerous though not quite so near; a third in their front as numerous as either . . . consisting of Guards and Horse, with troops which they would bring from the coast where they were quartered. So that there would be three armies made up of regular troops . . . The whole world would blame us as being rash and foolish to venture a thing that could not succeed, and the Prince's person, should he escape being killed in battle, must fall into the enemy's hands.'

Charles seemed initially not to hear this argument and carried on planning the march on London. When other officers backed Murray's assessment of the imminent danger, the Prince was said to be thunderstruck, apparently feeling betrayed and that his commanders did not want him to achieve victory. Finally, he agreed to follow the advice to retreat, but only after strong protest. When told of this decision, Sir Thomas Sheridan lamented: 'It is all over, we shall never come this way again.' His prophetic words serve as an epitaph to the Stuart cause.

History, until recently, has taken Murray's side, backing the decision taken at Derby as the only one to make military sense. As the Chevalier de Johnstone wrote in his memoirs:

> The enterprise was bold, nay rash, and unexampled. What man in his senses could think of encountering the English armies, and attempting the conquest of England with 4,500 Highlanders? It is true they were brave, resolute, and determined to fight to the very last, selling their lives as dearly as possible, and having no alternative but victory or death; but still the disproportion between this handful of men and the whole force of England was so great as to preclude the slightest hope of success.

The assumption has been that Murray was right and that any encounter with Cumberland's forces would inflict such severe casualties on the Prince's army that it would be disabled as a fighting force. Even if Cumberland had been defeated, the Prince would only have won a pyrrhic victory, given the likely casualties, and would have been unlikely to prevail a second time against the remaining Hanoverian forces. If a second battle had been avoided, the government forces would have still been strong enough to harry the Prince's army, whether it advanced against London or withdrew towards Carlisle. Derby was, therefore, the point of no return, beyond which the Prince's army could not extricate itself without total defeat.

In contrast to the Young Pretender, Lord George Murray was no daring 'Braveheart' but a man of caution who, by his own admission, felt personally responsible for the Prince's safety as heir-apparent to the Stuart throne. This caution dictated his strategy, which drew largely on eighteenth-century textbooks of military tactics. Although he proved a brilliant tactician, Murray had seen little action in the field, having only entered the service of Queen Anne in 1712, too late to take any great part in the long war with France (which was then drawing to a close). Although he had joined Mar in 1715, Murray had not actually been at the Battle of Sheriffmuir. Apart from the ineffective action at Glenshiel in 1719, when he commanded 150 men, Prestonpans was his real baptism of fire. He was then fifty years old.

Thirty years earlier, Murray had earned himself a reputation as a strict disciplinarian and an able organiser, but it was only now that his generalship was put to the test. He showed himself capable of outwitting Cumberland at almost every conceivable opportunity, especially during the retreat north from Derby, and his management of the entire campaign revealed him as a 'tactical genius of a high order', as Frank McLynn has argued convincingly in *The Jacobite Army in England 1745*. What he clearly lacked was the strategic insight that Charles Edward Stuart seemed to possess. Posterity has still to decide whether the Prince was the 'best officer in his army', as Sir Alexander MacDonald of Sleat thought, or merely a impulsive and headstrong young man, recklessly leading his men to certain disaster with his romantic dreams of heroic glory. However, Charles knew that only if he had decisively defeated a Hanoverian army on English soil were the Jacobites in England likely to risk rising in arms themselves.

In *Political Untouchables: The Tories and the '45*, Eveline Cruikshanks takes the view that, underlying the decision taken by Murray and his commanders to retreat from Derby, there was

> a narrow kind of Scottish nationalism. All along, they had complained that Charles Edward Stuart was 'occupied with England' to the exclusion of Scotland, the land of his ancestors, and some of them even told him 'they had taken arms and risked their fortunes and their hopes, merely to seat him on the throne of Scotland; but they wished to have nothing to do with England' . . . In his declaration, Charles Edward Stuart had promised to dissolve the Union, but he had no desire to be King of Scotland only, nor could he have been, for how could an independent Scotland be defended from King George and his allies? By forcing retreat, Lord George Murray and the others threw away the best chance there had been of a restoration of the Stuarts, together with all that the bravery of the Highlanders and their own military skill had achieved. The '45 was a gamble from beginning to end, but they threw in their hand when they held most of the trump cards.

It is difficult to argue against such a damning indictment.

What Murray did not know when he argued for withdrawing from Derby on 5 December was the actual state of the Hanoverian armies facing him in the field. Having left Newcastle, Wade and his cavalry were in Doncaster by 6 December, still more than fifty miles away from Derby, while his infantry were another fifteen miles farther north at Ferrybridge. He was forced to admit to Cumberland that 'the Rebels can greatly outmarch us', echoing the views of the Duke of Derbyshire: 'I have no notion of an army being able to march at the rate these fellows have come.'

In fact, Wade never even threatened the Prince's army as it withdrew north from Derby. He reacted to news of the Jacobite retreat by starting back north, planning to cross the Pennines and cut off the Jacobites before they passed through Lancashire. But, at 72 years of age, 'Grandmother Wade' made slow progress and was no longer able to campaign actively in the field. By 10 December, he was only in Wakefield, while the Prince had already reached Wigan, several days' march ahead of him. Wade, therefore, dispatched 500 cavalry, under Major-General James Oglethorpe, to cross the Pennines into Lancashire. They arrived at Preston on 13 December after an epic journey across difficult country in atrocious weather.

At the same time, Wade had sent Major-General John Huske from Ferrybridge to cut across the Pennines towards Penrith with all available men fit to fight – around 4,000 troops. Two days later, however, Wade cancelled this order, having decided, because of appalling weather, to march directly to Newcastle. In retrospect, Murray had been extremely fortunate that it was Wade who had had command of the Hanoverian army at his rear as he advanced into England.

Cumberland and his army posed a far greater danger to the Jacobite army at Derby. When Cumberland finally realised, late on 3 December, that Murray had outflanked him at Stone, he immediately tried to regain the initiative but evidently did not think his forces fit enough for a battle against the Prince's army. Writing to Newcastle on 4 December from Stafford, he said:

> Had the troops been as able as they seem to be willing, I should have marched directly for Derby, but [they] . . . had scarcely halted six hours these seven days, had been without victuals for twenty-four hours, and had been exposed to one of the coldest nights I have ever felt without shelter, for the country produced not straw sufficient for two battalions.

Instead of making for Derby, Cumberland now decided to fall back farther south to Northampton. Long before dawn on 4 December, he mustered his troops at Stone and marched back south-east towards Stafford, from where he dispatched half his infantry to Lichfield, which they reached the next day. Meanwhile, he had ordered his cavalry south to Coventry and then to Northampton, where they were to arrive on 6 December.

Although Cumberland was still confident of stopping the Jacobite advance south at Northampton, he warned London to muster all available forces on Finchley Common to defend the capital. Richmond was rather more alarmist, writing to Newcastle on 5 December:

> Are we all mad? that you do not send for 10,000 more forces, be they Hessians, Hanoverians or devils if they will but fight for us . . . The

whole kingdom is asleep. Our cavalry cannot be here [from Flanders] before February and the Pretender may be crowned at Westminster by that time.

There is little doubt that the Prince's army could easily have outstripped Cumberland's exhausted infantry in a march on the capital from Derby. Cumberland's cavalry posed more of a threat but may not have been able to intercept the Prince's army if it had continued south. In the event, Cumberland chased the Jacobites north with only his dragoons and 1,000 infantry mounted on horseback, catching up with their rearguard only because the Prince insisted on halting for two nights at Preston and Lancaster. The Jacobites moved almost as quickly on foot as Cumberland's on horseback, as Cumberland conceded in a letter of 9 December: 'I fear it will be fruitless for they march at such a rate that I cannot flatter myself with the hopes of overtaking them.' Cumberland obviously knew just how difficult it would be to stop the Jacobites on a victorious march south towards London.

The decisive factor which finally swung the argument against the Prince at Derby was the apparent presence of yet another army to the south of Northampton, blocking the way to London. In fact, this army never existed. It was the invention of Dudley Bradsteet, a Hanoverian agent in the pay of the Duke of Newcastle, who had reached Lichfield in mid afternoon on 5 December with dispatches for Cumberland. Cumberland sent him straight on to deceive the Jacobites at Derby, with orders 'to delay them but twelve hours'. Arriving in Derby around 6 p.m., he posed as a leading member of the English gentry, who had come to see Charles Edward Stuart. He was ushered into the Prince's council which was still arguing over strategy.

The 'news' Bradsteet brought totally undermined the Prince's position. He announced that Cumberland planned to cut off the Jacobites' line of retreat as soon as they marched south, while another army of 9,000 men lay in wait, barring the road south of Northampton. As Bradstreet later admitted: 'Observe that there was not nine men at Northampton to oppose them, much less 9,000.' Murray accepted his word without question for it reinforced his own strategy to withdraw north. Certainly, he referred to this apparent threat in his later account of the council meeting at Derby. So it was that the Jacobite army, closer to London than the two hostile Hanoverian armies and capable of out-marching them, chose to retreat back north, having been taken in by false intelligence from a Hanoverian agent.

The Defence of a Capital in Panic

Had the Prince won the argument at Derby, he might well have found himself languishing in Newgate Gaol within a fortnight, as Lord Elcho warned him. Yet matters might well have turned out very differently, as the authorities in London clearly feared. On Cumberland's advice, they were desperately trying to muster enough forces to defend the city. According to the *Scots Magazine*:

> It being apprehended that the rebels were coming forward from Derby for London, and that the Duke [of Cumberland] would not be able to come up with them, it was resolved to form a camp on Finchley Common; for which purpose the guard, Lord John Murray's (the old Highland) regiment, etc., marched on the 7th to Highgate, Enfield and Barnet; and a large train of artillery was sent from the Tower . . . But upon news of the rebels' retreat, the orders given the troops were countermanded.

The crisis had passed.

The regular troops called to defend London included five companies of Guards, (ordered to St Albans), five companies of Mordaunt's Foot, (ordered to Highgate and Hampstead), and Hawley's Troop of Dragoons, (ordered to Barnet). The inadequacy of this defence became obvious when they were joined by seven companies of the Black Watch, under Lord John Murray. Drawn from the Highland clans loyal to the government, they had mutinied in 1743, suspecting they were being sent to serve in the American colonies, rather than in Flanders. George II himself doubted their loyalty; if faced by their Gaelic-speaking countrymen in the Prince's army, he reckoned they would probably have all deserted.

The London militia might well have strengthened the army drawn up on Finchley Common, had it turned out in force. But, as the Lord Mayor of London later admitted, no more than 500 men were likely to volunteer to defend London, had the Jacobites advanced south beyond Derby. The fact that the Prince's army had marched almost halfway down England through country supposedly loyal to George II, without meeting any significant opposition, surely suggests the Hanoverian regime did not enjoy widespread popularity. London might not have proved any different, as William Pitt later said: 'If the rebels had obtained a victory and made themselves masters of London, I question if the spirit of the population would not have taken a different turn.'

Furthermore, Cope's defeat at Prestonpans suggests a full-blooded Highland charge would simply have swept aside any forces gathered on

Finchley Common, which might not have stayed to confront the Prince's army, whether or not George II kept his promise to place himself at their head. Admitting that his infantry might not be able to stop the Jacobites at Northampton, Cumberland still remained convinced his cavalry could fall back south in time to strengthen the defences of London at Finchley. His confidence was evidently not shared by the citizens of London, where 'the consternation upon the rebels slipping [past] the Duke was here very great'.

The news that the Young Pretender had reached Derby threw London into 'a panic scarce to be credited', according to the novelist Henry Fielding. Whig propaganda subsequently dismissed the alarm and consternation that swept the capital on 6 December 1745, later to be dubbed 'Black Friday' by Horace Walpole. Walpole wrote: 'There never was so melancholy [a] town . . . nobody but has some fear for themselves, for their money, or their friends in the army . . . I still fear the rebels beyond my reason.' The propertied classes packed up all their money, jewels and silver plate for safe-keeping, and the rush to withdraw money from the Bank of England was so great that it supposedly resorted to paying out in sixpences to stem the outflow of capital, just as it had done during the collapse of the South Sea Bubble in 1720. Especially vulnerable were the fundholders in the City of London, who had financed the National Debt by buying government stock. Faced with financial ruin, they might well have come to terms with Charles to safeguard their financial interests, had he entered London.

Moreover, the Prince's arrival in London would surely have forced his English supporters to finally declare themselves. Sir Watkin Williams Wynn and James Barry, fourth Earl of Barrymore, the leading Jacobites in England, did actually send a message to Derby, saying they were now ready to join the Prince, but it arrived on 8 December, two days after Charles's army had begun its withdrawal north. Marching south from Carlisle, the Prince had concealed the truth about commitments from the English Jacobites, merely claiming that they were certain to rally to his cause. Only at Derby was he forced to admit he had not even managed to contact them since landing in Scotland. This revelation finally made Murray and his commanders lose all confidence in the Prince's leadership. Whatever the Prince now suggested, his commanders would only consider an immediate rapid retreat towards Carlisle and the Border.

The determination of Charles's commanders to return north was merely reinforced when they heard that Lord John Drummond, brother of the Duke of Perth, had landed in Scotland on 22 November from France with more than 800 men. Drummond immediately sent a message south to the commander of the Dutch auxiliaries with Wade's army, demanding that they withdraw from the campaign against the Jacobites. The Dutch troops had been captured at Tournai and had only been released on condition that they did not take part in any future hostilities against France and its allies. Now that the Stuarts were allied to France by the Treaty of Fontainebleau, Charles had every right to hold them to this agreement and they did comply. They were eventually replaced by 6,000 troops under George II's son-in-law Friedrich Wilhelm, Prince of Hesse.

Charles seized on the news of Drummond's arrival in Scotland as clear evidence that France would now invade England, especially if he had already occupied London. Murray's view was that the French were now more likely to focus on Scotland and that, therefore, it would be far better to withdraw north across the Border where the Jacobite forces could be reinforced, instead of facing probable defeat in England – in that event, the French would then have no incentive to invade Scotland, let alone England. Meanwhile, although Drummond had orders to march south as soon as he landed in Scotland to reinforce the Prince's army in England, he decided to remain in Scotland, waiting for definite news of a Jacobite victory south of the Border.

It is highly ironic that French plans to launch a large-scale invasion of the south coast of England were already far advanced when the decision was made to withdraw from Derby. The Prince seemed to have actually succeeded in forcing the hand of Louis XV. The authorities in London were already acutely aware of the danger from across the Channel, since Newcastle wrote to Cumberland on 3 December, warning him that 'a great quantity of small boats and vessels [were gathered] at Dunkirk, in order to transport a considerable number of troops to some part of England'. By 12 December, the build-up of French forces at Dunkirk seemed so menacing that Newcastle wrote to Ligonier: 'We are under the greatest alarm of an immediate embarkation from Dunkirk and perhaps some other ports . . . we shall be but very ill-prepared to receive them until you come to our assistance, not having . . . 6,000 men in all.' There was even a report, albeit inaccurate, that 12,000 French troops had already landed at Hastings.

Ligonier was instructed to return south to strengthen the defence of London with all his forces, except Sempill's and Campbell's battalions, which were to go north to join Wade. Cumberland was then at Macclesfield but was ordered to stop pursuing the Young Pretender and return to London with all cavalry and mounted infantry. All Hanoverian troops stationed at Manchester were also ordered south, but this was counter-manded a few hours later by Newcastle, on the news that the Jacobites had given up their march upon London.

Two days later, a royal proclamation was issued, ordering 3,000 foot soldiers and 1,000 cavalry to defend the coasts of Essex and Suffolk, and a further 5,500 troops were to guard Kent and Sussex. All horses, oxen and cattle were to be driven twenty miles inland out of reach of a French invasion force. By then, the word was that 12,000 men were waiting at Dunkirk to cross the Channel in a large fleet of fishing vessels. Evidently, the government still did not realise that the real threat came from the French ports farther along the coast.

Meanwhile, Louis XV had appointed Louis de Plessay, Duc de Richelieu, to command the French invasion forces. Although it is often argued that the French never seriously intended to invade England, it was a threat that Newcastle took seriously:

> The Duke of Richelieu is to have the command of this embarkation. If so, the sending of an officer of his rank and quality shows plainly that the design is not only very serious but that the numbers of troops to be employed in it will be very considerable . . . all our advices agree that the Court of France intend now to support the Pretender in earnest.

Richelieu arrived at Dunkirk on 17 December to find that, although the winds were favourable, he did not have enough officers or artillery for the embarkation to go ahead. Next day, news reached France that the Prince's army had started to retreat from Derby.

Nevertheless, the French continued to build up forces at the Channel ports, apparently to 23,000 men. Voltaire wrote a 400-word manifesto, which declared that Louis XV was only answering the call of all true Englishmen in coming to the assistance of their rightful Prince, that French forces would not harm the people and would leave the country as soon as James Edward Stuart was safely established upon his throne. Far from being an act of aggression, the invasion would bring peace to all Europe, admittedly on Louis XV's terms. Three thousand copies were printed for Richelieu to distribute when he landed in England.

There is little doubt that this invasion force would have sailed if the British navy had not succeeded in wiping out much of the French fleet. The first losses occurred on 18 December when the British intercepted a convoy of eleven transports sailing out of Calais, sinking two ships and capturing another. British privateers seized another French ship lying at anchor off the harbour. At daybreak next day, sixty French ships loaded with arms, ammunition and other stores, sailed along the coast from Dunkirk, making for Calais. Seventeen ships were either destroyed by British privateers or brought as prizes into Dover. More losses occurred on 20 December, when the British navy attacked another French convoy and its escorts as they skirted the coast, making for Boulogne. British privateers were still active, capturing two more French ships, and driving several others ashore to be wrecked. When the French navy attacked later the same day, another ship was lost.

Despite these losses, Richelieu still persevered with his invasions plans as more and more troops poured into Channel ports from their winter quarters in Flanders. He eventually called a council of war, which agreed that the invasion fleet should sail on the afternoon of 26 December to allow a landing at Dungeness at high tide, before it was realised that the heavily-laden transports also needed a high tide to leave the harbour at Boulogne and, even then, could not all sail on the same tide. Worst of all, the British navy still commanded the English Channel, blockading the French at Dunkirk. After nearly five weeks, Richelieu finally dropped the invasion plans on 1 February 1746 and returned to Paris.

In *The Prince and the Pretender; a Study in the Writing of History*, A. J. Youngson concludes that:

> Had Louis [XV] acted with more promptitude and decision; had he arranged something less cumbersome than an armada; had he been able to trust the English Jacobites to rise when the French troops landed; had Charles made his plans clear to Louis before sailing from France; had reasonable secrecy been maintained about the invasion, compelling Vernon [Admiral of the British fleet] to disperse his ships, instead of being able to concentrate them as he did; had all sorts of things been different, the outcome would of course have been also – although how much different no one can say.

Nevertheless, the decision to retreat from Derby was arguably a massive strategic blunder, despite Murray's resounding declaration that 'had not a Council determined the retreat from Derby, what a catastrophe must have followed in two or three days!'.

Chapter Eleven

RETREAT TO SCOTLAND

The Chase North

The decision to retreat, once taken, was rapidly put into action. On 6 December 1745, the army itself was ordered to march before dawn, to conceal the direction from the troops and, a mile out of Derby, they were issued with powder and ball, amid rumours of imminent battle with Wade's army. But the deception could not last. According to the Chevalier de Johnstone:

> The Highlanders, believing at first that they were in forward march to attack the army of the Duke of Cumberland, testified great joy and alacrity; but soon as the day began to clear in the distance, and they perceived we were retracing our steps, we heard nothing but howlings, groans and lamentations throughout the whole army to such a degree as if they had suffered a defeat.

Morale plummeted among the troops and their iron discipline of the march south began to break down, while local militias plucked up enough courage to harass what was now an army in retreat.

The army marched back north almost as quickly as it had come, halting overnight at Ashbourne, Leek, Macclesfield, Manchester and Wigan, before reaching Preston on 11 December, where Charles insisted on spending two nights. Although Cumberland knew the Jacobites were retreating on 6 December, he did not start pursuing them north until early on 9 December, when he left Lichfield with his cavalry and mounted infantry. Deep snowdrifts hampered his forces, who took two gruelling days to reach Macclesfield, where he stayed until 13 December, on orders not to chase the Jacobites beyond Manchester until the French threat resolved itself. Cumberland then finally moved on, reaching Preston on 14 December.

Charles delayed for a full day at Preston, just to demonstrate that this was merely a strategic withdrawal north, rather than a full flight retreat before Cumberland. A stand at Preston was even suggested, where supplies of food and forage were plentiful for men and horses, which might dissuade the French from abandoning their invasion plans. But Murray still was worried that they might be cut off by Wade's army if it crossed the Pennines and, on 13 December, the decision was taken to continue the retreat north.

A party of 120 Hussars had left Preston, under the Duke of Perth, to collect Drummond's French reinforcements from Scotland and Charles hoped, when they returned, he would be strong enough to fight Cumberland and resume the march to London. However, Perth only got as far as Shap, before being driven back by local militias to rejoin the main army which, by then, was in Kendal.

On 13 December, the Jacobite forces arrived at Lancaster but not before Oglethorpe's cavalry had attacked Lord Elcho's Lifeguards at its rear. Oglethorpe had arrived at Preston, after covering over a hundred miles from Wakefield over snow and ice in just three days. Although his cavalry were exhausted, he set off with a small detachment in pursuit of the Jacobite army, which had left Preston a few hours ahead of him. He caught up with the Jacobite rearguard north of Garstang and the two sides briefly exchanged fire. Lord Elcho's men then withdrew as Oglethorpe's Dragoons lost four men to the covering fire of MacPherson of Cluny and his clansmen, who were hidding behind the roadside hedges.

That evening, Charles reached Lancaster and stopped for another day. Still hoping to confront Cumberland, he sent Murray out early next morning with John O'Sullivan to reconnoitre south of Lancaster for a suitable battlefield but, on their return, they were told that Oglethorpe's Dragoons had reached Preston the previous day. Murray naturally assumed that they were the vanguard of Wade's army, which must, therefore, be approaching Preston after crossing the Pennines. The news confirmed his worst fears that the Jacobite army faced the combined strengths of Wade's and Cumberland's forces. The Prince reluctantly agreed to withdraw farther north until the military situation was clearer.

Cumberland was in Wigan by late evening on 13 December, where he received a series of contradictory orders from London: firstly, Newcastle's order of 12 December was waiting for him, instructing him to return immediately to defend London against a French invasion; next, an express cancelling this order arrived early the following morning, so that he continued north towards Preston with his cavalry and mounted infantry; finally, yet another order came, instructing him to return south urgently, after reports of a French landing at Pevensey Bay, east of Beachy Head (which later turned out to be inaccurate). Cumberland received this order on the morning of 15 December, while still at Preston.

By then, the Prince's army had left Lancaster for Kendal, shadowed so closely by Oglethorpe's Dragoons that Murray taunted the Prince: 'As your Royal Highness is always for battles, be the circumstances what they may, I now offer you one in three hours from this time with the army of Wade, which is only three miles from us.' Four miles beyond Lancaster, Oglethorpe's Dragoons suddenly wheeled around and galloped off south, evidently after Cumberland had recalled them after his third set of orders from London. Back in Preston, Cumberland was furious at being forced to call off his pursuit, since the twenty-four hours lost in the town prevented him from catching up with the Jacobite army until three days later at the village of Clifton, just south of Penrith.

Cumberland only began chasing the Prince again on 16 December, heading out of Preston towards Lancaster. By then, Charles's army was leaving Kendal, toiling up the steep road over Shap Fell in driving rain to reach Shap village long after dark, before continuing next day towards Penrith. The artillery train under Murray lagged far behind as a rearguard, only reaching Shap after nightfall a day later, two days out of Kendal. Murray had strict orders from the Prince not to leave behind the heavy field guns, which had to be hauled by men and officers over the summit. Moreover, he found the road strewn with cannonballs, abandoned along the way by Cluny's clansmen. On the Prince's orders, Murray paid sixpence for every cannonball that the Glengarry clansmen carried over the summit to Shap.

Engagement at Clifton

By the evening of 17 December, Cumberland was in Kendal, leaving again long before dawn to try to overtake the rearguard of the Jacobite army under Murray. By midday, he had reached Shap, a few hours behind Murray and his lumbering column of artillery, who were, by then, moving slowly along the narrow lanes towards Penrith.

Cumberland's men first threatened Murray's column at Thrimby Hill, a few miles north of Shap, where a troop of Hanoverian cavalry was put to flight. A running fight began; Murray's rearguard was making slow progress but, as the narrow road was lined with hedges and ditches, the Hanoverian cavalry at the vanguard of Cumberland's forces could only mount a few ineffectual charges against the tail of Murray's column before it reached the relative safety of Clifton, under three miles from Penrith. By mid afternoon, reinforcements of cavalry had reached Clifton to act as Murray's rearguard. They included Pitsligo's Horse which, however, fled back humiliated to

Penrith after a failed attempt to ambush the vanguard of Hanoverian cavalry. Another 300 horsemen were more successful in decoying the main body of Cumberland's cavalry into Lowther Park, just south of Clifton, delaying its arrival in more open country on the outskirts of Clifton until dusk.

Murray was now told that Cumberland was only a mile away with 4,000 cavalry. Although Murray thought this a greatly exaggerated figure, the news allowed him to plead for more reinforcements from Penrith. However, the Prince evidently believed the threat only came from local militiamen, who had constantly harried the Jacobite army on its way north from Lancashire. At first he refused Murray any more men, promising to review the military situation with all his commanders before leaving for Carlisle in the evening. But, eventually, he sent troops to Clifton to save the rearguard, giving Murray strict orders to retreat to Penrith without engaging the enemy. Lord Elcho was scathing: 'As there was formerly a contradiction to make the army halt when it was necessary to march, so now there was one to march and shun fighting when there was never a better opportunity for it.'

The Prince sent Murray the Atholl Brigade from Penrith, under the Duke of Perth, to guard Lowther Bridge, just north of the long, straggling village of Clifton. Meanwhile, Charles Stewart of Ardsheil crossed the bridge with his Appin clansmen and 'raced off to Clifton like hounds', along with the MacPhersons, under Cluny. Murray placed the MacDonalds of Glengarry within the enclosed fields west of Clifton, making up his right flank as a line of defence stretching back from the village almost to Lowther Bridge. Murray's left flank was east of Clifton, where Roy Stewart's Regiment was backed by clansmen under Ardsheil and Cluny. As Frank McLynn comments: 'The subtlety of Murray's dispositions was that the most vulnerable part of his army, on his left, could be protected by flanking fire from Glengarry's [on his right] if the enemy attacked it.' Meanwhile, the Jacobites kept up a barrage of 'popping shots', to give Cumberland the impression that he faced far more men than Murray actually commanded.

As the terrain was quite unsuitable for cavalry, Cumberland ordered 500 of his dragoons to dismount. At around 5 p.m., after darkness had fallen, they advanced against Murray's troops in their strong defensive position. Cluny's men fired first, their shots going wide in the dark. Cumberland's dragoons replied with a more accurate volley, aiming at the musket flashes that revealed the presence of their enemy. The Highlanders drew their swords to charge the enemy, with Murray at their head, and Cluny's and Ardshiel's men rushed across the 150 yards separating them from Cumberland's forces to fall upon them in fierce hand-to-hand fighting. After barely two minutes, the dragoons broke, fleeing in panic towards the road and coming under fire from the MacDonalds of Glengarry. Meanwhile, Cumberland's men had attacked Roy Stewart's Regiment and the MacDonalds of Glengarry, but to little effect.

Murray now ordered a general retreat and Cumberland was left in possession of Clifton, giving him the victory. However he did not chase Murray towards Penrith in the darkness, deciding that his men were too cold and tired to face the enemy. Moreover, he had around forty dead and wounded, whereas Murray had lost only a dozen men. Cumberland considered the skirmish at Clifton a defeat, blaming it on the 'great, heavy boots [his men wore] and it being among ditches and soft watery ground'.

The rearguard action fought at Clifton on 18 December by Murray, against the express orders of the Prince, is usually dismissed as a mere skirmish. Yet, as A. J. Youngson emphasises in *The Prince and the Pretender: A Study in the Writing of History*, its importance was far greater. Cumberland clearly planned to overtake and destroy the Prince's army by pursuing it north from Derby, but signally failed to prevent it crossing the Border into Scotland, where the Prince joined forces with Drummond and Lord Lewis Gordon. Moreover, at Clifton, Cumberland proved an orthodox commander, who only understood the set-piece battles of the eighteenth century, where armies formed lines and advanced firing murderously at each another. One cannot imagine what he expected the Highlanders to do when he ordered his own men forward in the dark, still in their riding boots, unless he believed the Whig propaganda that they would simply run away.

The comparison with Murray is striking: once forced to stand and fight, the Jacobite commander took full advantage of the ground at Clifton, positioning his men where they could best defend themselves, before attacking the enemy. Moreover, Murray led them from the front after sizing up the situation in the heat of battle. Had Charles sent the 1,000 men Murray asked for, 'Clifton might have been as conclusive as Prestonpans, with incalculable consequences', to use Youngson's words.

Even at this late stage, a Jacobite victory might have convinced the French to invade the south of England, despite the losses they had already suffered at sea. It is doubtful if Murray could then have prevented a renewed advance into England, as Charles wanted. But events turned out otherwise and the Prince's army retreated back over the Border into Scotland without ever winning a full-scale battle on English soil.

Fate of the Carlisle Garrison

While Murray's men were fighting at Clifton, Charles set out on an overnight march to Carlisle with the rest of his army. Well before the last of his men had left Penrith at midnight, the rearguard, under Murray, had caught up with them, with the baggage train, artillery and all ammunition resting briefly before moving on to reach Carlisle by noon. Only four weeks earlier, the Jacobites had left the town, in a very different mood, to march 400 miles in the opposite direction, heading south to Derby.

On the following day, 20 December 1745 (which was the Prince's twenty-fifth birthday), the army moved north out of Carlisle. After his commanders had again refused to make a stand against Cumberland, Charles insisted on leaving behind a garrison to hold the town, in another gesture designed to demonstrate that he was merely making a tactical withdrawal and would return, as soon as possible, to England with further Scottish reinforcements.

To Murray, this was utter folly – Cumberland might not have heavy cannon to besiege the castle, but he could easily obtain artillery from Whitehaven, as, indeed, he did. Murray wanted to blow up the castle and the town gates to prevent the need to lay siege to the town if they ever came south again. He also insisted that Carlisle was militarily insignificant, since the Border could easily be crossed near Brampton, on better terrain for Highland warfare. As for the baggage and artillery, which the Prince wanted to leave behind at Carlisle, why not throw the whole lot into the River Eden?

However, the Prince was adamant and Murray was forced to give way. Colonel Francis Townley agreed to remain behind with the Manchester Regiment, with two companies from the Duke of Perth's Regiment and smaller detachments from Lord Ogilvie's, Gordon of Glenbucket's and Colonel Roy Stewart's Regiments, apparently a total of around 250 men. Another 100 men from the Irish Brigade joined them. As regular soldiers in the service of France, they would be treated as prisoners of war, not as rebels guilty of high treason. However, Townley was assured that Carlisle Castle could not be taken, so that he could obtain reasonable terms of capitulation if he was forced to surrender. Scotland held no attraction for Townley's men, many of whom had already deserted on the march north from Derby.

By 4 a.m. on 20 December, Cumberland was leaving Penrith for Carlisle. As Murray had predicted, he ordered up heavy cannon from Whitehaven to attack the 'old hen-coop' of Carlisle Castle and, within ten days, had destroyed its defences and accepted the total and unconditional surrender of the garrison. Townley was tried for treason, found guilty and executed with the full barbarity of the English law, being hung, drawn and quartered along with nine other officers, the regimental chaplain and seven sergeants. Nine men of lower rank were also tried and executed, and nearly all the others were transported to the colonies – except for those who died as prisoners, turned King's evidence or enlisted for George II.

There is no doubt that the Prince was directly responsible for the fate of the Carlisle garrison, stubbornly refusing to accept that the town could not be defended. His decision to leave the garrison behind seems perverse, unless he was supremely confident of a triumphant return south within a few weeks. The Chevalier de Johnstone described it later as a calculated act of vengeance against the English Jacobites, who had signally failed to support Charles, but this seems quite out of character. Even so, the decision was apparently taken in a fit of pique after Murray had again refused to make a stand against Cumberland. While probably not vengeful, Charles could not bear being thwarted.

The Jacobites Return to Scotland

The Prince's army crossed back into Scotland after wading through the swollen waters of the River Esk at Longtown. Once across, the men lit fires to dry themselves off, dancing reels to the bagpipes, or so it was said. Charles now made for Glasgow with his army, having left no garrison to hold Edinburgh, which had rapidly fallen to the government after his departure south for Carlisle. Having taken refuge in Berwick, the Lord Justice Clerk and other officials had returned to the capital on 13 November, followed by General Roger Handasyde with two foot regiments and two troops of dragoons. Reinforcements had quickly been sent to the Hanoverian garrison in Stirling Castle, guarding the crossing over the River Forth.

As the Prince's army moved towards Glasgow, it had split into two columns. Murray marched with the Lowland regiments, through Ecclefechan, Moffat, Douglas and Hamilton, to look as if he intended to attack Edinburgh, before turning west to enter Glasgow on 24 December. Meanwhile, the Prince took a more westerly route with the Highland regiments, spending successive nights at Annan, Dumfries and Drumlanrig, before reaching Douglas a day after Murray. In Hamilton, he spent a day or two hunting before entering Glasgow on 26 or 27 December, marching on foot at the head of his army. The Prince decided to use the next few days to assess the military situation. During this time, he dined sumptuously in public, dressed in the most elegant of French clothes, and danced the evenings away. Reviewing all his forces on Glasgow Green, he found that fewer than twenty-four men seemed to have lost their lives in the invasion of England, despite the engagement at Clifton.

Glasgow was a Whig town and Glaswegians lost no love whatsoever on the Jacobite cause. Their hostility only increased when they were presented with a demand for '6,000 cloth shortcoats, 12,000 linen shirts, 6,000 pairs of shoes, 6,000 bonnets, and as many tartan hose, beside a sum of money'. On 3 January 1746, the Prince's army marched out of Glasgow towards Stirling, where he planned to join any Jacobite forces raised in Scotland during his absence in the south.

After leaving Glasgow, the Highland regiments under Murray, together with Lord Elcho's Horse, headed via Cumbernauld to Falkirk. Lochiel's regiment was then sent to Alloa to escort the heavy guns brought from France. The largest gun weighed over one and three-quarter tons, needing twenty 'north country horses' to pull it. Two pieces of artillery were brought to Stirling 'with great labour', crossing the River Forth by the Fords of Frew, while the rest were ferried across the Forth estuary at Alloa, where the British Navy tried to intercept them.

Meanwhile, the Prince and the rest of his army marched towards Stirling, staying overnight near Kilsyth, before continuing to Bannockburn, where he stayed at Bannockburn House with Sir Hugh Paterson. Immediately he arrived there, Charles became seriously ill with influenza and a high fever. He was nursed back to health by Paterson's niece Clementina Walkinshaw, who later became his mistress and the mother of his daughter Charlotte, born in 1753. Clementina was the daughter of a staunch Jacobite, who had lived abroad in exile since the 1715 Rebellion, and she had been christened Clementina after the Prince's own mother, Clementina Sobieska.

The army itself was quartered in Bannockburn and the surrounding villages and was joined there by the forces under Drummond and all the men raised in the north-east by Lord Lewis Gordon, apparently a total of 4,000 men. Stirling was ordered to surrender on 6 January and it capitulated two days later, unable to put up much of a defence as its walls had fallen into disrepair.

The Prince now decided to lay siege to Stirling Castle, which was of little strategic value, rather than trying to reoccupy Edinburgh before its garrison could be reinforced. The siege was fraught with difficulty for there was only one suitable position to mount a battery. When the townspeople also objected, Charles gave in to their protests on the advice of Mirabel de Gordon, a French officer of Scots descent, who had arrived in Scotland with Drummond with the reputation of being one of the best military engineers in France. According to the Chevalier de Johnstone,

> it was supposed that a French engineer of a certain age and decorated with an order must necessarily be a person of experience, talents and capacity; but it was unfortunately discovered, when too late, that . . . he was totally destitute of judgement, discernment and common

sense. His figure being as whimsical as his mind, the Highlanders, instead of M. Mirabelle, always called him Mr. Admirable.

On 10 January, Mirabel opened trenches in order to place a battery on Gowan Hill, north of the Castle. But, as the soil was very shallow on top of solid rock, the works had to be protected by large numbers of sandbags and woolpacks. The Irish brigade did much of the labouring, which the Highlanders saw as beneath their dignity, while the Lowlanders were supposedly too lazy for it. On 14 January, the heavy guns that were needed to reduce the castle finally arrived after their laborious journey from Perth. Two days later, the siege was abruptly called off when news came that a Hanoverian army under General Henry Hawley was advancing from Edinburgh to threaten the Jacobites near Falkirk.

The Threat from General Hawley

After the fall of Carlisle on 30 December, Cumberland had been immediately recalled south. There, he took command of the government forces massing urgently in the south of England against the imminent threat of a French invasion. Cumberland had already recommended that Wade be relieved of his command, and Hawley was appointed in Wade's place as commander-in-chief of the Hanoverian forces in Scotland. A veteran of Sheriffmuir, Hawley had witnessed the collapse of the Jacobite right wing under the onslaught of the Hanoverian cavalry, which left him believing that Highlanders lacked the courage and resolution to withstand a cavalry charge. He held them in contempt as little more than a rabble, declaring: 'I do and always shall despise these rascals.' This proved to be a dangerous underestimation.

Hawley had arrived in Edinburgh on 6 January, bringing with him a well-deserved reputation of severity with his own men, who knew him as the 'Lord Chief Justice'. To his enemies, he was 'Hangman' Hawley, a nickname he immediately earned in Edinburgh, ordering two pairs of gallows to be set up, one in the Grassmarket and the other on the way to Leith. Over the next ten days, there was a rapid build-up in the government forces under Hawley to around 8,000 men, in twelve infantry and five cavalry battalions, comprised of the Edinburgh regiment, the Glasgow and Paisley militia, under Lord Home, and the Yorkshire Blues, raised by William Thornton at his own expense.

However, Hawley knew that the calibre of his troops left much to be desired. The infantry were exhausted by the recent campaign under Wade in which nearly all had taken part. The cavalry was not much better, as they included the dragoons, now under Hamilton and Ligonier, who had not only failed to protect Edinburgh in September 1745, but who had also fled so precipitately from the Battle of Prestonpans. They were, however, reinforced by Cobham's dragoons, fresh from the engagement at Clifton, bringing their strength up to 700. The artillery was even worse, as Hawley had to make do with ten assorted cannons from Edinburgh Castle, along with a few small mortars, since there were no horses to haul an artillery train from Newcastle. The gunners consisted of two bombardiers, fourteen under-gunners and twelve 'country people'.

Although he complained about the state of this army, Hawley nevertheless shared the overweening self-confidence of Cumberland himself, who wrote to Hawley on 11 January: 'You and I being of the same opinion with regard to that despicable enemy . . . that far from besieging Stirling they will retire to Perth upon the first appearance of the King's troops.' Hawley replied that he intended 'driving the rascally scum out of Stirling' since he thought 'as your Royal Highness does that they will go off or else they are mad'.

On 13 January, Hawley began by sending forward his second-in-command Major-General John Huske, who left Edinburgh for Linlithgow with five regular battalions, the Glasgow Militia and Ligonier's Dragoons, followed by three more regiments. Before reaching Linlithgow, they met Lord Elcho's Dragoons reconnoitring the country west of Edinburgh. Meanwhile, Murray had also moved towards Linlithgow with all his forces to try to capture stores and equipment left there by the government forces. However, when Elcho reported that 'there was a very large body of horse and foot advancing as fast as they could' from Edinburgh, Murray started to withdraw. Crossing the bridge over the River Avon, just west of the town, he waited for the Hanoverian vanguard to reach the bridge. Any exchange between the two sides was, however, limited to much verbal abuse, as Huske's men did not try to advance further and Murray was unable to attack them on the bridge as he had planned. Instead, he withdrew first to Falkirk and then, on the following day, to Bannockburn, to rejoin the rest of the Jacobite army.

By now, nearly all the expected Jacobite reinforcements from the north had arrived. Of the clans that had marched south to Derby, Lochiel's Regiment received another 450 men and Glengarry's Regiment was brought up to 1,200 men, divided into two battalions. As James Maxwell of Kirkconnel wrote in his *Narrative of Charles Prince of Wales' Expedition to Scotland in the Year 1745*:

They looked mighty well, and were very hearty. The MacDonalds, Camerons and Stuarts, were almost double the number that had been in England. Lord Oglivie had got a second battalion much stronger than the first . . . The Frasers, the MacIntoshes and Farquharsons, were reckoned 300 men each. The Irish Piquets and a part of Lord John Drummond's regiment [Royal Scots], were already at Stirling; the rest of the regiment, and Lord Lewis Gordon's men, were within a day's march. The Earl of Cromartie and his son Lord MacLeod were at Alloa, at the head of their own men. In fine, all were at hand in high spirits, and expressed the greatest ardour upon the prospect of a battle.

On 15 January, the Prince chose a battlefield and reviewed his army the following day, hearing that evening that Hawley's whole army was in Falkirk, camped between the town and the River Carron. The following morning, Hawley was joined by the Argyll Militia under Lieutenant-Colonel John Campbell.

Hawley spent the night of 16 January at Callendar House as the guest of Lady Kilmarnock, although her husband was actually serving with the Prince's army a few miles away. After visiting his troops in camp early next morning, he rode to Torwood, a few miles from the Jacobite camp at Bannockburn. Apparently reassured, Hawley returned to Callendar House for a leisurely lunch, not even bothering to send out cavalry patrols to keep the enemy under surveillance. He was quite convinced that the Jacobites would not have the nerve to attack, although they had moved forward from Bannockburn to muster on Plean Moor.

Battle of Falkirk

The Prince, however, had reviewed his forces on Plean Moor at midday, before calling a council of war. Since Hawley looked like staying put for the rest of the day, Murray suggested that the Jacobite army should take the offensive. Drummond was despatched along the main road from Bannockburn to Falkirk, with a detachment from his own regiment, along with the Irish Piquets and all the cavalry. They would act as a decoy while the bulk of the Prince's army made a detour farther west, heading south towards the River Carron. Twelve hundred men were left behind, under the Duke of Perth, to guard Stirling Castle, while the Prince's standard was left flying on Plean Moor. After fording the River Carron at Dunipace, three miles west of Falkirk, the Jacobite army swung east in a wide circuit to approach the so-called Hill of Falkirk from the south-west. The coming battle would be fought on this long ridge of barren moorland, forming the higher ground south-west of Falkirk, just a mile from the enemy's camp.

These movements did not go entirely unnoticed, but Hawley refused to be alarmed at his lunch, merely giving permission that 'the men might put on their accoutrements, but there was no necessity for them to be under arms'. Only when Huske heard that the Jacobite army was rapidly approaching the River Carron from the north, hardly two miles from the Hanoverian camp, did Hawley sound the call to arms. An eye-witness recorded how he was 'surprised to see in how little time the regular troops were formed (I think in less than half an hour)'. Confusion reigned among the officers until Hawley eventually arrived at a gallop from Callendar House, giving 'the appearance of one who has abruptly left an hospitable table'. Only now did he realise the extreme danger. He urged forward his cavalry, followed by the infantry and what artillery he possessed, to try to gain the high ground south-west of Falkirk before the Jacobites could occupy it. The Glasgow Militia formed a rearguard on Hawley's far left, with the Argyll Militia on his right at the foot of the hill, where they took no part in the action.

The Jacobite forces were now approaching the Hill of Falkirk from the south-west, marching uphill in two columns with the wind on their backs. As they reached the flat crest of the hill, they saw the Hanoverian dragoons for the first time, approaching uphill from the opposite direction. Even so, the Jacobite army had enough time to assemble into two lines lying north to south across the hill, before the Hanoverian infantry, lagging behind the dragoons, formed up in line of battle, farther down the ridge to the east. The Jacobites were protected by a steep ravine to their left, and marshy ground to their right.

The Highland regiments under Murray were in the front line of 4,500 men: on the right wing were the MacDonalds of Keppoch, Clanranald, Glengarry and Glencoe; in the centre, the Farquharsons, the MacKenzies, the MacIntoshes and the MacPhersons; while the left wing was made up of the Frasers and Chisholms, the Camerons and the Stewarts, together with detachments of MacGregors, MacKinnons, Grants and MacLeods. Behind them in the second line were 3,000 troops: the three battalions of the Atholl Brigade; and five other battalions under Ogilvie, Gordon and Drummond, as well as the MacLachlans. The rearguard apparently consisted of nearly 750 cavalry and the Irish Piquets, who acted as the Prince's bodyguard. With a total strength of over 8,000 men, it was the largest army the Prince ever commanded, almost matching Hawley's numbers.

Hawley drew up his own infantry two lines deep, in preparation for the full impact of a Highland charge, while all his cavalry were strung out widely on his left wing, facing the MacDonalds on the Jacobites' right wing. A violent storm of wind and driving rain descended from the west upon the two armies facing one another in the fading afternoon light of 17 January 1746.

Battle began when Hawley's dragoons, after several attempts against the MacDonalds, were ordered to advance against the enemy across the 200 yards of rough ground separating them. Their commanding officer was incredulous, having only 700 men who faced 4,000 Highlanders in the Jacobite front line backed by another 4,000 men. Murray reacted by ordering his men to advance slowly against the dragoons, holding their fire until within pistol shot. Then he fired his own musket as the signal for his men to open fire. In a single lethal volley delivered at a range of ten to fifteen yards, 80 dragoons fell dead on the spot. An eye-witness ghoulishly claimed that he 'saw daylight through them in several places'.

According to the Chevalier de Johnstone,

the most singular and extraordinary combat immediately followed. The Highlanders, stretched on the ground, thrust their dirks into the bellies of the horses. Some seized the riders by their clothes, dragged them down, and stabbed them with their dirks; several again used their pistols; but a few of them had sufficient space to handle their swords. MacDonald of Clanranald . . . assured me that whilst he was lying upon the ground, under a dead horse, which had fallen upon him, without the power of extricating himself, he saw a dismounted horseman struggling with a Highlander: fortunately for him, the Highlander, being the strongest, threw his antagonist, and having killed him with his dirk, he came to his assistance, and drew him with difficulty from under his horse. In short, the resistance of the Highlanders was so incredibly obstinate, that the English cavalry . . . were in the end repulsed, and forced to retreat. But the Highlanders not slacking the fight, pursued them vigorously with sabre strokes, running after them as quick as their horses, and leaving them not a moment's respite to be able to recover from their fright; in so much, that the English cavalry rushed through their own infantry in the battlefield behind them; there it immediately fell into disorder, and dragged the army with them in their rout.

Within thirty seconds, nearly all the survivors of the first devastating volley had fled, pursued by the MacDonalds of Glengarry and Clanranald, despite Murray's orders to remain on the field. Their poor discipline lost Charles Edward Stuart a complete victory over Hawley's army, whose cavalry was in panic. Sixty of Hamilton's Dragoons galloped off through the Glasgow Militia at the rear of Hawley's left wing, carrying away a whole company. Worse still, Ligonier's Dragoons caused utter confusion by wheeling right to escape, cannonading into the front line of Hawley's infantry. Only

Cobham's dragoons managed to avoid collision with their own infantry as they galloped away between the lines of the two armies, attracting a hail of fire from the Highlanders on their left.

In what John O'Sullivan claimed was 'perhaps one of the boldest and finest actions, that any troops of the world could be capable of', the Highlanders then attacked Hawley's infantry. Throwing down their muskets, which the rain had rendered useless, they drew their swords and charged the enemy, followed closely by many men from the second-line regiments, who broke ranks to follow up their attack. The Hanoverian infantry had the wind and the rain in their faces and few were able to fire their muskets effectively. All but two of Hawley's front-line regiments gave way, leaving only Ligonier's and Price's Foot to stand their ground. Then his second line broke as well, so that only Barrel's Foot was fighting. 'It seemed a total rout; and for some time General Hawley did not know that any one regiment of his army was standing . . . The disorder and confusion increased, and General Hawley rode down the hill.'

Of the Jacobite army, only the left wing under Drummond was seriously at risk during the battle, coming under sustained musket fire from the three Hanoverian regiments that stood firm on Hawley's right wing, protected by the ravine between the two armies. These regiments apparently moved uphill to pour a flanking fire into the ranks of the Highlanders charging downhill after Hawley's other regiments as they fled the field. The sound of this musket fire so alarmed the Highlanders who had already chased Hawley's dragoons and the rest of his infantry downhill, that they returned to their original lines to find disorder and confusion with 'a considerable space altogether void and empty'. Thinking the Hanoverian forces must have gained the upper hand, they promptly fled west, bringing the misleading news of a Jacobite defeat.

By now, Huske had managed to rally Cobham's Dragoons and, along with the three infantry regiments on Hawley's right wing, they formed an effective rearguard. Murray still had command of some men on the extreme right of the Jacobite army and he now joined the Prince and his bodyguard of Irish Piquets, near the brow of the hill. Although Cobham's Dragoons seemed briefly to threaten the Prince's position, they almost immediately retreated downhill in good order towards Falkirk, along with the three infantry regiments that were all that remained of Hawley's army as a fighting force.

The Battle of Falkirk had hardly been underway for twenty minutes before Hawley and all of his forces were driven from the field. Between five and six hundred of his troops were killed or wounded, including a high proportion of officers, while several hundred were taken prisoner.

By contrast, fifty Jacobites were killed and seventy wounded. Rather than seek shelter from the driving rain, Murray decided to enter Falkirk to prevent its occupation by the Hanoverians. Hawley, however, fell back to Linlithgow with his humiliated army, before returning to Edinburgh the next day.

Chapter Twelve

THE HIGHLAND CAMPAIGN

Acrimonious Disagreement between Murray and the Prince

Although Charles Edward Stuart had won a resounding victory at Falkirk, it was followed by passionate recriminations within his camp. Having lost control of their men right at the start of the fighting, Murray and his commanders had failed to crush Hawley's defeated army. They had made no attempt to chase it to Edinburgh, as demanded by several of the Prince's advisers, where the city might well have fallen into their hands. This was arguably as serious a failure of nerve as the decision to retreat north from Derby, since the Jacobites had again squandered the initiative. The Chevalier de Johnstone argued, albeit with the benefit of hindsight:

> We ought to have pursued the English with the rapidity of a torrent, in order to prevent them from recovering from their fright. We should have kept continually at their heels; we should never have relaxed until they were no longer in a condition to rally . . . But with fatal blindness, instead of pursuing a vanquished and routed enemy, the Prince resolved to continue the siege of Stirling Castle. This determination was the result of a consultation with M. Mirabelle, the senseless individual who promised to reduce it in the course of forty-eight hours . . . The absurd wish to possess an insignificant castle which could be of no use to us produced a series of effects which ruined the prince's enterprise and brought a great many of his partisans to the scaffold.

The morale of the Jacobite forces was not improved when Angus MacDonald of Glengarry was accidentally killed the day after Falkirk, shot dead by a MacDonald of Keppoch as he was cleaning his musket. The unfortunate man was hanged and the episode provoked widespread desertions from the Prince's army, especially among the MacDonalds.

Charles now fell ill and, on 19 January, retired to Bannockburn House with all the Lowland troops, while Murray stayed at Falkirk with the Highland regiments. The siege of Stirling Castle was resumed, but still made no headway, and the battery itself had to be abandoned with the loss of many lives when it was fired upon from the castle. Despondency took hold of the Jacobites.

Towards the end of January, news came that Cumberland had arrived in Edinburgh to replace Hawley as commander-in-chief of the Hanoverian forces in Scotland. They had already been strengthened by an artillery train from Newcastle, together with another two or three infantry regiments, battle-hardened from service on the Continent, and three squadrons of dragoons.

The Prince now asked Murray to prepare a plan of battle, which he received on 28 January with evident approval. But, the very next morning, Charles was astonished to receive a letter, signed by Murray and the seven Highland chieftains, namely Lochiel, Keppoch, Clanranald, Ardshiel, Lochgarry and the Master of Lovat, advocating an immediate withdrawal to the Highlands. Faced with desertions from among the Highlanders and doubting if Stirling Castle could ever be captured, Murray wrote:

> there is no way to extricate your Royal Highness and those who remain with you, out of the most imminent danger, but by retiring immediately to the Highlands, where we can be usefully employed [for] the remainder of the winter.

Murray said that the Hanoverian forts along the Great Glen could be captured, and sufficient men kept in arms to 'hinder the enemy from following us in the mountains at this season of the year'. Then, in the spring, an army of 10,000 Highlanders could be brought together, particularly if there was support from France. He continued, 'We think that it would be the greatest imprudence to risk the whole [enterprise] . . . when there are such hopes of succour from abroad, besides the resources your Royal Highness will have from your faithful and dutiful followers at home'. In a letter to John Hay of Restalrig, who delivered Murray's letter to the Prince, Murray also wrote: 'We are sensible it will be very unpleasant but in the name of God what can we do?' Murray was apparently at the end of his tether after five months of fruitless but arduous campaigning. He confided to his wife: 'What would I not do for a little rest.'

Charles Edward Stuart was completely stunned at Murray's recommendation of the same strategy he had proposed three months earlier, before it was decided to invade England. According to John Hay, the Prince 'struck his head against the wall until he staggered, and exclaimed most violently against Lord George Murray'. But he calmed down enough to reply in what can only be described as bitter exasperation at Murray's defeatism. He wrote:

> Is it possible that a victory and a defeat should produce the same effects, and that the conquerors should flee from an engagement, whilst the conquered are seeking it? Should we make the retreat you propose, how much more will that raise the spirits of our enemies and sink those of our people? Can we imagine, that where we go the enemy will not follow, and at last oblige us to a battle which we now decline? Can we hope to defend ourselves at Perth, or keep our men together there, better than we do here? We must therefore continue our flight to the mountains, and soon find ourselves in a worse condition than we were at Glenfinnan. What opinion will the French and Spaniards then have of us, or what encouragement will it be to the former to make the descent [invasion] for which they have been so long preparing [against England], or the latter send us any more succours? I am persuaded that if the descent be not made before this piece of news reaches them, they will lay aside all thoughts of it, cast the blame upon us, and say it is vain to send succours to those who dare not stay to receive them.

Nevertheless, after an acrimonious meeting with Cluny and Keppoch, the Prince was forced to accept Murray's strategy of withdrawal. He complained vehemently that:

> I have an army that I cannot command any further than the chief officers please, and therefore if you are all resolved upon it I must yield; but I take God to witness that it is with the greatest reluctance, and that I wash my hands of the fatal consequences which I foresee but cannot help.

Murray evidently thought the Jacobite forces could hold out in the Highlands for several years, if necessary, but only by waging a guerrilla war against the Hanoverian forces. However, Charles would adamantly reject these tactics, insisting instead on fighting a conventional battle against Cumberland's army at Culloden on 16 April 1746, where the Jacobite cause would be irretrievably lost.

Retreat to Take Inverness

With the decision to withdraw taken, the Jacobite army had to act on it quickly. Cumberland was in Edinburgh by early 30 January and he lost no time, advancing first to Linlithgow with his army and then on to Falkirk over the next two days. Murray's regiments had by then withdrawn from Falkirk to rejoin the rest of the Jacobite army at Bannockburn. The Prince then agreed with Murray to muster their forces on the morning of 1 February and choose a hundred men from each regiment for a strong rearguard. But, without waiting, the rank and file had already begun a disorderly retreat towards the Fords of Frew. Indeed, in Lord Elcho's words,

> never was there a retreat [that] resembled so much a flight, for there was nowhere 1,000 men together, and the whole army passed the river in small bodies and in great confusion, leaving carts and cannon upon the road behind them.

The climax to the day's chaos came with the accidental destruction of St Ninian's Church, which had been used as a magazine. There were not enough carts to carry away fifty barrels of gunpowder, so the Prince ordered them to be taken outside to a piece of waste ground where they could be destroyed to prevent them falling into Cumberland's hands. However, the villagers doing the work took to pilfering from the barrels, opening them up and hiding parcels of gunpowder under the seats of the church, no doubt for sale later to Cumberland. A sentinel who spotted them fired a warning shot in the air and a piece of glowing padding fell on to a trail of spilt gunpowder. A huge explosion left only the church tower standing amid the ruins of the church and surrounding buildings. The Prince himself had a lucky escape, having left the area only a few minutes earlier, as did Lochiel and the young wife of John Murray of Broughton, who were riding past in a carriage.

By nightfall on 1 February, the Jacobite army was quartered on Dunblane, Doune and the surrounding villages, while the Prince stayed at Drummond Castle. Next day, the cavalry and advance guard continued to Perth, while the clan regiments and nearly all the Lowland infantry marched north to Crieff.

Murray now insisted on another council of war, during which he gave vent to all his pent-up anger and frustration, blaming John O'Sullivan especially for the breakdown in discipline among his own men during the retreat from Stirling. After a great deal of heated argument, it was decided that the cavalry and Lowland regiments would march to Inverness along the coast by way of Montrose and Aberdeen, while the Prince and the clans would head there through the Highlands. Murray agreed to take command of the contingent following the coastal route and he left immediately for Perth. He would be followed north by the Hanoverian army under

Cumberland. Meanwhile, Lord Ogilvie's Regiment and the Farquharsons left Perth to visit their own country.

The Highland regiments used Wade's road north through the Sma' Glen to Aberfeldy and then over the hills to Dalnacardoch, while the artillery and baggage train went round by Dunkeld and Blair Atholl, before heading north over the Drumochter Pass into Strathspey, where an advance party, under Glenbucket, had seized Ruthven Barracks on 10 February. Two days later, the Prince arrived with the rearguard of his army. He then left Ruthven on 15 February to stay overnight with Grant of Dalrachney, disregarding his Whig sympathies, reaching Moy Hall in Strathnairn the next day, a mere eight miles from Inverness. There, he was entertained by the redoubtable Lady MacIntosh, the 'Colonel Anne' of Jacobite legend.

The government forces in Inverness under Loudon had taken little or no action since the engagement at Inverurie on 23 December 1745. However, three more Independent Companies had been raised since the New Year, from the MacKays, Rosses and MacKenzies. Once Loudon heard that the Jacobite army was marching north, he began to fortify the town. The Inverness garrison now had around 2,000 men, while three British navy ships had anchored off the harbour on 9 February, bringing £5,000–£6,000, together with much-needed arms and ammunition. One of them was HMS *Speedwell* under the command of Captain Porter. This was the position when Grant of Dalrachney informed Loudon that the Prince had left his house to spend the night of 16 February at Moy Hall, with only a small bodyguard. It seemed an ideal opportunity for a surprise attack.

Long after nightfall, Loudon marched out of Inverness with 1,500 men, leaving the town ringed by the rest of his troops to prevent the alarm being raised. According to legend, an inkeeper's fourteen-year-old daughter heard about Loudon's plans while serving officers at her father's tavern. She promptly warned the dowager Lady MacIntosh, who sent off Lachlan MacIntosh, a youth of fifteen, to warn the Prince. Lachlan slipped through the cordon around Inverness and reached Moy Hall without meeting any government troops. Shouting out the alarm, he woke the Prince and the rest of the household, who thought, at first, they were under attack. Amid some confusion, the Prince and his bodyguard were quickly hustled away to take refuge on the shores of Loch Moy with Lochiel and his Cameron clansmen.

Lady MacIntosh had earlier sent Donald Fraser, the Moy blacksmith, and four others to watch the road from Inverness. As Loudon approached, the five men started shouting out a series of orders, naming the various Jacobite clans to give the impression they were all drawn up, waiting to ambush. Finally, they fired several volleys, adding to the turmoil, during which Donald MacCrimmon, famous as the piper to the MacLeods, fell dead from a stray shot. According to Bishop Robert Forbes, author of *The Lyon in Mourning* and the collector of eye-witness accounts of the events of 1745-6, 'This so struck Lord Loudon's men with horror that instantly they wheeled about, after firing some shots, and in great confusion ran back with speed to Inverness'. However, the Highlanders were equally confused, running off in the opposite direction. Loudon later wrote: 'If it had pleased God that the accident had not happened in the march, I flatter myself that I should have had the happiness at one blow to have broke the neck of the present rebellion.' This extraordinary intimidation of such a strong force by only five men must suggest that the troops of the Independent Companies had no real commitment to the Hanoverian regime.

This 'Rout of Moy' gave a much needed boost to Jacobite morale and the Marquis d'Eguilles wrote back to France in glowing terms, praising Lady MacIntosh, *La Belle Rebele*, and her heroic blacksmith. After consulting Duncan Forbes among others, Loudon decided to withdraw from Inverness. Several hundred men had already deserted after the Rout of Moy and many more would probably change sides if he tried to defend Inverness. He also risked losing all his arms and ammunition to the Jacobites if they took the town. Loudon, therefore, planned to cross the Beauly Firth to the Black Isle, landing his troops at Kessock from a flotilla of small boats.

The Hanoverian forces abandoned Inverness in disorder on 18 February, after Loudon had first pretended to march out to meet the advancing Jacobite army. This ploy nearly backfired, so delaying their departure that Loudon's men were still leaving Inverness by the bridge over the River Ness just as the Jacobites entered the town from the opposite direction. Nonetheless, Loudon managed to reach Kessock without losing a single man, despite coming under fire from three cannon which the Jacobites had captured. After marching across the Black Isle the next day, Loudon ferried his troops across the Cromarty Firth and continued north towards Tain. The garrison holding Inverness Castle with its valuable supply of ammunition and provisions surrendered after only two days.

Guerrilla Tactics in the North

The fall of Inverness to the Jacobites on 18 February marked the beginning of nearly two months of successful campaigning in the Highlands. Murray pursued his own strategy of guerrilla warfare so effectively that Kirkconnel later described the next few weeks as without dispute the finest part of the Prince's expedition, and what best deserves the attention of the judicious reader. The vulgar may be dazzled with a victory, but in the eyes of a connoisseur, the Prince will appear greater about this time at Inverness than either at [Preston-pans] or at Falkirk. It's certain an army of eight thousand men could not be more extensively and more usefully employed.

Unfortunately the Prince cannot actually be credited with these smaller triumphs, in which he played little part, falling seriously ill with scarlet fever after a bout of pneumonia. Moreover, whatever successes the Jacobite forces achieved, they made no real attempt to counter the threat posed by Cumberland's army, which was then building its strength in Aberdeen.

Murray arrived in Inverness the day after its capture by the Jacobite forces. On 4 February, he had left Perth for Aberdeen, where he stayed for two or three days, waiting for Lord Ogilvie's Regiment and the Farqu-harsons. He then marched towards Inverness in blinding snowstorms, passing through Cullen, Fochabers, Elgin, Forres and Nairn. Along the way, he left behind detachments of the Lowland regiments quartered in such towns as Elgin and Nairn.

On 22 February, two French ships docked in Aberdeen with what proved to be the last reinforcements to reach Charles Edward Stuart. The two ships had sailed from France with two other transports, which had been captured by the British navy, so that the Jacobites lost nearly 400 men of FitzJames's Cavalry and all their horses, while the 120 men who did arrive safely had no mounts. Kilmarnock's troop of cavalry gave up their horses to the new arrivals, forming itself into an infantry company.

From Inverness, Murray set out for Tain, where he joined George MacKenzie, Earl of Cromartie, who had already chased the Hanoverian forces under Loudon into Easter Ross. Cromartie and his MacKenzie clansmen were with the MacDonalds of Glengarry and Clanranald. Also with them were as well as the Stewarts of Appin, the MacGregors and the MacKinnons. Loudon was so threatened by their advance into Easter Ross that, on 23 February, he crossed the Dornoch Firth into Sutherland. He set up his headquarters at Dornoch for a month, while Duncan Forbes stayed nearby at Overskibo. By now, Loudon's forces were much reduced, after a great many desertions on the way north from the Independent Companies, whose men were proving once again to be some of the most reluctant Government conscripts.

For the time being, Murray broke off his chase of Loudon's forces north, knowing that, had he moved into Sutherland around the head of the Dornoch Firth, Loudon could have cut him off by ferrying his own men back across into Easter Ross. Murray, therefore, went back to Inverness, leaving the Jacobite forces in Easter Ross under the command of the Duke of Perth. In the meantime, Loudon received an order from Cumberland, sent from Aberdeen on 7 March, to cross the Moray Firth with all his forces to a rendezvous at Banff, but he did not have the boats to comply. He had himself instructed Captain Porter of HMS *Speedwell* to cruise off the coast of the Moray Firth, where he could supply him with arms and money if needed. Bad weather forced Porter to take shelter at Cromartie for five days, before setting sail for Dornoch, only to run aground at Tarbat Ness. HMS *Speedwell*'s keel was so damaged that it had to head south to Sheerness for repairs.

At Findhorn, the Jacobites had been amassing a large flotilla of fishing boats from all along the Moray coast and, on 20 March, Murray exploited his opportunity, using them to convey 800 men, under the command of the Duke of Perth, across the Moray Firth. The operation only succeeded because a thick fog hid the flotilla from the British warships blockading Inverness. The fishing boats landed at Tain, before sailing north across the Dornoch Firth. Reaching Sutherland, 300 men marched to Overskibo in an unsuccessful attempt to capture Duncan Forbes who escaped. So did Loudon, who had left Dornoch earlier that morning to visit the outposts on the River Shin at the head of the Dornoch Firth. However, the government forces scattered at the Jacobite attack and 200 were taken prisoner, so that, when Forbes and Loudon joined up with one another, they could only retreat. Meanwhile, realising the Dunrobin Castle could not easily be defended, the Earl of Sutherland escaped by sea, along with several others, to be picked up by HMS *Vulture* the following day. The bulk of Loudon's Regiment went north to Strathnaver with Lord Reay.

Loudon and Forbes then had to make their way, next day, up Strathoykel with their remaining men, eventually reaching Loch Carron on the west coast on 23 March, 'after a distressing and fatiguing march . . . in want of money, ammunition and provisions'. Three days later, they crossed to Skye in small boats, to be joined there by MacLeod of MacLeod and MacDonald of Sleat. Altogether, they still had 800–900 men. They sat out the rest of the rebellion on Skye and were still there when they heard news of Cumberland's victory at Culloden on 16 April 1746.

Jacobite Losses and Gains: the *Prince Charles* and the Great Glen Forts

Although HMS *Speedwell* had sailed south for repairs in early March, other British warships were still patrolling the northern waters. They included HMS *Sheerness* and three other vessels, all under the command of Commodore Smith. Sailing through the Pentland Firth on 25 March, they encountered the sloop *Hazard*, which the Jacobites had captured in the harbour at Montrose in November 1745. Renamed the *Prince Charles*, it had then sailed for France, where it took on a valuable cargo of men and supplies for the Prince's army. Pursued by the British warships along the northern coast of Sutherland, the *Prince Charles* was finally driven aground in the shallow waters of the Kyle of Tongue. All of its crew, together with 140 men from Berwick's Regiment of the Irish Brigade, were captured by the MacKays, under Lord Reay, and its cargo was also seized. This consisted of arms destined for the Prince, mostly pistols and broadswords and thirteen barrels of gunpowder. But an even greater blow was the loss of the sum of £13,600 in English gold and 1,500 guineas, which the Prince desperately needed to pay his army.

To set against this loss, Jacobite successes in March 1746 were not limited to the operation against Loudon. Shortly after capturing Fort George at Inverness, they decided to force the surrender of the two other forts in the Great Glen still garrisoned by Hanoverian troops – Fort Augustus and Fort William. A detachment of the Royal Scots, commanded by Brigadier Walter Stapleton, marched out of Inverness around the end of February, heading for Fort Augustus. Lochiel and Keppoch went with them, while Colonel James Grante was in charge of siege operations. At Fort Augustus, trenches were opened, and the garrison surrendered on 5 March, after the magazine had been blown up.

Fort William now came under attack. Two additional companies of Hanoverian troops had already reinforced its garrison a few weeks earlier and its Governor ordered 'all the gardens, and part of the town of Maryburgh to be destroyed, as they may not harbour our enemies'. The fort was surrounded by hostile country and marauding parties of around 600 Highlanders had been sighted on the nearby hills – or so Captain Alexander Campbell, the deputy-governor, reported to General John Campbell at Inveraray. He responded by sending His Majesty's sloop *Serpent*, under Captain Robert Askew, and the vessel anchored off Fort William on 15 February. Ten days later, HMS *Baltimore*, under Captain Robert Howe, also arrived having passed through the Corran Narrows, where it had been fired on from the shore. On 4 March, a raiding party from Fort William landed at Corran Ferry to deal with this threat in a surprise strike against the Highlanders, killing two and scattering the rest. The ferry houses were burnt down and a nearby hamlet destroyed to deprive the Highlanders of cover.

After the Jacobites had taken Fort Augustus, their commander, Stapleton, marched down the Great Glen to besiege Fort William but could not begin in earnest until the arrival of the artillery on 19 March, delayed by the lack of heavy enough horses to haul the guns from Fort Augustus. By then, three companies of Guise's Regiment had reinforced the garrison on Cumberland's orders and another fifty government troops arrived shortly by sea, sailing up Loch Linnhe from Dunstaffnage now that the Corran Narrows were safe.

Fort William proved much more challenging than Fort Augustus for the Jacobites, even though they had more than 1,000 Highlanders, together with 200 troops of the Irish Brigade. On 27 March, its deputy Governor reported:

> The rebels began firing this morning at five from a four-gun battery opened on a little hill within 300 yards from us and have given us a great number of shot from its six-pounders, which do only penetrate our roofs. No other harm is yet done. This day they also fired from their three-gun battery and have thrown in a few cohorn [mortar] shells. We have damaged their four-gun battery by our mortars and guns . . . and have blown up some of their powder . . . Not one man is killed only a man of Balnaby's company who had his leg shot and cut off last night.

Unfortunately for the Jacobites, however, Colonel James Grante was wounded early in the siege by a spent cannonball and the siege operations were then put in the incompetent hands of Mirabelle de Gordon. Then on 31 March, 'Captain Caroline Scott, at the head of 150 men, sallied out from the fort and attacked the works at the craigs . . . demolishing the battery', which was near the old burial ground, close to the River Nevis. Three of the Jacobite four-pounders were hauled back to the fort, along with two six-pound mortars and a bellows for heating up bullets.

This was a turning point, as the siege had to be abandoned a few days later, after the Jacobites had loosed off a final night bombardment. When a party of Hanoverian troops ventured out on the morning of 3 April, they found the trenches deserted. Although the fort was badly damaged, only six men had been killed and twenty-four wounded. All the Jacobite artillery had been taken, including five brass four-pounders, four iron six-pounders and nine mortars.

Raid on Atholl and Siege of Blair Castle

Meanwhile, Murray had mounted a daring raid against the Hanoverian outposts that Cumberland had established in Atholl. Three days after arriving at Perth on 6 February, Cumberland had dispatched Sir Andrew Agnew with a detachment of the Scots Fusiliers to garrison Blair Castle in the very heart of Atholl. The Argyll militia was also pressed into service, sent to various outposts around Loch Tay, Loch Rannoch, Glen Lyon and the Braes of Balquhidder, as well as to Dunkeld. Murray knew that this was likely and he was also aware that several thousand Hessian troops had arrived at Perth and Stirling from the Continent. If Cumberland marched on Inverness from Aberdeen, while the Hanoverian forces penetrated north into Badenoch, the Jacobite forces in the north could be cut off by a pincer movement.

Accordingly, on 12 March, Murray, with 600–700 men of the Atholl Brigade set out for Rothiemurchus in Strathspey, where Lord Nairne's Regiment was quartered, in order to keep the Grants subdued. His first target was Castle Grant, whose defenders thought that the castle was surrounded by 1,600 men armed with heavy cannon and promptly surrendered. Murray then crossed the hills to Dalwhinnie, where another 300 men joined him, under Ewan MacPherson of Cluny. Advance parties were sent ahead to guard all the passes through the mountains into Atholl, before Murray and his men made their way over the Drumochter Pass to Dalnacardoch in a heavy snowstorm. Having talked to Cluny, Murray now took all his officers into his confidence – dividing their forces into separate detachments, they were to attack the government outposts in Atholl. In fact, these outposts were mostly the private residences of Murray's own officers from Atholl, who were each to lead the attack upon their own property. The raids were to be launched well before daybreak on 17 March.

Apparently this complex military operation was perfectly executed. Not a single Highlander was killed or wounded, while some 300 Hanoverian troops and militiamen were sent back as prisoners under heavy guard to Inverness. Cluny described the Jacobite jubilation in a letter to Lochiel:

> We seized, killed and took prisoner every private man and officer upon the different commands without the escape of a single person . . . Not one of the commands smelt the design till they were fallen upon. There was not one of the Prince's men so much as wounded . . . We are all in great spirits.

In fact, the regular troops garrisoned at Coshieville did have sufficient warning to retire to Castle Menzies, while the officers commanding the garrison in the village of Blair Atholl managed to fight their way back to the castle to raise the alarm.

Just before daybreak, the victorious raiding parties were at Bridge of Bruar, two miles north of Blair Castle, heading back to a rendezvous there with Murray. Murray was waiting anxiously for their return with only twenty-five men, when Sir Andrew Agnew suddenly rode out of Blair

Castle with a strong force to check what was happening. Retreat was out of the question, as the raiding parties could be picked off one by one as they returned. Murray, therefore, drew up his small company concealed behind a turf wall. By flying the regimental colours above the wall at intervals along it, while playing the bagpipes at full blast, he managed to convince Agnew that he faced a much larger force. Agnew's nerve was finally broken when the Highlanders flashed their claymores in the light of the sunrise, and he promptly retired to Blair Castle. After Murray's men had joined him at the rendezvous, the reunited company followed Agnew back. When the news reached Perth, the local Hanoverian commanders seriously considered withdrawing all their forces to Stirling, much to Cumberland's contempt.

For the next fifteen days, Murray laid siege to Blair Castle, his own ancestral home, in what was to be the last operation of its kind in British history. The defenders were short of food and water and depended on supplies brought up every four days from Perth. More seriously, Cumberland had not expected the castle to be attacked, so had not sent any guns or ammunition for its defence. But Murray was making little progress in reducing his own castle. He had hauled two four-pounder cannons with great difficulty through the mountains from Inverness, but they made little impact on its walls, which were seven feet thick. Moreover, he had no sappers to undermine the foundations so he was reduced to trying to set the roof alight with red-hot bullets, heated in a bellows.

Even so, he was within a few days of starving out the castle's garrison when he had news that a force of troops, under the Prince of Hesse, was advancing towards Dunkeld from Perth, followed by a troop of dragoons, under the Earl of Crawford. Murray promptly raised 500–600 men from his brother's estates in Atholl and urged the Prince to send him an additional 1,000 Highlanders. But the request was overruled, it seems, by those in Inverness, who were 'quite bent upon reducing all in the north in order to bring out the clans and leave no enemy behind'. According to Lord Elcho, the Prince claimed he could not spare the 1,000 troops Murray had asked for.

By now, apparently, the Prince was so suspicious of Murray that he did not trust him with more men, in case Murray defected to the government as so many of his closest advisers had already done. Murray, therefore, could not act on his plan to entice the Hessian troops into the Pass of Killiecrankie, which he now controlled and where he could ambush them. If the tactic had worked, Cumberland would have been threatened from behind and forced to withdraw south from Aberdeen, relieving the pressure on the Prince's army at Inverness. However, the Hessians apparently refused to enter the Pass of Killiecrankie, believing its narrow defile to be the 'Gates of Hell'. Moreover, the Prince of Hesse was reluctant to engage the Jacobites without a formal agreement on the exchange of prisoners, which Cumberland would not contemplate, considering the Jacobites to be guilty of high treason. Hesse refused to move beyond Pitlochry, stating baldly that he was 'not enough interested in the quarrel between the Houses of Stuart and Hanover' to risk the lives of his own subjects in 'combating with men driven to despair'.

Without the reinforcements he needed to bring the Hessians to battle, Murray could only withdraw north, abandoning the siege of Blair Castle in the early hours of 2 April. He marched back into Strathspey, while Cluny's clansmen stayed in Badenoch to guard the passes from Atholl. The rest of the Atholl Brigade headed down the River Spey to Elchies, to guard the river crossings near Craigellachie. Murray was back in Inverness on 3 April but, by now, his relations with the Prince had reached their absolute nadir, poisoned by 'Irish intriguers and French politics', as a junior officer later noted. The Prince now so distrusted Murray that he had him watched night and day for fear of betrayal.

Chapter Thirteen

CONFRONTATION APPROACHES

Cumberland Prepares with a
Policy of 'Military Authority and Severity'

While the Jacobites under Murray were enjoying such a remarkable run of successes after recapturing Inverness, Cumberland had begun to muster his own forces for what would be the final campaign of the 1745 Rebellion. When he arrived back in Scotland to replace Hawley after the fiasco at Falkirk, Cumberland was intensely disappointed to find the Prince's army had withdrawn into the Highlands, rather than preparing for battle. He considered the morale of his own troops was so high that it 'made me wish the rebels would have ventured an action, and I doubt not but then I should have shared in their glory of giving them a total defeat, and crushing at once this band of robbers'. But, instead of launching into an immediate engagement, he was now forced to chase the Prince north into the Highlands.

Leaving Edinburgh on 31 January, Cumberland spent the first night in Linlithgow, where his troops accidentally set the Palace ablaze. He then moved on through Falkirk and Stirling to Perth, where he arrived on 6 February, two days after Murray's forces had left the city. Over the next fortnight, Cumberland stayed in Perth, raising money for food and other supplies for his army. On 20 February, he left for Aberdeen, which he reached a week later.

For nearly seven weeks, Cumberland remained in Aberdeen, resting his men after their arduous if ineffectual winter campaigning under Wade. By 4 April, his secretary was confidently claiming that:

> our troops are [now] in exceedingly good condition, their fruitless marches under Marshal Wade, in the dead of winter, and always encamped, had quite worn them down, but they have recovered strength as well as spirit by the rest they have had here . . . Since the Duke's departure from Edinburgh, at least 1,000 recovered men are joined the army from the hospitals.

Cumberland would eventually build up his army to a total of around 9,000–10,000 men, with fifteen regiments of infantry, two regiments of cavalry and a body of Argyll and other militia. Many were battle-hardened veterans who had seen service against the French in Flanders. The Scottish regiments included the Royal Scots of St Clair's Regiment, the Royal Scots Fusiliers of Campbell's Regiment and the King's Own Scottish Borderers of Sempill's Regiment, as well as the Argyll Militia and Loudon's Independent Companies, raised from the Highland clans loyal to the government.

Cumberland now trained his troops to deal with the hand-to-hand fighting that broke out in the aftermath of a Highland charge, when they were faced by men wielding broadswords and targes (shields). By now, the plug-bayonet of the late seventeenth century had been replaced by the socket-bayonet. This new weapon meant that a soldier no longer needed to push the blade into the muzzle of the musket, which was fitted with a collar to hold the blade in place, allowing him to fire it with bayonet fixed. Cumberland taught his men to strike an opponent on his right as he raised his right arm to deliver a blow with his broadsword, making him especially vulnerable there to a bayonet thrust.

The fall of Inverness to the Jacobites on 18 February 1746 had greatly alarmed the government in London, given the military reverses that Britain had already suffered in Flanders. Just a week earlier, Marshal de Saxe had taken Brussels, leaving the way open for the French to conquer the Austrian Netherlands, so that they were able to capture Antwerp, Mons, Charleroi and Namur during the spring and summer of 1746. Meanwhile, Britain could make no contribution to stem the French advance, having recalled all its troops in Flanders to deal with the Jacobite threat. The crisis was so great that, from the Hanoverian standpoint, 'every hour produces some new cause to curse the vile authors of all our misfortunes', so that 'delay at this time harms all Europe'.

Cumberland now decided against sending the Hessian troops back to Flanders as he had intended, retaining them instead for a spring campaign against the Jacobites. This decision antagonised Britain's allies on the Continent. Austria had already come to terms with Bavaria, while making peace with Prussia in December 1745 under the Treaty of Dresden. Moreover, the French were now involved in peace negotiations with the Dutch and also with the Austrians. If France could reach agreement with both of these countries, all French military might could then be concentrated against Britain. The country, therefore, looked in danger of being isolated at the very time when the Hanoverian regime was struggling to suppress 'this accursed rebellion at home'.

To the British government, speed was, therefore, essential in stamping out the Jacobite rebellion if the international situation was not to deteriorate any further in France's favour. Cumberland's correspondence at this time demonstrates his determination to subjugate the Highlands once the rebel army had retreated north of the Forth, using whatever means necessary. Before leaving Edinburgh, he had addressed his army with the words:

> The only apology I can make for troubling you with this short address is the hearty and sincere zeal I have for the noble cause we are now engaged in. Many of you, after severe campaigns abroad, in defence of the liberties of Europe, wherein you have gained immortal reputation, are now called home to confirm it in defence of your king, your religion, and the liberty of your country . . . After what you have already done, you will find it an easy matter . . . to crush the insolence of a set of thieves and plunderers, who have learned from their fathers to disturb every government they have lived under . . . Remember you are the free soldiers of a free people . . . Go forth, show yourselves like men, and your enemies will as snow in the sun melt before you.

Despite these resounding words spoken in praise of a constitution that supposedly upheld the right to life, liberty and property by due processes of the law, Cumberland was convinced that 'nothing will cure this [rebellion] but some stroke of military authority and severity'.

A few days later, as the Prince's army was withdrawing into the Highlands, Cumberland assured Newcastle that 'the rebellion is now crushed, and nothing [is] left but the punishment due to their crimes'. If he could not bring the rebels to battle, he saw no alternative but 'to burn and destroy that nest of robbers. And orders shall be given to kill all that have arms in their houses as that will be the only trace of treason left'. This 'disagreeable hunting of those wild beasts', as Ligonier described it, would destroy forever the threat posed to the regime by these 'barbarians, enemies to all civil society'.

Nevertheless, there were Scots courageous enough to challenge this policy of repression. When Cumberland drafted a proclamation in Aberdeen against 'rebels and disaffected persons', threatening them with 'military execution' for engaging in any treasonable activity, Andrew Fletcher, Lord Justice Clerk, changed 'military execution' to 'the utmost rigour of the law'. However, he explained in a letter to Cumberland that he was especially concerned to protect the legal rights of 'his Majesty's lawful subjects as happen to be creditors'. They had a prior claim to the 'rebel's just and lawful debts', which could not be seized by the Crown 'until the rebels are attainted or convicted'. Needless to say, such legal niceties were lost on

Cumberland, who proceeded to issue instructions that 'all provisions, cattle, forage, or arms which shall be taken from the rebels shall be given to the people', while 'all methods . . . [were to be] used for disarming the disaffected people in the hills [and] they shall be destroyed if they resist'. Even so, Cumberland was sufficiently worried about such actions possibly being illegal that he wrote to Newcastle, asking him to consult the king.

The government in London evidently did not want to incriminate itself, and passed back responsibility to its commander-in-chief. Newcastle wrote back to Cumberland, assuring him that,

> as General of His Majesty's army, your Royal Highness has authority to do whatever is necessary for suppressing this unnatural rebellion . . . His Majesty apprehends that no general rule can be given for your Royal Highness's conduct in this respect as that must depend on the circumstances that attend the particular case.

But, suspecting that Cumberland might not be satisfied by such vague advice, Newcastle wrote another 'most private' letter, in his 'own illegible hand for greater secrecy', to be opened by Cumberland alone and then burnt. It instructed Cumberland to do everything in his power to quash the rebellion as quickly as possible, provided he did not give 'any just cause of complaint to a country so ill disposed to the King, and so willing to find fault with everything that is done for His Majesty's service'.

Cumberland replied that he 'could have wished the King's order had been fuller. Yet I will take the hint, and will do all in my power to put an end to this unhappy rebellion'. He even added a postscript, asking Newcastle not to 'imagine that threatening military execution and many other things are pleasing to me'. Nevertheless, in giving Cumberland such a free hand, the government and the king himself, were obviously condoning extreme measures, just as William of Orange had done at the time of the Glencoe Massacre in 1692. In Scotland, Cumberland would long be remembered as 'The Butcher' for his brutality in suppressing the Jacobite clans in the months after the Battle of Culloden.

In March 1746, British navy ships, cruising north of the Sound of Mull, began to carry out Cumberland's policy of fire and sword. Two, the *Greyhound* and the *Furnace*, had already sailed and were joined a few days later in the Sound by the *Terror* and the *Princess Anne*, which anchored off Mingary Castle on the south coast of Ardnamurchan, where they took on board men from the castle's garrison. After heading back south along the coast of Morvern, they landed raiding parties on 10 March to carry out Cumberland's orders. As Captain Duff of the *Terror* reported to General John Campbell at Inveraray:

I landed Lieutenant Lindsay with the detachment of your regiment, Captain Campbell with twenty men from Mingarry Castle, a lieutenant and fifty-five [men] from my ship with orders to burn the houses and destroy the effects of all such as were out in the rebellion. They began with Drimnin MacLean's town, and by 6 o'clock at night had destroyed the Morvern coast as far as Ardtornish, except a town belonging to the MacDougalls, and the houses of those men who . . . declared they had never been out, which were very few. While the men marched along the coast I covered them with my ship. This service was performed without the loss of a man on our side, although they were often fired at by parties of the rebels from behind the hills.

Captain John Hay of the *Princess Anne* added that fourteen miles of the coast had been ravaged, while 'near 400 houses amongst which were several barns well filled with corn, horses, cows, meal and other provisions were destroyed by fire and fire-arms'. The Jacobites were outraged and Lochiel and Keppoch signed a manifesto, threatening retribution upon the Campbells.

During the second half of March, Cumberland began to probe the Jacobite defences along the lower reaches of the River Spey, before advancing in strength from Aberdeen in early April. Lord John Drummond had command of these defences and he had established his headquarters at Gordon Castle near Fochabers, just east of the River Spey, forcing the Duke of Gordon to join Cumberland in Aberdeen. A contingent of Jacobite cavalry under Lord Strathallan held Cullen, farther along the coast to the east, while John Roy Stewart's Edinburgh Regiment and Lord Elcho's Lifeguards, held the inland district of Strathbogie around Huntly.

Although Cumberland had arrived in Aberdeen by 27 February, it was not until 16 March that he ordered forward four infantry battalions and two cavalry squadrons under the command of Major-General Humphrey Bland, reinforced the following day by four more battalions of infantry under Brigadier Mordaunt, armed with artillery. Bland had orders to attack John Roy Stewart's Regiment, said to be 1,000 strong, at Strathbogie. However, his vanguard was observed by Stewart's own patrols, giving the Jacobites enough time to retire west across the River Deveron at Huntly and withdraw in good order.

In fact, Bland did not follow the Jacobite forces across the River Deveron but, instead, sent forward sixty men of the Argyll Militia, under Alexander Campbell, together with twenty men from Kingston's Horse. After occupying Keith on 19 March, they were joined next day by another detachment of the Argyll Militia, under Captain Colin Campbell the younger of Ballimore. They all spent the night of 20 March in the church at Keith, where they were surprised in the early hours of the morning by a Jacobite detachment, under Major Nicholas Glascoe, a French officer of the Irish Brigade.

Glascoe's men had entered Keith undetected and attacked the Camp-bells inside the church, who surrendered, after perhaps half an hour's fighting, on the promise of quarter being given. Nine men were killed and seventy were wounded, including Campbell of Ballimore, while there were twelve Jacobite casualties. After this setback, Bland withdrew all his forces to Strathbogie. William Keppel, first Earl of Albermarle, now took over Bland's command, ordering 900 Argyll Militia under Barcaldine's brother, Alexander Campbell, to reconnoitre the country around Keith. Although the Jacobite forces defending the River Spey were still strong enough to repulse the Campbell Militia, it was only a matter of time before they would face the full might of Cumberland's army when it finally marched out of Aberdeen.

Cumberland Crosses the River Spey

In fact, Cumberland was only waiting for the spring floods to abate so that the River Spey was low enough for his army to cross. On 8 April, having received final reinforcements, he marched out of Aberdeen through Old Meldrum and Banff to Cullen, where he was joined by Albemarle's forces from Strathbogie. At midday on 12 April, Cumberland crossed the Spey, fording the river in three places just below Fochabers. The infantry had to wade up to their waists and a dragoon, his wife and three other women were swept away by the current. But the crossing went unchallenged by the 2,000 Jacobites on the far bank, who merely fired a few shots before falling back.

Next day, Cumberland's army passed through Elgin, to camp at Alves, and then moved on to Nairn through Forres, crossing the River Findhorn unhindered. Although the Jacobite forces tried to cut off an advance guard sent by Cumberland to reconnoitre a camp site for the night, they were repulsed by a troop of Hanoverian cavalry under Bland. Entering Nairn, Cumberland's troops almost caught up with the Irish Piquets, the rear-guard of the Jacobite forces, withdrawing towards Inverness. Shots were exchanged across the bridge, before the Piquets retired in good order under covering fire from the Jacobite cavalry. Cumberland's army then crossed the River Nairn to pitch camp at Balblair, a mile south-west of the town. April 15 was Cumberland's twenty-fifth birthday, and his army rested 'after four hard days' marching'. Meanwhile, a naval force had sailed round the coast from Aberdeen, under Commodore Smith, carrying food and provisions for them.

It is difficult to understand why the Jacobite forces under Lord John Drummond did not try to stop Cumberland's army crossing the Spey, especially as the river is wide and fast flowing in its lower reaches and they could probably have done so easily. Equally, they could have opposed the crossing of the River Findhorn or even the River Nairn. They were all natural obstacles 'where thousands must have fallen' if a determined attempt had been made to block the advance of Cumberland's army towards Inverness. Moreover, Lord John Drummond and his brother, the Duke of Perth, still had enough men along the Spey to hold off Cumberland's army until they could be reinforced. Cumberland's aide-de-camp, Joseph Yorke, was damning in his assessment of what was a serious blunder by Lord John Drummond:

If the rebels had defended this river, we should have found some difficulty to have passed so cheap; for I never saw a stronger post in my life by nature, and a very little art would have rendered it very strong and tenable. The rebels here, who were chiefly the Low-landers, complain bitterly of the Pretender and the clans for not coming down to them which, joined to the entire want of money, renders them mutinous and fearful. The greater part of the Mac-Intoshes left them some days ago and the men desert in droves . . . our men are in high spirits and showed the utmost alacrity in fording the river, though up to their waists.

Clearly, the morale of the Jacobite forces was starting to break, after the sieges of Blair Castle and Fort William had been lifted early in April.

Murray had returned to Inverness to find the rank and file being paid in kind and surviving on a diet of oats. Many Highlanders had already left for home, where they could at least feed themselves. The capture of the *Prince Charles* had proved a disaster, since the loss of its precious cargo of bullion and gold coin meant no money to pay the troops. In a desperate attempt to recover the treasure and to obtain more recruits, the Prince had already dispatched a large force of possibly 1,500 men north into Caithness and Sutherland, but this ended in disaster when around 200 men were surprised at midday on 12 April at Dunrobin Castle. Cromartie, the officer in command, was taken prisoner, along with 178 of his men. It was the day before the Battle of Culloden.

In truth, the price of the Jacobite successes during March was that the Prince's forces were spread far too thinly through the Highlands from Atholl in the south, Badenoch and Lochaber in the west, and Caithness and Sutherland in the north. As Frank McLynn points out, they should surely have been deployed along the River Spey east of Inverness, where they could have opposed the inevitable advance of Cumberland's army from Aberdeen. Even when the Atholl Brigade under Murray returned from laying siege to Blair Castle, they were not used to strengthen the defences along the Spey but were sent, instead, with John Roy Stewart's Regiment into Strathspey in a fruitless attempt to bring out the Grants. Meanwhile, Lochiel and Keppoch had lingered in Lochaber with their clansmen after the siege of Fort William was abandoned, trying to avert attacks on their own estates, like those which had already devastated Morvern.

This widespread dispersal of the Prince's forces during March 1746 meant that none of his senior officers were present in Inverness to advise him. The only exception was the Duke of Perth, whose regiment acted as the Prince's bodyguard. Moreover, although Murray had returned to Inverness on 3 April, his relations with the Prince were close to breaking-point, so that he was no longer in effective command. Charles turned, instead, to John O'Sullivan, who toured the lower reaches of the Spey and decided that the river could not be defended except in force, since it could be crossed at so many points. This may have persuaded Charles not to try to prevent Cumberland's army fording it. In any event, the Prince refused to sent any cannon to defend the Spey, while his commanders were apparently under orders to retreat without engagement.

Astonishingly, the Prince and the small coterie of sycophantic courtiers now advising him were apparently caught unawares by Cumberland's sudden advance from Aberdeen because of a fatal lack of intelligence. The Prince did not actually hear that Cumberland had crossed the River Spey on 12 April until the following day. Whatever the reason, the Jacobites, under Drummond and Perth, fell back from their defensive positions along the Spey as Cumberland advanced and a crucial opportunity was lost. In retrospect, the failure to challenge Cumberland's army as it crossed the River Spey marked a final turning point in the Prince's fortunes, from which they never recovered.

The Prince's Fatal Decisions

Even at this late stage, the Jacobites could still have grasped the initiative, if only they had chosen to fight on ground where a Highland charge had the best chance of breaking the Hanoverian lines. But Charles Edward Stewart would not listen to his military advisers, especially to Lord George Murray. As Lord Elcho wrote later, the Prince seemed in a sanguine and exalted frame of mind, and said that he had no doubts as to the issue of the approaching conflict with . . . Cumberland; he believed that the English soldiers would with difficulty be got to attack him. He refused to listen to any suggestion . . . When a rendezvous in the event of defeat was spoken of, he replied that only those who were afraid could doubt his coming victory . . . As he had consulted with only his favourites everything was in the greatest disorder. The persons capable of serving him were suspected or neglected, and those in whom he had placed his trust had not the ability to be useful to him.

Murray, for his part, thought that

His Royal Highness had so much confidence in the bravery of his army, he was rather too hazardous, and was for fighting the enemy on all occasions. What he had seen them do, and the justice of his Cause, made him too venturous.

Charles's blind optimism was accompanied by an extraordinary capacity for self-delusion, convinced as he was that Cumberland's men would desert the Hanoverian army in droves rather than fight against their 'true Prince'.

Once the Prince learnt that Cumberland's army was camped at Balblair within striking distance of Inverness, he sent Murray to reconnoitre the country for a suitable battleground. Murray selected a stretch of rough and boggy terrain near Dalcross Castle, a few miles north-east of Culloden Moor. This was ideal ground for the Highlanders, where they could launch a Highland charge from a position of strength, and it would also be a difficult place for Cumberland to use his artillery and cavalry at all effectively. Inexplicably, when O'Sullivan was sent to inspect the proposed site, he reported that the ground was quite unsuitable.

Charles accepted O'Sullivan's advice to meet Cumberland's army on the open terrain of Culloden Moor, a mile south-east of Culloden House. Its only advantage was that a morass would protect the Jacobite left flank. Otherwise, as Murray wrote later:

not one single soldier but would have been against such a field, had their advice been asked. A plain moor where regular troops had . . . full use of their cannon so as to annoy the Highlanders prodigiously before they could possible make an attack.

Indeed, the place was ideally suited to cavalry tactics. Murray had grave misgivings: 'I did not like the ground. It was certainly not proper for Highlanders.'

Subsequently, when Murray made a closer inspection of the proposed battlefield on the day before Culloden, it only confirmed his worst fears. He, therefore, sent Stapleton and Colonel James Ker to reconnoitre another field of battle, which he had previously inspected. Lying to the south of the River Nairn, they judged it 'very strong ground', ideally suited to the Highlanders' way of fighting, and likely to bring them victory 'had the Duke of Cumberland ventured to have passed the water of Nairn in their sight, and attack them there'. Moreover, Murray thought that, if Cumberland did not cross the Nairn to attack the Jacobites there, they could retire farther, drawing him up to the mountains, to attack him 'at some pass or strong ground'.

A. J. Youngson, in *The Prince and the Pretender*, comments that the Jacobite army, by withdrawing into the Highlands, could have constantly harassed Cumberland and a single error by him might well have led to a Highland charge like the one which gave victory to Viscount Dundee at the Battle of Killiecrankie in 1689. But nothing would sway the Prince from deciding to fight Cumberland on Culloden Moor, dismissing the advice of Murray, whom he now insisted on seeing as the architect of all his misfortunes. The Marquis d'Eguilles complained that the Prince, 'proud and haughty as he was, badly advised, perhaps even betrayed, forgetting at this moment every other object, could not bring himself to decline battle for even a single day'.

The Prince, therefore, took the fatal decision to fight on ground that was more favourable to the enemy. However, not only did he decide to fight the battle in the wrong place, but he also chose the wrong day. Had he fallen back to a defensive position, in line with Murray's advice, substantial reinforcements would have arrived over the next two days for the Jacobite army. Instead, it was seriously understrength when it met Cumberland's forces at Culloden on 16 April. The forces under the Earl of Cromartie were still in Caithness and Sutherland, while the MacPhersons of Cluny had not returned from Badenoch, where they were threatened by Hanoverian forces advancing into Atholl.

Moreover, Lochiel did not join the Jacobite army at Culloden until the evening of 14 April, bringing only half his regiment, while Keppoch only appeared the following day and his regiment was short of numbers too. Three hundred Frasers, under Charles Fraser the younger of Inverallochy, appeared on the morning of the battle itself, while the other Fraser regiment, under Lovat, arrived too late, perhaps deliberately. Only by delaying the battle could the Jacobite army be brought up to strength. Meanwhile, lack of provisions would have forced it to withdraw into the Highlands and the Prince absolutely rejected what he saw as a retreat.

Murray later claimed that:

there was above ten days' provisions in Inverness . . . and a vast deal of bread had been baked, but whether it was an ill-timed economy or that in the confusion for two days before the battle they had neglected to provide horses to bring out the provisions . . . Had provisions been distributed as they ought to have been, there would have been no obligation to have given . . . battle when two thousand more men would have joined in a day or two.

The responsibility for provisioning the Jacobite army had been with John Murray of Broughton but he fell ill with scarlet fever in early April. His place as the Prince's secretary was taken by John Hay of Restalrig and he proved totally incompetent. The troops in the field were forced to survive on half rations, despite the provisions supposedly stored at Inverness.

Abortive Last-Minute Marches with Starving Troops

On April 14, two days before the battle itself, as Cumberland was advancing towards Nairn, Charles Edward Stuart in Inverness ordered the drums to beat and the pipes to play. The hungry men in the town were assembled, the cannon was ordered forward and the Prince rode out at their head to Culloden House, while Murray mustered troops quartered outside the town. Next day, the whole army marched up to the moor, where they were drawn in battle order to await the arrival of the Duke of Cumberland. Cumberland, however, stayed in camp at Nairn with his army, having more important things to do – he was celebrating his birthday.

Throughout 15 April, the Jacobite army waited in readiness for an enemy move that did not happen and, at the end of the day, it was forced to stand down. With mounting impatience, the Prince now suggested a surprise dawn attack on Cumberland's camp. Although Murray was very aware of the risks of failure, he grasped at this plan – anything would be better than fighting on Culloden Moor, his only condition being that the attack should be launched before 2 a.m. while it was still pitch dark. With any luck, Cumberland's men might also be blind drunk after his birthday festivities (although in fact they had only been issued with half a pint of brandy). It was, therefore, decided to march towards Nairn as soon as darkness fell. But, mustering the men, the officers found that many had gone off looking for food. While Cumberland's soldiers had been celebrating his birthday, the Jacobite troops had only had a single biscuit as their daily ration. When they refused to return, saying that they would rather be shot for desertion than starve, they were left behind.

The Prince, however, still insisted on an attack and gave the order to march. Murray set off first, at the head of the Camerons and the other Highland regiments, followed by Lord John Drummond with the Lowland regiments, while the Prince brought up the rear with the Royal Scots and the Irish Piquets, under the Duke of Perth. They avoided the roads for fear of running into Cumberland's patrols, marching instead across Culraich Moor towards Nairn. By 1 a.m., the vanguard under Murray had only covered six miles in the pitch darkness over rough and very boggy ground. The troops behind were even slower, stumbling 'through trackless paths, marshes and quagmires'. The heavily-equipped French units at the rear found it particularly hard going.

Eventually, Murray's advance guard reached the farm of Knockanbuie near the Muir of the Clans, under three miles from Cumberland's camp at Balblair on the outskirts of Nairn. By then, he realised that the attack could not be launched before dawn, with his men clearly exhausted from lack of food, and he, therefore, sent Lochiel back to the Prince, advising him to call off the attack. Charles's anger was rising, however, and he would not hear of retreat. Instead, he ordered Lochiel to return to Murray, with Lord John Drummond, John O'Sullivan and the Duke of Perth, to try to persuade him to press on with the attack. At around 2 a.m., the commanders of the Highland regiments joined them to report that many of their own men had fallen back, from sheer exhaustion, along the way, faint with hunger. All but John O'Sullivan agreed that they could not reach Cumberland's camp in time to launch an attack before dawn, when all surprise would be lost.

While Murray and his commanders were arguing with O'Sullivan, the detested John Hay of Restalrig arrived with urgent orders from the Prince – Murray was to attack Cumberland at once with whatever forces he had under his command. Murray had a maximum of 1,000 men, as against Cumberland's 8,000 – but he was instructed that he was not even to wait for the rest of the Jacobite forces to catch up so that a simultaneous attack from two different directions could be launched, as originally planned. When Murray refused to obey, Hay galloped back to warn the Prince that 'unless he come to the front and ordered his Lordship [Murray] to go on, nothing would be done'.

At that point, a drum beat was heard in Cumberland's camp, raising the alarm, and Murray ordered his troops to return as quickly as possible to Culloden House, marching along the main road now that secrecy was pointless. Perth galloped back to the second column, ordering them to go back the way they had come. They had hardly gone a hundred yards when the Prince passed them, riding furiously to the front, demanding to know what was happening. When Perth's officers told him that they were ordered to return to Culloden House, the Prince was distraught, shouting,

'I am betrayed! What need have I to give orders when my orders are disobeyed'. Perth could not be found in the confusion but, when he did appear, he told the Prince that 'Lord George Murray . . . turned back with the first column three-quarters of an hour ago'.

The Prince was incredulous and demanded that Murray be called back. Eventually, he accepted the inevitable, however, especially after hearing that Lochiel had been party to the decision. His Irish officers blamed Murray for the debacle, reinforcing the suspicions of the Prince, who apparently made his closest associates promise to watch Murray, particularly during battle, and to shoot him if they found that he was intending to betray the Jacobite cause. This was the state of relations between Charles Edward Stuart and Lord George Murray, his commander-in-chief, on the morning of Culloden.

Chapter Fourteen

BATTLE OF CULLODEN

By 6 a.m. on 16 April 1746, nearly all the Jacobite forces had returned to Culloden House in a sullen and dejected state, after the aborted attack upon Cumberland's camp. They were exhausted after marching almost to Nairn and back, and the senior officers rested in the house, while their men sheltered in its grounds. The Prince himself started off towards Inverness to demand food from the townspeople for his hungry troops but returned after the Duke of Perth had persuaded him that his troops needed him at their head, especially as he had now decided to command them in person. Colonel Robert O'Shea was sent instead to Inverness with a hundred troopers of FitzJames's Horse to carry back whatever provisions they could find. It is not certain whether or not he succeeded, although a soldier in Cumberland's army claimed later that, before the battle, the Jacobite forces had 'a double portion of oatmeal and whisky for encouragement'.

The Marquis d'Eguilles tried once more to dissuade Charles from giving battle on Culloden Moor. He later wrote to Louis XV:

> In vain I represented to him that he was still without half his army; that the greater part of those who had returned had no longer their targets – a kind of defensive armour without which they were unable to fight to advantage; that they were all worn out with fatigue by the long march made on the previous night; and for two days many of them had not eaten at all for want of bread. In the end, finding him immovable in the resolve he had taken to fight at any cost, I made my desire yield to my duty. I left him for the first time. I retired in haste to Inverness, there to burn all my papers and there to think over the means for preserving your Majesty that portion of the [Franco-Irish] troops which might survive the action.

Call to Arms

At 8 a.m., the Prince, at Culloden House, heard that Cumberland's army was now only four miles away, having struck camp at daybreak. Amid scenes of confusion, the Jacobite troops were roused and marched up to Culloden Moor. Many had gone off foraging for food, while others were left behind, still fast asleep on the ground. Although the nominal strength of the Prince's army was 8,000 men, according to the muster rolls fewer than 5,000 men fought at Culloden. They faced a regular army under Cumberland of 8,000 or 9,000 men who were well trained, well fed and strong in artillery and cavalry.

Only 1,000 men were ready to march when the alarm was first raised. Reaching Culloden Moor, they were drawn up further back than the day before and on much less advantageous ground. The Jacobite army was no longer protected by marshy ground to its left, while a boggy hollow in front of the Highlanders would have to be crossed when charging the enemy. Charles was now so desperate to draw up his troops for battle that he curtly refused Murray 'a little time to view the ground', so the boggy area went unnoticed.

Struggling against time, the Jacobite commanders under the supervision of John O'Sullivan drew up their men to face Cumberland's army approaching from the east. The Highland regiments made up the first line of over 3,000 men but their exact disposition is uncertain. Contrary to custom, the MacDonalds did not take their traditional place on the right wing, having probably arrived late on the field to find the Atholl Brigade, under Murray, occupying this position. Flanking the Atholl Brigade on its left were the Camerons of Lochiel and the Stewarts of Appin. The centre of the front line was made up of the Frasers, the MacIntoshes of Clan Chattan and the Farquharsons, all under the command of Lord John Drummond. Beyond them were the MacLeans, the MacLachlans, the MacLeods and the Chisholms, as well as John Roy Stewart's Regiment. The left wing was formed by the MacDonalds of Glencoe, Clanranald, Keppoch and Glengarry, together with the Grants of Glenmoriston and possibly the Duke of Perth's Regiment (if it was not in the second line).

The second line had fewer than 2,000 men, under the command of Stapleton. They included Lord Ogilvie's Regiment on the right wing, flanked by the regiments of Lord Lewis Gordon, Glenbucket and possibly the Duke of Perth, in the centre, while Lord John Drummond's Regiment and the Irish Piquets made up the left wing. What cavalry the Jacobites possessed was mostly concentrated behind the second line of infantry regiments.

After riding among his men to exhort them to victory, the Prince had retired with a small party of FitzJames's Lifeguards to a small hillock behind the right wing of his army. There he had a good view of the battlefield but he was not far enough forward to command his army in person, as he had wanted. Moreover, occasional showers of sleet and snow, blown on a stiff easterly wind, obscured his view and, once the battle began, the smoke from the guns drifted towards him, hiding the action.

As Cumberland advanced across the open ground into battle, he also drew up his men in two lines. Seven regiments of infantry made up his front line, with another six regiments in the second. Three other regiments were in reserve towards his rear. His troops outnumbered the Jacobites, out-flanking them on both wings. He also left a gap of fifty yards between the two lines, so that any Highlanders breaking through his front line would then have to charge the second line across this exposed ground. This defence in depth meant that any Highland charge had to penetrate both infantry lines if it was not to be overwhelmed.

Cumberland's army advanced in good order to within 600 yards of the Jacobite lines, when his artillery pieces became bogged down in the marshy ground. Seeing this, the Prince sent O'Sullivan forward to Murray with orders to attack while the Hanoverian troops struggled to extricate the cannon. It seemed an ideal moment to take the initiative but the Jacobite army had still not all arrived on the battlefield. Murray judged that he had insufficient troops for an effective attack over such a long distance since 'what vigour the men had left would be spent before they could reach the enemy'.

Moreover, Murray was uneasily aware that a series of enclosures to his right would provide ideal cover for Cumberland's troops to encircle the Jacobite army from the south. Lochiel had already reported that a large body of Argyll Militia and some cavalry had drawn away from the main body of Cumberland's army with exactly that intention. On first arriving on the battlefield, Murray had wanted to pull down the drystone walls of the enclosures, which would have been easy enough. But the Prince and O'Sullivan had refused on the grounds that it would break the Jacobite lines. They were concerned that Cumberland would attack before their own forces were ready, although his troops had not yet appeared. Instead, detachments of Stoneywood's Regiment from Aberdeen were moved from the far left of the second line to defend the right flank of Murray's Atholl Brigade.

Battle Begins

When the battle began in the early afternoon of 16 April 1746, the two armies were still several hundred yards apart. The guns of the Jacobite artillery opened fire first but did negligible damage, as the gun-crews were poorly trained and the artillery itself varied in quality, making the effective supply of ammunition difficult.

By contrast, the efficiency of Cumberland's artillery decided the ultimate outcome of the battle. He had placed his artillery batteries between the regiments in his front line but also slightly behind them, where they could be swung round and discharged against any Highlanders who had managed to break through towards the second line. Once his ten three-pounders opened up, they maintained a well-directed and ferocious bombardment, which lasted anything up to half an hour. At first, they fired cannonballs towards the rear of the Jacobite lines, aiming for the Prince and the troopers around him. Then, Cumberland ordered his gunners to switch to grapeshot, which swept the field like a hail storm, devastating the Jacobite lines and cutting huge swathes through them. Cumberland found that his guns were rapidly thinning out the Jacobite ranks without a corresponding loss in return. A volunteer in his army later wrote: 'Their lines were formed so thick and deep that the grapeshot made open lanes quite through them, the men dropping down by wholesale.' When Cumberland's infantry moved forward, they 'could hardly march for bodies'.

Because of the many conflicting accounts of the battle itself, it is not clear exactly why the Jacobite army faced the Hanoverian artillery for so long without attacking the enemy. Cumberland himself had no need to order his infantry to attack the Jacobites, when his artillery was so effective. The Prince, on the other hand, is frequently accused of being stricken with indecision and delaying orders to his troops to charge the enemy. One account suggests that he was waiting for the return of officers sent to reconnoitre the ground to the south for a pincer movement attacking the enemy lines from the rear. Others claim that he did issue orders for an immediate attack which either failed to get through or were disobeyed – a messenger from the Prince to Murray was supposedly decapitated by a cannonball. After further delays, Murray finally received a belated order to advance against the Hanoverian lines at the head of the Atholl Brigade. Only when 'the Highlanders were much galled by the enemy's cannon and were turned so impatient that they were like to break their ranks' were they finally ordered to attack.

Quite a different version of events states that Jacobite indiscipline may have contributed to the chaos: the right wing, seeing the MacDonalds on the left wing advance, followed their example without orders from Murray; whereas the MacIntoshes in the centre of the front line probably broke into a full-blooded Highland charge, unable to endure the bombardment any longer.

Charging into Slaughter

Only as the Jacobite right wing advanced did it become clear just how bad its position was. The Campbells had already taken cover behind the drystone walls that Murray had wanted demolished, firing at the Atholl Brigade as it charged past towards the enemy lines. Worse, Cumberland had moved the musketeers of Wolfe's Regiment forward to a position on his left wing at right angles to his front line and slightly in advance of it. Lying behind a wall of turf, they could fire volley after volley at the Atholl Brigade as it passed in front of them, inflicting such heavy casualties that very few Athollmen even reached the Hanoverian lines before falling back in retreat.

To the left of the Atholl Brigade, the Camerons of Lochiel and the Stewarts of Appin were veering sharply to their right as they rushed forward, perhaps trying to avoid the boggy ground directly in front of them, exposing themselves to salvo after salvo of devastating enemy fire. Only the MacIntoshes of Clan Chattan, under Alexander MacGillivray of Dunmaglass, charged straight at the enemy lines, close to their centre. But their attack ground to a halt just short of the Hanoverian lines, having suffered heavy losses including the death of Dunmaglass.

Consequently, the Highlanders' charge was hopelessly concentrated upon the two regiments on Cumberland's left wing. The Jacobite ranks became tightly packed together against the turf wall running along their right flank. Nevertheless, the Camerons of Lochiel and the Stewarts of Appin, pressed their charge forward, fighting hand-to-hand with Cumberland's infantry and breaking through to face his second line. The Hanoverian infantrymen advanced in good order for fifty yards against the Highlanders, before kneeling down to pour a devastating volley of musket fire into them.

The impact of the Jacobite attack was shattered. Only a few Highlanders managed to cover the intervening ground to fight the enemy and nearly all died on Hanoverian bayonets. One of Cumberland's officers later boasted: 'Our lads fought more like Devils than men . . . no one that attacked us, escaped alive, for we gave no quarter, nor would accept of any.' Of the 500 men who probably broke through Cumberland's front line, very few escaped alive, attacked from nearly every direction. Those who managed to retreat towards safer ground were still exposed to a hail of musket fire from Wolfe's Regiment and the Argyll Militia, who were now positioned to their left. The Campbells even mounted a small charge from behind the walls of the enclosure, losing eight men and two officers.

Even while his men retreated, Murray still managed to mount a rear-guard action. The Hanoverian cavalry had broken through the walls of the enclosure south of the battlefield and had actually reached a lane running behind the Prince's position. Realising the danger, Murray ordered Lord Elcho's Lifeguards and FitzJames's Horse, along with the infantrymen of Lord Ogilvie's Regiment, to confront this new threat. Although heavily outnumbered, they managed to hold off the enemy cavalry for a precious ten minutes. This action allowed the surviving Jacobite forces on the right wing to escape total destruction. Murray himself 'had behaved . . . with great gallantry, lost his horse, his periwig, and bonnet . . . had several cuts . . . in his coat, and was covered in blood and dirt'.

Exactly what happened on the Prince's left wing is equally confused. The two armies were positioned somewhat obliquely to one another, so that the left wing of the Jacobite army had to cover an even greater distance than its right wing to attack the Hanoverian lines. But, instead of advancing before the right wing had begun its charge, the left wing seems to have hesitated, so that the Jacobite attack was uncoordinated, failing to strike the whole front line of the Hanoverian army simultaneously, which was virtually its only chance of success. Moreover, the MacDonalds, slighted at losing their accustomed place of honour on the right wing, were probably reluctant at first to charge the Hanoverian lines, ignoring Lord John Drummond and the Duke of Perth when they eventually received the order from the Prince to advance.

Alexander MacDonald of Keppoch seems to have broken the impasse. Yelling out in frustration, '*Mo Dhia, an do threig clann mo chinnidh mi?*' (My God, have the children of my clan forsaken me?), he rushed forward alone, brandishing his pistol and broadsword, to be hit almost immediately by a musket ball which shattered his right arm. Goaded into action, his clansmen dashed after their wounded chief, along with the other MacDonalds. Now at the head of his clansmen and still advancing against the enemy, Keppoch received a chest wound which killed him outright. Another shot killed his brother Donald.

Although the MacDonalds on the Jacobite left wing probably only hesitated momentarily before obeying the Prince's belated order to attack, they never mounted a full-blooded Highland charge against Cumberland. Instead, they seem to have advanced slowly and cautiously across the boggy ground, hoping no doubt to provoke the Hanoverian infantry into charging. The tactic did not work. Cumberland wrote that the Highlanders

came running on in their wild manner, and upon the right [that is, the Jacobite left wing] where I had placed myself . . . they came down there several times within a hundred yards of our men, firing their pistols and brandishing their swords, but the Royals and Pultenay's hardly took their fire-locks from their shoulders, so that after those faint attempts they made off; and the little squadrons [of cavalry] on our right were sent to pursue them. General Hawley had by the help of our Highlanders beat down two little stone walls [around the

Culloden enclosures], and came in upon the right flank of their second line.

Even so, this attempt to encircle the MacDonalds was thwarted by covering fire from the Irish Piquets, at the extreme left of the Jacobite second line. However, they eventually fell back towards Inverness, carrying the wounded Stapleton with them. He died a few days later from his injuries.

By now, as Kirkconnel later wrote, 'the day was irretrievably lost; nothing could stop the Highlanders once they had begun to run'. Cumberland ordered his infantry to halt and they dressed their ranks, not taking possession of the battlefield until later. Meanwhile, the Hanoverian cavalry chased the fleeing Jacobite survivors from the field, running down and butchering them with sword and pistol. Cumberland entered Inverness at 4 p.m. at the head of his army and took the surrender of the Royal Scots and the Irish Piquets, who, as French citizens, were treated as prisoners of war.

Escape of the Prince

Charles Edward Stuart left the battlefield once it was clear that the day was lost. As John Home reported in his near-contemporary account, *The History of the Rebellion in the Year 1745* (which was not published until more than fifty years later in 1802):

> When Charles saw the Highlanders repulsed and flying, which he had never seen before, he advanced, it is said, to go down and rally them. But the earnest entreaties of his tutor, Sir Thomas Sheridan and others, who assured him it was impossible, prevailed upon him to leave the field.

Home admitted in a footnote that

> the persons who attended Charles on the day of the battle did not agree exactly in their accounts of what passed; most of them . . . gave the same account that is given above. But the cornet who carried the standard of the second troop of horse guards, has left a paper, signed with his name, in which he says, that the entreaties . . . would have been in vain, if General O'Sullivan had not laid hold of the bridle of Charles's horse, and turned him about. To witness this, says the coronet, I summon mine eyes.

Charles himself apparently said he 'was forced off the field by the people about him, who refused to allow him to sacrifice his own life for a cause that was now clearly lost, however he may have wished for martyrdom'. He rode off with FitzJames's Cavalry, and a small party of his closest followers, including Lord Elcho, Sheridan, Hay of Restalrig and O'Sullivan.

At the Ford of Faillie over the River Nairn, some miles upstream from Culloden Moor, Charles dismissed the Franco-Irish cavalry, who turned back to surrender to Cumberland. He then rode up Strathnairn to the Fraser country of Stratherrick, where he stopped at Gortuleg (now Gorthleck) House. There, quite fortuitously, he met Lord Lovat, who had sought refuge with his kinsman, Fraser of Gortuleg, after escaping from Loudon's custody. It was an unfortunate meeting for Lovat, which sealed his fate when he was later captured by the government. But Gortuleg offered little sanctuary to the Prince and his party, and Charles continued his flight, finally reaching the security of Glengarry's castle at Invergarry at 2 a.m. on 17 April. Charles Edward Stuart would spend the next five months evading Cumberland's forces before eventually escaping to France.

Casualties at Culloden

The casualty figures are a stark illustration of the scale of the Jacobite defeat at Culloden. Of Cumberland's army of over 8,000 men, fewer than 100 men were killed and just 259 were wounded, all but six of the dead being infantrymen. They were mostly killed or wounded in stemming the Highland charge that broke upon Cumberland's left wing.

Hardly surprisingly, the Jacobite army suffered far worse casualties, although the exact numbers of dead and wounded are very uncertain. Lieutenant-Colonel George Stanhope, veteran of Fontenoy and Falkirk, declared: 'I never saw such dreadful slaughter . . . I reckon two thousand of them killed in the field besides a full thousand killed in the pursuit by the horse and dragoons with a great many of their chiefs.' According to the *Newcastle Journal* of 26 April 1746, '1,700 [bodies] were buried from the field of battle . . . and it appears in all that 3,600 have been killed'. Jacobite sources suggest that around 4,000 men were killed, half the total strength of the Jacobite forces, had they all been present at Culloden.

These casualty figures are just possible, given that Highland armies under Montrose and Dundee inflicted equally heavy losses on their opponents in the seventeenth century. However, as only 5,000 men fought for the Prince at Culloden, while at least 1,500 men from the remnants of his army mustered at Ruthven a few days later, the numbers seem too high. More likely, as A. J. Youngson has suggested, the total casualties were around 2,500 men at the very most, with 1,000 killed upon the battlefield and another 1,500 cut down in flight. They tally with the figure of 1,000, left dead on the battlefield, given by Colonel John

Campbell, while 750 bodies were counted by a surgeon in Cumberland's army. Such losses imply that, of the men who actually fought for the Prince at Culloden, nearly, if not quite, half were slaughtered in the battle or in flight from it.

The manner in which many met their deaths is equally disputed. There is so much anecdotal evidence, mostly collected by Bishop Robert Forbes of the Episcopalian Church, that it leaves no doubt that the Hanoverian forces committed widespread atrocities in the immediate aftermath of the battle itself. Doubtless, many Jacobites were killed by Cumberland's men as they lay wounded upon the ground, dispatched in the heat of the action or just afterwards. However, others appear to have been killed in cold blood wherever they were found still asleep after their exhausting march to Nairn of the previous night. Even a Whig historian later admitted that:

> the soldiers, warm in their resentment, stabbed at some of the wounded . . . The troops were enraged at their hardships and fatigues during a winter campaign; the habit of the enemy was strange, their language still stranger, and their mode of fighting unusual; the fields of Preston[pans] and Falkirk were still fresh in their memories.

This may well explain the absence of wounded among the hundreds of Jacobite prisoners held at Inverness after the battle, although wounded men were not usually listed separately at the time.

There are allegations that Cumberland issued actual orders on the day of the battle that the rebel troops in the Prince's army should be given no quarter, but these remain unsubstantiated. Even so, Cumberland openly snubbed those Hanoverian officers who did offer quarter. Of Cumberland's commanders, Hawley apparently encouraged his men to bayonet any Jacobite still alive on the battlefield. He even ordered Brevet-Major James Wolfe (who would later achieve fame upon the Heights of Abraham) to kill Charles Fraser, the younger of Inverallochy, as he lay wounded on the ground. Wolfe refused but a private soldier obliged instead.

Many more were evidently killed in flight. However, it must be remembered that nearly every Highland charge during the previous century had ended in the hot pursuit of men fleeing in panic, who were cut down and killed, often by troops of Royalist cavalry; now it was the Highlanders who suffered the same fate as they ran in headlong flight from Culloden Moor. As Cumberland later wrote:

> Lord Ancram was ordered to pursue with the horse as far as he could, and which he did with so good effect, that a very considerable

number were killed in the pursuit . . . Major-General Bland . . . also made great slaughter and gave quarter to none but about fifty French officers and soldiers he picked up in his pursuit.'

The Hanoverian cavalry 'cut down every thing in their way' as they mercilessly harried the fleeing Jacobites, so that 'for near four miles from where the pursuit began, the ground is covered with dead bodies'. Even the streets of Inverness were said to run with the blood of victims, while, according to John Ray, 'the misery and distress of the fugitive rebels was inexpressible, hundreds being found dead of their wounds, and through hunger, at the distance, fourteen, or twenty miles from the field of battle'.

Claims of Atrocities

This bloodletting by Cumberland's troops might be put down to pent-up frustration in facing an enemy who fought by a different and more elemental code of honour. But, as W. A. Speck has emphasised, the plan to attack Cumberland's camp at Balblair the night before Culloden depended on equal remorselessness from the Highlanders. According to O'Sullivan, no separate orders were issued before the troops set out, while Murray later stated that 'there was no need of orders. Everybody knew what he was to do . . . the order of battle was sufficient'. However, halfway to Cumberland's camp, Murray sent back instructions for his officers 'to order their men to make attack sword in hand, which would not alarm the enemy so soon'. Moreover, the troops entering the camp were not

> to make use of [their] firearms, but only of sword, dirk and bayonet, to cut down the tent strings [guys], and pull down the poles, and where [they] observed a swelling or bulge in the fallen tent, there to strike and push vigorously.

Doubtless, every man on the night march to Nairn knew that success depended on striking at Cumberland's troops in cold blood as they lay asleep, without giving them time to surrender.

In the immediate aftermath of Culloden, the Hanoverian troops probably felt justified in giving the rebels no quarter, knowing how narrowly they had escaped a similar fate the previous night. When Lord Bury brought the news from Culloden to London, he was asked if the Duke of Cumberland gave the order that no quarters should be given. To which he answered that he had not but that his men, 'knowing the day before the action, the orders of the rebel generals, [he] believed they gave the rebels no quarter'. The troops were not restrained by Cumberland and his officers, who turned a blind eye to their atrocities on the day of the battle, and some of whom, like Hawley, actually encouraged them.

It is more difficult to explain away the following written order that Cumberland issued on 17 April, the morning after Culloden:

A captain and fifty foot to march directly and visit all the cottages in the neighbourhood of the field of battle, and to search for rebels. The officers and men will take notice that the public orders of the rebels yesterday was to give us no quarter.

Although the wording seems almost deliberately unspecific, doubtless Cumberland's own troops took it as a licence for merciless slaughter. It is hard to believe that he simply intended 'to warn those detailed for the work that they had to deal with desperate men from whom no quarter was to be expected', as one apologist for Cumberland claimed.

Cumberland seems to have issued this order in retaliation for what he believed were similar written orders to the Jacobites before Culloden, an assumption widely shared by the Hanoverian forces. William Oman wrote from Inverness on 23 April: 'Their mock Prince gave out orders not to give quarters to the English, which caused a great many lives to be taken.' A letter in the *Newcastle Journal* explained that Wolfe's Regiment had taken more prisoners in the thick of the fighting than it 'should have done, had we known their orders, which was to spare neither man, woman or child.' Then, just ten days after the Battle of Culloden, the *Newcastle Journal* published what purported to be a 'copy of the rebels' orders' to 'give no quarter to the Elector's troops on any account whatsoever'. Another version, printed in the *Gentlemen's Journal*, was said to bear Murray's signature.

Several copies of the orders issued by Murray do exist, all signed by him. None carry the words 'and to give no quarters to the Elector's troops on any account whatsoever', except for one copy, supposedly found in the pocket of a Highlander, captured after the fighting. It was not in Murray's handwriting, was not signed by him and was written on the bottom half of a copy of a declaration published by Lord John Drummond at Montrose on 2 December 1745.

Whoever wrote this document can hardly have been attempting a serious forgery. It was certainly not Cumberland nor one of his staff, even if Kirkconnel, in his memoirs, accused the Hanoverian general of producing

an impudent forgery of an order from the Prince . . . for no other purpose but to execute what was intended, and to divest the common

soldiers of all sentiments of humanity and compassion and harden
them for the execution of such bloody designs.

A. J. Youngson's view is that 'it is virtually certain no such orders were ever
issued; but they were believed to be issued, and Cumberland used this
belief to encourage his men to spare no one'.

Apparently, Cumberland's order was only carried out two days after the
battle, following reports from burial parties that many Jacobites still lay
wounded upon the battlefield. According to contemporary accounts given
to Bishop Forbes, Culloden Moor was scoured by detachments of
Cumberland's army over the next two days and all Jacobite wounded
systematically put to death. An account in the *Newcastle Journal* of 3 May
even claimed that the Jacobites brought retaliation upon themselves
because of 'the treacherous behaviour of some of the rebels who, after
quarter was given, fired at the officers who had given it'.

One of the worst atrocities recorded was the fate of 'a multitude of
prisoners, all gentlemen, [who] lay under strong guards' at Culloden
House. Seriously wounded, the officers were there for three days without
any medical attention before eighteen were taken away in carts. They
included John Fraser, an ensign in Lovat's Regiment and they were all
supposedly shot and left for dead. Only Fraser survived and recorded the
event in a pamphlet entitled *An Account of the Signal Escape of John Fraser*,
published in 1749. When it appeared, his story was challenged by two
Hanoverian officers, who had fought at Culloden. They gave an assurance
under oath that Fraser's account was 'absolutely false and groundless'. One
of them, who had spent fourteen weeks recovering from his wounds in
Culloden House, declared

> to his certain knowledge, none of the wounded rebels were carried to
> Culloden House; that a few of the common soldiers were there and
> two sergeants but not one Ensign nor any of superior rank. He added
> that not one of those had received any hurt and that they did not
> remain in the House above two hours.

This may be quite untrue, but it certainly casts doubt on the episode.
Equally, John Fraser's account cannot be substantiated by independent
evidence, like so many statements recorded by Forbes in *The Lyon in
Mourning*.

However, there are other versions of this account which have the ring of
truth. William Rose, grieve to Duncan Forbes of Culloden, described to
Bishop Forbes how twelve wounded men had sheltered in his house after
the battle. A party of Hanoverian soldiers under an officer had taken them

out of the house that Friday, saying a surgeon would dress their wounds. A few minutes later, Rose's wife heard musket fire and rushed out to find their bodies. Apparently, George II later asked Duncan Forbes if it was true that 'a party of the Duke's army had killed certain supposed rebels, who had fled for safety into the court of Culloden House'. Forbes replied that he wished he could say 'No'. His honesty lost him all favour at Court.

Whether or not individual reports of atrocities are true, the Jacobite wounded at Culloden were certainly left untended for two or three days. Yet, almost incredibly, the Hanoverian wounded seem to have been almost as callously neglected, as W. A. Speck has emphasised. After the battle, it took Cumberland three days to order a sergeant and six men to take fifteen or twenty carts

> as soon as possible to the houses in the neighbourhood of the field of battle in order to bring to the hospital here [in Inverness] the poor wounded soldiers who through the negligence of the officers and surgeons were left there without care.

The order clearly referred only to the Hanoverian wounded, since it also required that their regimental name and number should be established.

Such acts of common humanity, even if delayed, apparently earned Cumberland the devotion of his troops, despite the harsh discipline he exercised over them. He was 'our dear Bill' to 'his brave boys' and he returned to London a national hero. However, in Scotland, especially in the Highlands, he left behind a reputation as 'The Butcher' for the atrocities he allowed his soldiers to commit in the aftermath of Culloden. Over the subsequent months, he put into effect a savage policy of brutal repression in the Highlands, directed against the Jacobite clans.

Nevertheless, the General Assembly of the Church of Scotland praised Cumberland's 'illustrious name, so dear to us', while hoping that he might 'share the happiness and glory bestowed by Divine Mercy on those who have been eminent examples of virtue and the happy instruments of communicating public blessings to mankind'. He was even appointed Chancellor of the University of St Andrews. Nothing demonstrates so clearly the religious schism that then divided Scotland, separating the Presbyterian Lowlands from the Episcopalian Highlands, north of the River Tay.

Chapter Fifteen

AFTERMATH OF CULLODEN

A Defeated Army

After the Jacobites' catastrophic defeat at Culloden, Lord George Murray rallied the shattered remnants of his forces, falling back through Balvraid to the Ford of Faillie, which the Prince had crossed a little earlier. There he met Aeneas MacDonald, who had stayed behind with money from the Prince in the form of 500 Spanish *pistoles* (a gold coin worth slightly less that a pound sterling), which he gave to Murray to pay his followers. Murray and the other survivors then moved on, sleeping out that night near Loch Moy, before being joined there, the morning after the battle, by 300–400 clansmen from Badenoch, under MacPherson of Cluny. Worried about a surprise attack by the Grants, Murray ordered them to act as a rearguard as the defeated army marched south-west along Strathspey on the Prince's instructions, making for Ruthven in Badenoch.

Next day, Murray was outraged to receive a demand from the Prince for the return of the Spanish *pistoles*. Burning with indignation 'that the Prince carries away the money while so many gentlemen who have sacrificed their fortunes for him are starving', Murray gave vent to his frustrations in a long letter, castigating the Prince and resigning his commission. This outburst seems merely to have stoked the Prince's suspicions of his former commander-in-chief to the point of paranoia.

By 20 April, what remained of the Jacobite rank and file had mustered at Ruthven along with many of their officers – probably a total of just 1,500 men. This disregards the over-optimistic estimate given by the Chevalier de Johnstone that there were

4,000 or 5,000 Highlanders, all in the best disposition possible for renewing the contest, and having their revenge . . . breathing with impatience for the moment to be led back to the enemy . . . Everyone beseeched the Prince most earnestly to come thither quickly to put himself at their head.

Elcho and Lovat had put the option of further military action to Charles at Gortuleg but, by then, he had taken the advice of Sheridan and O'Sullivan to try to escape to the Continent. If the Scots had failed him, the French would surely help him with yet another army. He must have known for certain that the war-weary French had already discounted any further armed support but he chose to totally ignore that.

There are widely varying accounts of the dismissal of the Jacobite forces at Ruthven: Lord Elcho, who was with the Prince, claimed that the men were told on the way there to 'disperse and everybody shift for himself as best he could'; Andrew Lumisden, who was at Ruthven, stated that the Prince eventually sent a message of thanks to his followers for their bravery and devotion, advising them 'to do what they thought was best for their own preservation, till a more favourable opportunity of acting presented itself'; the Chevalier de Johnstone's version was that, in response to a message from Murray, the Prince sent the well-known, laconic reply: 'Let everyone seek the means of escape as well as he can'; while Ker of Graden claimed that the Prince did not bother to reply, so that the army just dispersed after waiting a few days.

Yet another account has the Prince behaving much less honourably, getting his aide-de-camp to write to Cluny on the evening after the battle:

> We are to review tomorrow at Fort Augustus, the Frasers, Camerons, Stewarts, Clanranald's and Keppoch's people. His Royal Highness expects your people [the MacPhersons] will be with us at furthest Friday morning [18 April]. Dispatch is the more necessary that His Highness has something in view which will make ample amends for this day's ruffle [at Culloden].

Since the bearer of the letter let slip that Charles was, at that moment, heading along the Great Glen in the opposite direction to Fort Augustus, this version of events suggests that he was trying to use his followers as decoys in order to deceive Cumberland about his own whereabouts.

Cumberland now made Inverness his headquarters for the next five weeks. Orders were given that the Jacobite leaders were to be detained, while the ordinary Highlanders still in arms were required to surrender their weapons on pain of execution. They would then be issued with certificates, allowing them to 'return unmolested to their homes until his Majesty's pleasure is known'. Nevertheless, Lochiel, along with Stewart of Ardshiel and Cluny, tried to maintain the momentum of the Rebellion, calling a meeting at Murlaggan near the head of Loch Arkaig in late April. It was attended by Lovat, MacDonald of Barisdale, MacDonald of Lochgarry, Glenbucket and John Roy Stewart and several others. Ranald MacDonald, younger of Clanranald, was absent, having returned home severely wounded after Culloden. They all agreed to muster under arms a week later for a summer campaign of guerrilla warfare against Cumberland's forces but had to abandon their plans after a poor response. Instead, they were threatened by Cumberland, who by then controlled the Great Glen.

Their threat of further insurrection must have finally convinced Cumberland, if he needed any convincing, that only a savage policy of widespread repression would end the 1745 Rebellion, especially while the Prince still remained at large. By refusing to accept the inevitable after such a decisive defeat at Culloden, the chiefs of the Jacobite clans had merely made a desperate situation far worse for themselves and, more especially, for their clansmen.

Cumberland's Policy of Repression with Fire and Sword

Cumberland was now absolutely determined, in his own words, 'to bruise those bad seeds spread about this country so as they may never shoot again'. He shared the anti-Scottish prejudice of many who held high office in England, that 'the Jacobite principle is so rooted in this nation's mind that this generation must be pretty well worn out, before this country is quiet'. But by mid-May, when he moved to Fort Augustus, only the Fraser country at the head of the Beauly Firth had felt the full force of Cumberland's repression.

His first orders were to Brigadier John Mordaunt to march into the Fraser country with 900 volunteers, 'to destroy all the rebels he finds there'. In the plunder, Mordaunt brought back were 1,000 bottles of wine, a substantial amount of oatmeal, a large quantity of malt, salmon in abundance and even a fine library of books (said to be worth £400). The wine from Lovat's cellars was sold to Cumberland's officers at two shillings a bottle for Madeira and one shilling and eight pence for claret, with profits divided among the men and officers. What could not be carried away was destroyed and the houses of the Fraser clansmen were burnt to the ground.

Cumberland also dispatched Lord Ancram to Aberdeen, with most of his cavalry, followed later by a battalion of infantry who were replaced by another four battalions from London. Ancram reported back that he had 'burnt two Roman Catholic meeting-houses and five Episcopal, not forgetting two libraries of Popish and Jacobite books' on the way to Aberdeen. Another officer 'burnt the Popish academy at Scanlan [in Aberdeenshire] four mass-houses and two priests' houses', a task that Sir Harry Monro was given, 'as I know he has a particular regard for that sect, for which I have christened him *Flagellum Ecclesiae Romanae*

[Scourge of the Roman Church]'. Other raiding parties destroyed the chapels and meeting houses of the non-juring Episcopalians.

John Campbell, Earl of Loudon, after taking refuge on Skye from Murray's Highlanders in late March, was still on the island, having missed the Battle of Culloden. On 22 April, Cumberland ordered him to march all his men to Fort Augustus, where he was to 'drive the cattle and burn the ploughs of all those . . . out in the rebellion . . . and to burn the houses of their leaders'. Cumberland advised Loudon that he should 'constantly have in mind to distress whatever country of rebels you may pass through, and to seize or destroy all persons you can find who have been in the rebellion or their abetters'. Cumberland's initial draft of Loudon's orders mentioned the taking of prisoners, but this nicety was subsequently omitted. Two days later, Loudon crossed to the mainland with around 500 of his men, together with MacDonald of Sleat, MacLeod of MacLeod and 1,200 of their clansmen who made up their Independent Companies. That night, they accepted the hospitality of Grant of Glenmoriston, before burning his house down in the morning, 'destroying at the same time all the ploughs, harrows and other such-like utensils they could find'.

With the arrival of good weather in mid-May, Cumberland felt ready to occupy Fort Augustus, in the very heart of Jacobite country, which had been 'hitherto deemed inaccessible to an army'. He began by dispatching three battalions of infantry from Inverness on 16 May, following himself a week later with eight more battalions and Kingston's Light Horse. Four additional battalions of infantry were left behind to garrison Inverness under Major-General William Blakeney, while a further three under Mordaunt had marched to Perth to relieve the Hessian troops, who were finally sent back to the Continent. Later, Mordaunt and his troops would harry the MacGregor country in the Braes of Balquhidder, burning down Glengyle's house and driving off all the cattle they could find, while his clansmen took refuge in the hills.

Since the Jacobites, in capturing Fort Augustus, had destroyed the barracks built by Wade, the Campbells in Loudon's Regiment now

> made a pretty place for the Duke [of Cumberland] to reside in, with handsome green walls. They built a fine hut with doors and glass windows, covered at the top with green sods of boughs, so that His Royal Highness['s life] resembled a shepherd's life more than that of a courtier.

So wrote Michael Hughes, a volunteer in Bligh's Regiment, in his *Plain Narrative or Journal of the Late Rebellion*. The troops lived in a tented city pitched beside the River Oich. Their temper was not improved by the discovery of nine bodies of their comrades floating in a well or cistern, 'drowned by the rebels after having been made prisoner' – or so it was claimed.

Now established at Fort Augustus, Cumberland could take the submission of the Jacobite clans from the surrounding districts. Loudon's regiment marched into Badenoch, where nearly all the MacPherson clansmen surrendered their arms under an amnesty, apparently avoiding the brutal repression later meted out to the Jacobite clans farther west beyond the Great Glen. Even so, the house of their chief, Ewen Mac-Pherson of Cluny, was burnt in June 1746, while Cluny himself would spend the next nine years as a fugitive in his own country, supported by his loyal clansmen. His hiding places included 'Cluny's Cage', high upon the slopes of Ben Alder, where he would entertain Charles Edward Stuart during the Prince's wanderings after Culloden. Eventually Cluny did escape to France in 1755, dying in abject poverty at Dunkirk in 1764.

Another Jacobite clan which apparently escaped the worst of the savagery was the MacIntoshes of Clan Chattan, who had answered the call to arms of 'Colonel Anne', the Jacobite wife of their Hanoverian chief. She was arrested immediately after Culloden, where many of the regimental officers had died, including MacGillivray of Dunmaglass. Nearly all the surviving officers fled abroad into exile, while the other ranks surrendered to the government during May and June. There is little evidence that the MacIntoshes were subsequently targeted by Cumberland, although the troops who arrested Colonel Anne did commit atrocities, killing more than a dozen MacGillivrays, including several women and children, on their way to Moy.

In May 1746, the MacDonalds of Keppoch surrendered en masse. Alexander MacDonald of Keppoch and his brother Donald had both been killed at Culloden, leaving Alexander's natural son Angus Ban to act as tutor to his young son Ranald until he came of age. Their lands in Lochaber were plundered and burnt by Hanoverian troops under Sackville, who reported with grim satisfaction:

These hills will now have been thoroughly rummaged, and the inhabitants will have learned that they have placed a vain trust in them [as a place of safety]. Those who have submitted have been spared, the others have borne the reward of their own wickedness and obstinacy.

The Jacobite clans living west of the Great Glen felt the full brunt of Cumberland's mercilessness to those rebels who refused to submit, probably because they were the first to rise in support of the Prince and afterwards gave him sanctuary while he waited for a ship to France. Their still defiant chiefs had also sworn the oath at Murlaggan to continue with the Rebellion, no doubt hardening Cumberland's resolution to stamp out its dying embers. This was justification enough for a series of punitive expeditions, led by Lieutenant-Colonel Edward Cornwallis, Lord George Sackville and Captain Caroline Scott, Governor of Fort William, during which the country still held by the western clans was systematically devastated.

By these means, Cumberland wanted to show the Jacobite clans that they were no longer beyond the reach of the law, since 'it is as much in his Majesty's power to march his forces into that country which they have hitherto boasted as inaccessible as into another part of his domains'. The *Scots Magazine* reported that he offered 'a promise of pardon and protection to all common people that would bring in their arms and submit to mercy'. Cumberland did warn Newcastle that this policy might not fully suppress the Highlanders: 'I hope his Majesty will not imagine that by these people's laying down their arms the country is a jot surer from any fresh rising for at this time almost every Highlander is possessed of two or three sets of arms'. Indeed, he 'trembled for fear that this vile spot may still be the ruin of this island and our family'.

Often the clans surrendered arms that were mere tokens, handing over those that were rusty and obsolete. This only encouraged Cumberland to order further brutal raids, such as those against Glenmoriston and Glengarry, where, according to Cumberland's secretary, 'the people . . . trifled, and their country has been laid waste and the cattle driven away', despite their prior submission to the government. Moreover, although their chief, MacDonald of Glengarry, had taken no part in the rebellion, his house was burnt down and he was held prisoner in Edinburgh Castle until 1749, on suspicion of harbouring Jacobite sympathies.

This repression was, therefore, not only targeted at Highlanders who had risen in arms against the government. Others, who had stayed at home, suffered equally. Even clans known to be loyal to the government were harried, although this was the exception not the rule. The Earl of Seaforth complained that Sackville's men had devastated his country of Kintail, taking his tenants prisoners, while

> their houses [were] plundered and burnt to ashes, their wives and daughters ravished, the whole of their cattle violently carried away, and even a little house I had there for my own convenience first rifled and then hacked to the ground.

Unsurprisingly, many Jacobite fugitives refused to surrender without a fight, knowing the atrocities committed immediately after Culloden. According to Michael Hughes of Bligh's Regiment, the expedition under Cornwallis against Moidart 'did great execution amongst those who were still in arms, obstinately refusing to submit and accept of pardon'. Resistance was not confined to the Highlands, as Captain Berkeley of St George's Dragoons reported from Arbroath in June: 'We have been dismounted these past two months and taken a great many rebels, both in the Highlands and Lowlands; numbers refused to surrender which caused many skirmishes wherein several of the rebels have been killed.'

Cumberland's forces also took to cattle raiding, which threatened the rebels with starvation. A report from Fort Augustus stated that:

whilst our army stayed here we had near twenty thousand head of cattle brought in, such as oxen, horses, sheep and goats taken from the rebels (whose houses we also frequently plundered and burnt) by parties sent out from them, and in search of the Pretender; so that great numbers of our men grew rich in their shares of the spoil.

Fort Augustus became a great market for cattle and other livestock, and drovers and cattle dealers flocked north, from as far afield as Galloway and even Yorkshire, attracted by the large profits to be made. The proceeds from these auctions were often divided among the officers and men who had brought in the cattle, although the officers usually received the lion's share.

The profiteering reached such a pitch that Cumberland decided to regulate the market. He ordered best beef and mutton to be sold at no more than twopence-halfpenny a pound, rum at eight shillings a gallon, brandy at seven shillings a gallon, porter at six pence a bottle, cheese at five pence a pound, butter at six pence a pound and meal at ten pence a pound. However, he would not allow his men to plunder indiscriminately, ordering them 'to behave with discretion, and to plunder none but by order, and then [only when] there is an officer and party to do it'. Men found looting were severely punished. Even so, officers would turn a blind eye wherever their men came across empty or abandoned houses since 'these our soldiers commonly plunder and burn so that many of them grow rich from their share of the spoils'.

However, much depended on the individual officers who carried out Cumberland's orders. Kirkconnel readily admitted there were

officers of all ranks whom neither the prospect of ingratiating themselves, and making their fortunes, nor the contagion of bad

examples, were able to corrupt. Some of those [officers] that had
done the Government the most essential services were as conspicuous
now for their humanity as formerly for their courage and conduct.

Kirkconnel withheld their names for fear they would be victimised for
acting too leniently and compassionately.

Acts of Atrocity and Summary Justice

Even so, Cumberland's commanders often exceeded strict legitimacy in
military terms, encouraging their men to commit acts of undoubted atrocity
and summary justice. According to an anonymous report in the *London
Magazine*, an officer justified burning and killing, since 'the people are
deservedly in a most deplorable way, and must perish either by sword or
famine, a just reward for traitors'. Wanton bloodshed was frequently
encouraged. Typical was the attitude of Bland, who ordered Cornwallis
to raze Lochiel's fine mansion at Achnacarry and 'to destroy as many of
them [rebels] as he can, since prisoners would only embarrass him . . .
[and to put] the men to death, being pretty well assured it will be difficult
for him to shed innocent blood on that count.'

The repression became even more severe as the hunt for the Prince
intensified, tempting Cumberland to stay at Fort Augustus until mid-July.
No doubt, he saw the Prince's capture as the ultimate prize, after his
victor's laurels from Culloden. No effort was spared and anyone known to
have hidden the Prince was killed and their lands ravaged. By June, Hawley
was claiming that the scale of the destruction had reached 'about seven
thousand houses burnt already, yet all is not done'. He went so far as to say
that if his infantrymen were bribed with 'a guinea and a pair of shoes for
every rebel's head they brought in, I would still undertake to clear this
country'. Huske went even further, suggesting £5 for each head, although
he did not have the brutal reputation of 'Hangman' Hawley. Some
commentators have described Hawley as a sound soldier, whose deep
offence at the Jacobite challenge to the values of God, King and Country
had pushed him towards savage retribution. However, such measures, last
used against the MacGregors during the early 1600s, were too barbaric for
the times. Even the proposal that whole clans should be transported to the
colonies did not meet with approval.

Prejudice against the Scots

English officers and their men were not the only ones wreaking vengeance
on the Highlanders. Because even the most loyal of Scots, Lowlanders as

well as Highlanders, were viewed by Cumberland and his senior officers with such suspicion and prejudice, some were tempted to prove their loyalty by acts of excessive severity. Lieutenant-General John Campbell admitted this when writing to the Deputy Sheriff of Argyll:

> You cannot imagine what pains are taken to lessen the service done by our people, and to put bad constructions upon all our endeavours. For which reason I have cautioned Bar [whom he had just ordered to Tiree] to be as active as possible in disarming those concerned in this rebellion and to . . . apprehend some of the leading men and drive their cattle, nay I should be glad if he would even burn some of their houses. For these measures, though in my opinion of no service to the cause, suit the taste of the times more than you can imagine . . . If you send him any instructions I beg you would let him act with as little leniency as possible.

The worst of all the Scots officers were three Lowlanders who went far beyond the letter of the law. Although very little is known of him, Major Lockhart of Cholmondeley's Regiment was apparently a fiery and bad-tempered Lowlander, who, in late May, led his first raiding party of 180 volunteers against the Grants of Glenmoriston and Glenurquhart. Over eighty clansmen had already surrendered their arms to Sir Ludovic Grant of Grant, only to be arrested and taken to Inverness, against Cumberland's orders. Quite possibly, they had failed to surrender their best weapons. Nearly all were transported, probably at the instigation of their own chief, whom they had offended by supporting the Prince, while he had maintained a studious neutrality. Then Lockart and his volunteers harried the remaining inhabitants of Glenmoriston – men were shot quite arbitrarily, their wives and daughters raped, all their cattle driven off, and their houses burnt. Lockhart meted out the same treatment to the Chisholms of Strathglass, who were Roman Catholics, as well as to their Fraser neighbours. Survivors had to take refuge in the hills, where many died from hunger and starvation. In late July, Glenmoriston was the scene of more atrocities, committed this time by the men of the Kingston Light Horse.

Captain Caroline Scott of Guise's Regiment, the Governor of Fort William, was another Lowland Scot whose savage brutality rivalled that of Lockhart. Soon after the siege of Fort William was lifted, he ventured into Glen Nevis with a raiding party. The Camerons living there had taken no part in the rebellion, so they did not expect reprisals. Nevertheless, Scott hanged three clansmen whom he had captured, before going on to sack the house of Alexander Cameron of Glen Nevis, who was away seeking the protection of Campbell of Mamore. Later in the summer, Scott raided Appin, where he demolished the house of Charles Stewart of Ardshiel in full view of its owner who was hiding in the hills, before selling the timber and slates for his own profit.

Meanwhile, Scott had joined Captain John Fergussone of HMS *Furnace*, which was cruising off the Western Isles. Bishop Forbes described Fergussone as

> a fellow of very low extract, born in the country of Aberdeen, who, being naturally of a furious, savage disposition, thought he could never enough harass, misrepresent, and maltreat everyone whom he knew, or supposed to be, an enemy of the goodly cause he was embarked in.

Terrorising the Western Isles, Fergussone had already raided Canna and Barra before the Battle of Culloden and then, in late May, he visited Raasay, burning the house of Malcolm MacLeod of Raasay, before sailing to Morar and Arisaig. Anchoring off Loch Moidart, he burnt down the house of Donald MacDonald of Kinlochmoidart, another leading rebel like MacLeod of Raasay. He then sailed to the Isle of Eigg, where he took thirty-eight rebels prisoner, burning their homes and killing their cattle.

However Captain Fergussone claimed the capture on 4 June of Simon Fraser, Lord Lovat, as his greatest triumph (although it was actually Captain Dugald Campbell of Achrossan who found Lovat, hiding in a hollowed-out tree trunk on an island in Loch Morar). The captive 'was put into his litter, and the soldiers made a run with him to the sea-side, the pipers playing Lovat's march, with which he seemed well pleased'. Among his written papers in a locked chest was enough incriminating evidence of treason to bring him to the block.

Later in July, after finding that the Prince had spent a single night on Raasay, quite unknown to its surviving inhabitants, Fergussone and Scott raided the island of South Rona, just to the north, and then Raasay itself, driving off what few cattle remained after Fergussone's earlier visit. Yet this was not the end of its people's suffering, since the island was subsequently visited by the Independent Company raised by MacLeod of MacLeod. Although he was a distant kinsman to MacLeod of Raasay, his militiamen killed 280 cows, 700 sheep and 20 horses and destroyed 32 boats and burnt 300 houses.

Among the Highland commanders of the Independent Companies there was the occasional officer who behaved with the same barbarism as these Lowlanders. The worst of all was Colonel George Munro of Culcairn, whose Independent Company was with Bligh's Regiment when it sacked

Lochiel's house at Achnacarry. It then marched into Moidart, 'burning . . . houses, driving away cattle, and shooting those vagrants who were to be found in the mountains'. Much of the carnage and destruction was undoubtedly committed by Culcairn's own men. Culcairn himself was eventually murdered on the shore of Loch Arkaig, apparently the victim of mistaken identity, since it seems Alexander Grant of Knockando was the intended victim. Grant had command of another Independent Company responsible for various atrocities in the Cameron country and he ordered the summary execution of a Cameron trying to surrender his weapons after taking to the hills with his family. Culcairn's murder may well have been a mistargeted act of revenge for this death. His killer was never caught.

Garrisoning the Highlands and Raising the Highland Regiments

Leaving Fort Augustus on 18 July, Cumberland arrived in London a week later to a hero's welcome, including Handel's celebratory work *See the Conquering Hero Come!*, which was composed in his honour. His place as commander-in-chief of the Hanoverian army in Scotland was taken by William Keppel, Earl of Albermarle. On 13 August, Albermarle ordered all troops still at Fort Augustus to march south into the Lowlands, while the Argyll Militia reached Inveraray on 17 August, where they were disbanded. Only Loudon's Regiment and the remaining Independent Companies were left to patrol the Highlands.

In February 1747, Albermarle was replaced by Bland but, long before then, nearly all the Prince's senior officers, if still at liberty, had escaped abroad, their exile making it unlikely that the Jacobite clans would ever again rise against the government. Moreover, those clansmen who had survived Cumberland's repression were now struggling to feed their families after a disastrous harvest in 1746. Peace in the Highlands was now more at risk from an upsurge in lawlessness, especially cattle thieving – hardly a surprising development after the devastating losses under Cumberland. A government agent reported: 'The inhabitants of the rebellious countries begin to be in misery for want of provisions; steal they must or leave their country, which is as bad as death.'

The cattle raiding was partly contained by guarding the passes and glens through which the stolen cattle were driven into the Highlands from the Lowland districts at their fringe. The government also tackled the problem by extending Wade's network of military roads, so that the Highlands could be patrolled by small detachments of the regular army or the militia. Eventually these roads would cover nearly 1,200 miles, criss-crossing the Highlands. Two small barracks were converted from fortified tower houses at Braemar and Corgarff on the military road now running north from Blairgowrie.

Fort Augustus was repaired at the same time, but the Hanoverian barracks in Inverness were abandoned in favour of a massive new fortification at Ardersier. Nine miles east of Inverness, it occupied a barren spit of flat land jutting out into the Moray Firth on its southern shore. The construction of Fort George, as it came to be called, was started in 1748 and took twenty-one years to complete. The building was a fine example of state-of-the-art eighteenth-century military engineering. Its masonry-faced ramparts were flanked by polygonal bastions, designed so that they could be defended by covering fire from all directions. However, Fort George's defensive capabilities were never tested, since the need for such a military stronghold to guard the Highlands had passed by the time it was finished.

Within six months of Culloden, the Independent Companies were disbanded, after acting as guides to the detachments of regular soldiers scouring the Jacobite country west of the Great Glen. The Companies were only revived in 1760 during the Seven Years War with France, to be incorporated soon afterwards into the Highland regiments then being raised for service abroad in the regular army. This well-calculated policy was apparently first suggested to George II by William Pitt the Elder, who gained power in December 1756, and it was supported by Archibald Campbell, third Duke of Argyll, as a means of securing the loyalty of the still disaffected clans. At first, it was decided to raise two Highland regiments of 1,460 men each. One regiment was recruited by Archibald Montgomerie, a Lowlander with family connections in the North, while the other was raised by none other than Simon Fraser, son of the eleventh Lord Lovat, whose long and disreputable life had ended in execution in 1747.

The experiment was such a success that the Highland regiments became a permanent feature of the British army. The remaining years of the eighteenth century saw the raising of twenty-seven regiments of the line and another nineteen battalions of militia acting as a reserve for the regular army – around 32,000 men in all. Most recruits came from the estates of the Whig magnates and landowners, including such well-known regiments as the Argyllshire Highlanders (1794), the Perthshire Highlanders (1789), Lord Seaforth's Highlanders (1778) and the Sutherland Highlanders (1800). However, a substantial number came from the Jacobite clans. They perhaps made up a third of the total and included over 2,000 MacDonalds. Another sixty-five infantry battalions were recruited from the Highlands during the Napoleonic Wars. Some commentators have regarded this policy as a cynical ploy, whereby Highlanders were allowed to sacrifice their lives for the greater good of the British Empire, but others have seen it as marking the final integration of Gaeldom into British society.

Legislation Against the Customs,
Churches and Jurisdiction of the Highlands

Immediately after Culloden, the Government in London enacted legislation intended to root out disaffection in the Highlands, once and for all. In an Act of Attainder, passed by Parliament against the leading figures who had fought for the Young Pretender, forty-one persons were declared guilty of high treason. Other Acts receiving the Royal Assent in August 1746 included a 'measure for disarming and undressing those savages', as Henry Pelham described it. This Disarming Act banned the possession of weapons of any sort (except by cattle drovers, who needed them to defend themselves) and it also forbade the wearing of Highland dress. Highlanders were required under the Act to swear a bizarre oath:

I do swear, as I shall answer to God on the great day of Judgement, I shall not, nor shall I have, in my possession a gun, sword, pistol or arm whatsoever, and never use tartan, plaid or any part of the Highland garb; and if I do so may I be cursed in my undertakings, family and property – may I never see my wife and children, father, mother or relations – may I be killed in battle as a coward, and lie buried without burial in a strange land, far from the graves of my forefathers and kindred; may all this come across me if I break my oath.

Anyone found guilty was liable to six months in prison for a first offence, with transportation to the colonies for seven years for a second.

The prohibition of the wearing of Highland dress made the Disarming Act a source of much resentment because it applied indiscriminately to loyal and disaffected clans alike. It seems a curious piece of legislation until it is remembered that the soldiers of the Prince's army had worn Highland dress in marching south into England. Ironically, the kilt and its accoutrements were later adopted as part of the uniform of the Highland regiments and it has even been claimed that men would enlist in these regiments rather than abandon the kilt and plaid. The ban against Highland dress was finally lifted in 1782, when it was declared:

to every man, young and old, Commoners and Gentles [Gentry], that they may after this put on and wear the Trews, the little Kilt, the Doublet and Hose with the Tartan kilt, without fear of the Law of the Land, or the jealousy of enemies.

By then, however, the plaid was no longer worn by the common people. When the Romantic Revival of the 1820s revived Highland dress, it was a fashion that was only popular at the highest levels of society.

Punitive legislation designed to undermine the Episcopalian Church in Scotland was equally significant, although hardly surprising, given the religious affiliations of those Jacobites who had rallied to the cause of Charles Edward Stuart in 1745. Their faith was blamed for having

> greatly contributed to excite and foment a spirit of disaffection . . . in that part of the Kingdom against his Majesty's person and government; which has been one of the causes of the wicked and unnatural rebellion lately raised . . . against his Majesty.

No more than five Episcopalians were allowed to worship together and, then, only if their ministers had taken the Oaths of Allegiance and Abjuration. They had to pray for George II by name, so making it clear that James Edward Stuart was not intended. They were then given certificates to fix to the doors of their meeting houses, declaring they had submitted to the Act. Anyone attending an Episcopalian service taken by a minister who had not taken the Oaths was liable to be deprived of their civil rights, so that they could not vote in Parliamentary and other elections, and they could also be imprisoned for six months if they did not pay a £5 fine.

Other legislation was directed against teachers in private schools, who were required to take the same oaths as the Episcopalian clergy to prevent 'the rising generation being educated in disaffected or rebellious principles'. If the teachers refused, they could be transported to the colonies for life, while the parents or guardians of children who knowingly sent their children to such schools could be imprisoned for two years.

The legislation against the Episcopalian Church was not repealed until 1792, by which time its hierarchy had been reduced to four bishops and forty clergy. Penal laws had long ago been enacted against Catholics, so that they could not inherit or bequeath property. Nor could they even recover debts owing to them, while their children were removed from their homes to be brought up as Protestants.

There was an equally far-reaching Act to abolish heritable jurisdictions in Scotland. These varied from courts of regality, with wide powers to try all criminal cases (apart from high treason), to courts of barony and even sheriffdoms, which were hereditary to many of the great Scottish families. These private courts were regarded with suspicion by such leading figures of the English establishment as Lord Hardwicke, the Lord Chancellor. He 'could not help thinking from the two formidable rebellions, which have broken out there within the last thirty years, that the cause must arise from some peculiar defect in the constitution and government of that kingdom [of Scotland]'. Judicial powers exercised by landowners over their tenants were abolished by the Heritable Jurisdictions (Scotland) Act, despite the guarantee of their continued existence under the 1707 Act of Union. This meant that the great landowners, especially in the Highlands, could no longer abuse their powers as they had done in the recent past by keeping 'the common people there in such a state of bondage, and [given that they had] erected themselves into petty tyrants over them . . . able to compel them into a rebellion . . . under the threat of fire and sword'. More specifically, the Act abolished ward-holding as a military form of feudal tenure peculiar to the Highlands, which had allowed the Jacobite chiefs to call out their clansmen in arms against the government.

Meanwhile, the estates of all Jacobite landowners convicted of treason were forfeited to the Crown. The administration of these forfeited estates was placed in the hands of Commissioners, mostly Edinburgh lawyers, who introduced new methods of landholding and cultivation, which were to transform the rural economy of the Highlands over the next century. Although the forfeited estates were restored in 1784, mostly to the descendants of their original owners, only Francis Farquharson of Monaltrie lived long enough to get back his own estates. Otherwise, several estates went to officers serving in the Highland regiments. Ten years earlier, Simon Fraser had had his family's estates restored as a reward for his role in 'calling forth from a corner of the Kingdom, many thousand soldiers' to serve the Hanoverian regime.

Fate of the Jacobite Prisoners

While this legislation was passing through Parliament, rough justice was meted out to the Jacobite prisoners. By May 1746, the Privy Council in London had decided that no trials should take place in Scotland and all prisoners held in Inverness were to be sent south by ship to the Thames. Three hundred were transferred to the fort at Tilbury, while the rest were left on board what were prison hulks. Other prisoners were taken to Carlisle and York for trial. Held in dreadful conditions, many died of hunger and disease.

Of the more prominent rebels captured, four peers were beheaded, since hanging was reserved for mere commoners as a more degrading form of execution. Charles Radcliffe, who had assumed his brother's title as the Earl of Derwentwater, was already under sentence of death for his part in the 1715 Rebellion but had escaped to France from Newgate

Prison. When he was recaptured on board a ship from France, it was only necessary to prove his identity for the sentence to be carried out. Four other peers were tried by Parliament and all were condemned to death for high treason. Balmerino and Kilmarnock had been taken prisoner at Culloden and appeared before the House of Lords in July 1746, along with the Earl of Cromartie, captured the day before the battle at Dunrobin. Balmerino and Kilmarnock were executed but Cromartie was reprieved after his wife had fainted at the feet of George II while pleading for her husband's life. Simon Fraser, Lord Lovat, was impeached by the House of Commons in March 1747 on the evidence of Murray of Broughton and of Lovat's own secretary, who had both turned King's Evidence to save their own lives. Although he used all his wiles to obtain a reprieve, Lovat was said to have finally accepted the inevitable with dignity.

Commoners were tried by lesser courts. Thirty-eight deserters from the British army and two suspected spies were court-martialled immediately after their capture, found guilty and shot by firing squad. Little mercy was shown to the Englishmen who had enlisted in the Manchester Regiment and twenty-four officers and men, captured after the fall of Carlisle, were executed in a deliberate act of exemplary justice. Another fifty-two were put to death. They were apparently mostly landed or professional gentlemen with a place in society who were seen as the ringleaders of the rebellion. Most held commissions as officers in the Jacobite army.

The great majority of Jacobite prisoners actually escaped with their lives. However, they were subjected to what now seems a bizarre form of justice that was arbitrary in the extreme. It was applied in particular to the Jacobite rank and file, 'not being gentlemen or men of estates, or such as shall appear to have distinguished themselves by any extraordinary degree of guilt'. They drew lots among themselves so that only every twentieth prisoner actually came to trial. Apart from a few acquittals, these men were mostly found guilty of high treason and condemned to death, although virtually all had their sentence commuted to transportation for life. The rest were allowed to petition for mercy, but only if they pleaded guilty to the same offence, whereupon they too were transported to the colonies as indentured labour. Nearly all of these prisoners, therefore, shared the same fate, whether or not they had drawn the unlucky lot.

Some 936 men were transported and another 222 men forbidden to return from exile. Many of their descendants fought for the British Crown during the American War of Independence. However, a further 905 prisoners were eventually released under an Act of Indemnity, passed by Parliament in June 1747, while another 382 had already been exchanged for prisoners of war who were being held by France, so they too obtained their freedom. Of the 3,471 prisoners who can be identified by name from the official records, it is not known what happened to 648 of them. Most likely, they died from hunger and disease while held in captivity.

Chapter Sixteen

ESCAPE OF THE PRINCE

Charles Edward Stuart's Flight to the Outer Isles

While Cumberland's forces were brutally suppressing those Highlanders still in arms after Culloden, Charles Edward Stuart was a fugitive with a price of £30,000 on his head. Desperately looking for an escape to France, he was finally rescued by two privateers from Saint-Malo after spending five long months in the Highlands and Western Isles, evading capture by government forces. This 'summer hunting' of the Prince was the final prerequisite for his transformation to the status of romantic hero, especially after he had received the help of Flora MacDonald to escape 'over the sea to Skye'. Flora was only the best known of the many Jacobite sympathisers who risked their lives and fortunes for the Prince in his wanderings. All refused to betray him, spurning the £30,000 offered for his capture. Even so, Charles was extremely lucky to avoid capture as he doubled back and forth in a tangled trail, dodging the troops sent to hunt him down.

After fleeing the battlefield at Culloden, the Prince had reached Invergarry Castle by the early hours of 17 April 1746, leaving in the middle of the next afternoon to ride west along the north-western shore of Loch Lochy towards Loch Arkaig. He was accompanied by Father Allan MacDonald, Edward Burke and John O'Sullivan. Turning west, he reached the head of Loch Arkaig, where he found shelter for the night with Donald Cameron of Glenpean and he lingered there until 5 o'clock the following afternoon, apparently waiting for news of his army.

Having received a message from Lochiel, the Prince continued westwards overnight through Glen Pean, tramping through eighteen miles of the wildest country to Meoble on the southern shores of Loch Morar. There he was sheltered by Angus MacEachan, a surgeon in Glengarry's Regiment. The journey had taken eleven hours and the Prince was so exhausted when he reached a small shieling that he had to be helped into bed. Next night, he crossed the hills by way of Glen Beasdale to the shores of the sea loch, Loch nan Uamh, returning to the very place where he had landed nine months earlier.

The Prince stayed nearby for the next five days, sleeping in a cottage in Glen Beasdale, while he recuperated from his exertions over the past week. He was now so desperate to escape to France that he was ready to ask for the help of MacDonald of Sleat or MacLeod of MacLeod. However, Donald MacLeod, a seventy-year-old boatman from Skye sent to act as his guide, absolutely refused to take him to the island, believing that the two chiefs would simply betray him to the government. Instead, he offered to take him to the Outer Hebrides.

The Prince, therefore, set sail on the evening of 26 April with Donald MacLeod and his crew of seven boatmen, accompanied by O'Sullivan, Captain Felix O'Neill, Burke and Father MacDonald. Donald MacLeod had already warned the Prince of a storm brewing and, indeed, a south-easterly gale blew up an hour after they had left Loch nan Uamh. Despite a broken bowsprit, Donald MacLeod steered the boat around the Point of Arisaig, hoisted the sail to run before the wind and took a course between Skye and the Small Isles of Rhum, Eigg, Canna and Muick. Only his superb seamanship brought them all safely across the Minch, landing at Rossinish on the east coast of Benbecula after a night at sea.

The Prince would spend the next two months in the Outer Hebrides, before eventually escaping to Skye with the help of Flora MacDonald. For the first two days, he stayed in a deserted hut at Rossinish and was visited by Ranald MacDonald, known as Old Clanranald, whose eldest son had led out their clansmen in support of the Prince. Although the old chief had stayed at home over the past nine months, he now did everything in his power to protect the Prince while he remained within Clanranald country.

The Prince decided to make for Stornoway, where he hoped to charter a ship to take him, posing as the survivor of a shipwreck, to Orkney and then to Norway. The party, therefore, sailed north along the coast from Benbecula. However a south-westerly wind forced them to land on the small island of Scalpay, which lies off Harris. They were given shelter by Donald Campbell, the only tenant on the island, while Donald MacLeod set off for Stornoway to hire a suitable boat. After a few days on Scalpay, the Prince sailed to Lewis, landing with O'Sullivan and O'Neill at the head of Loch Seaforth. As they crossed overland towards Stornoway, their local guide lost his way and it was eighteen hours before the exhausted party reached Arnish on the outskirts of Stornoway.

The plan to sail to Orkney collapsed when the townspeople suspected that the Prince was among the party who were so anxious to charter a boat. Prompted by Aulay MacAulay, the Presbyterian minister of Harris, they refused to let them enter the town or to hire a boat. The Prince spent the next twenty-four hours in Arnish, before setting sail once again with Donald MacLeod, hoping to land at Poolewe on the mainland. However, the sight of two warships in the Minch forced them to land on the deserted island of Eilean Iubbard, farther south off the coast of Lewis, where they stayed for four days sheltering in a 'low, pitiful hut', using the boat's sail to keep out the rain.

On 7 May, while on Eilean Iubbard, the Prince climbed to its highest point to see if he could spot any ships of the British Navy. Instead, he was astonished to see two French vessels whose nationality he could clearly identify from the nature of their rigging. But he could not persuade Donald MacLeod and his boatmen to put out to sea to confirm the ships' identities and so lost his last chance of reaching France for some time. The ships were the French privateers *Le Mars* and *La Bellone*, sent by the French government to rescue the Prince, after hearing of his retreat into the Highlands. They had left France before news of his defeat at Culloden had arrived and they were carrying arms and other supplies as well as 40,000 Louis d'Or in gold coin for the Jacobite cause. The two ships had dropped anchor at Loch nan Uamh on 30 April but were surprised four days later by three British men-of-war, the *Greyhound*, the *Baltimore* and the *Terror*. The French ships only escaped after a ferocious six-hour engagement, in which they were so badly damaged that they were now heading back to France. David Lord Elcho, Lord John Drummond and many other Jacobite fugitives were on board, including the Duke of Perth, who died on the voyage.

Having lost the opportunity, the Prince and his party left Eilean Iubbard on 10 May and sailed back south to Scalpay, where they found Donald Campbell had gone into hiding. They, therefore, continued along the east coast of the Outer Isles, evading Captain Fergussone in the *Furnace* near the southern tip of Harris, as well as another British warship anchored off North Uist at Loch Maddy. The Prince finally landed at Loch Uskavagh on Benbecula after another night at sea, sleeping for the next three nights at a 'poor grass-keeper's hut or bothy', where Old Clanranald visited him again, with welcome supplies of food and brandy, as well as even more welcome news of a safe refuge at Corodale on the east coast of South Uist.

Late on 13 May, Charles and his companions left their miserable shelter on Benbecula for Corodale, where they were to stay for the next twenty-two days in a crofter's cottage, in comparative comfort and safety. It was a remote spot, lying between the tall peaks of Heaval and Beinn Mhor, and they passed the time hunting and fishing. During this time, Charles's companions were able to observe his behaviour closely, and this revealed personality traits that would later destroy his life. He was prone to violent swings in mood, from high spirits and even euphoria to profound despondency and gloom, and his heavy drinking merely aggravated this manic depression. Neil MacEachan, the Clanranald parish schoolmaster who acted as his guide, recorded that he 'took care to warm his stomach every morning with a hefty bumper of brandy, of which he always drank a vast deal; for he was seen to drink a whole bottle of a day without being in the least concerned'.

By the first week of June, Cumberland had assembled a powerful fleet to patrol the waters around the Western Isles, while detachments from the Independent Companies, raised by MacDonald of Sleat and MacLeod of MacLeod, had already landed on Barra. It was just as well that Charles had listened to the advice of his boatman, Donald MacLeod, when he had insisted that MacDonald and MacLeod were not to be trusted, as they evidently intended to sweep from south to north through the Outer Hebrides. The Prince, therefore, left Corodale on 6 June, sailing north to the small island of Wiay, off the east coast of Benbecula, before returning to Rossinish on Benbecula three days later.

Hearing that Cumberland's forces were patrolling the nearby coast, he tried to double back to Corodale, hoping it had already been searched. However, the weather was so stormy that he was forced to land at Uishness Point on the east coast of South Uist, where the party spent the night of 13 June huddled in a rocky cleft at Acarseid Fhalaich. Next day, they sailed south past Corodale to Kyle Stuley, just north of Loch Boisdale, where they hid until 15 June, before moving on to Loch Boisdale in the hope of meeting Alexander MacDonald of Boisdale. He, however, had been arrested by Captain Caroline Scott.

By now, fifteen government ships were cruising off the coast and the country around Loch Boisdale was swarming with militia. For the next five or six days the Prince was 'skulking up and down the loch, sleeping in the open fields with only the boat-sails for shelter'. As dawn broke on 21 June, the alarm was raised by a man

> running down the hill . . . as fast as it was possible to go . . . [to warn] that all the boats of the seven men-of-war were coming towards the land, full of soldiers . . . and he did not doubt but they were informed of the place where the Prince was.

Seven hundred men were landing from the *Baltimore* within a mile of the Prince's hiding place.

Flora MacDonald and the 'Fantastical' Scheme

The Prince escaped by fleeing inland, with only O'Neill and Neil MacEachain, reaching a shieling near Ormaclett on the west coast of South Uist. Here, at midnight on 21 June, the Prince first met Flora MacDonald. She was the stepdaughter of Hugh MacDonald of Armadale who was a secret Jacobite supporter, despite serving as a captain in MacDonald of Sleat's Independent Company. It was his plan to smuggle the Prince across the sea to Skye, disguised as the Irish maid servant of his stepdaughter. Flora MacDonald had known nothing about this scheme, which she thought 'fantastical' when it was first explained to her. However, she eventually agreed and her name has passed into legend as a figure of romance, linked irrevocably with that of 'Bonnie Prince Charlie'.

The plan was only feasible since Flora had already arranged to visit her brother in South Uist, so that she already held a passport allowing her to return to her stepfather's house at Armadale on Skye. Two more passports, made out in the names of her two 'servants' were needed. While the Prince went into hiding, Flora set out next day for Clanranald's house on Benbecula with Neil MacEachan, to be detained overnight by a militia patrol commanded by her stepfather. Next morning, he released her and made out the additional passports in the names of Neil MacEaichan, posing as her manservant, and Betty Burke, her 'maid-servant' – more usually known as Charles Edward Stuart.

The Prince now had to cross heavily guarded country to reach Rossinish on Benbecula, where Flora would meet him. With MacEaichan and O'Neill, he walked to the head of Loch Skipport and crossed to the island of Wiay in a small fishing boat, before rowing next day across to Benbecula and reaching Rossinish around midnight. But the country was teeming with government militia and the fugitives had to retrace their steps to shelter in a cowherd's bothy. The Prince stayed there for three nights, hiding out in the open whenever government troops approached.

On the afternoon of 27 June, the Prince met up with Flora Macdonald who was accompanied by Lady Clanranald. Over supper, they heard that Campbell of Mamore was a short distance away with 1,500 men. Lochiel later claimed in *Memoire d'un Ecossais* that Campbell had 'told the chief of the locality on landing [presumably Clanranald], "Tomorrow we are going to carry out some thorough searches. If there is any contraband I think you would do well to get it under cover tonight" '. At the news, the 'contraband' Prince and his companions hastily crossed Loch Uskavagh by boat to the shelter of another bothy, where they finished their meal at 5 a.m. Some days later, Clanranald and his wife were taken prisoner by Campbell, by which time the Prince had reached the relative safety of the mainland.

However, the Prince had first to reach Skye. He dismissed O'Neill, who was not a Gaelic speaker, keeping only Flora MacDonald, MacEachan and four boatmen with him. After lying low during the day, they embarked for Skye after sunset. The Prince had disguised himself as Betty Burke, stripping to his underclothes and putting on women's clothes including shoes and stockings, with a wig and cap to cover his whole head. There was no wind at first and it seems they had to row north-east along the coast until a stiff westerly wind rose around midnight and this carried them to Waternish Point at the north-western tip of Skye by early morning. Waternish was MacLeod country and the boat came under fire from government troops as it rounded the headland, after they ignored an order to come ashore. Instead, they sailed across Loch Snizort to land near Kilbride in Trotternish, where a small headland is still known as Prince Charles's Point.

While the Prince lay hidden, Flora MacDonald went to Mugstot (now Monkstadt) House, where Lady Margaret MacDonald of Sleat was living alone, as her husband was then stationed at Fort Augustus with his Independent Company. A staunch Jacobite herself, she summoned help from Alexander MacDonald of Kingsburgh and Captain Donald Roy MacDonald. But a detachment of militia was actually occupying the house under Captain Alexander MacLeod of Bracadale. While Flora distracted the Captain, a hurried decision was taken outside that the Prince should shelter for the night at Kingsburgh's house, before taking refuge with MacLeod of Raasay, who was himself in hiding. Lady Margaret and Flora then had to entertain Captain MacLeod to dinner.

Finally the odd party was able to set out and 'Betty Burke', the maidservant, walked along the road with MacDonald of Kingsburgh and MacEachan, while Flora rode on horseback. The Prince's disguise as a woman left much to be desired and he had great difficulty in managing his petticoats, especially when fording streams. James Boswell was later told by Flora that:

> his size was so large, and his strides so great, that some women whom they met reported that they had seen a very big woman, who looked like a man in woman's clothes, and that perhaps it was (as they expressed themselves) the *Prince*, after whom so much search was making.

Kingsburgh's wife thought him an 'odd muckle trollop' before being told his real identity. Nonetheless, the party reached Kingsburgh House safely and, after a hearty dinner and a good night's sleep, Charles set off again late the next day for Portree.

He was accompanied along part of the way by Kingsburgh but, when Kingsburgh was arrested after a few days, a young boy called MacQueen took his place as the Prince's guide. They kept to the byways, while Flora took the main road with MacEachan. Halfway to Portree, the Prince lost patience with his petticoats and put on a tartan shortcoat and waistcoat, with a kilt or philibeg and short hose, a plaid and a wig and bonnet. A boat was waiting at Portree to take him to Raasay and he left in the early hours of 1 July, after taking his leave of Flora MacDonald. She was subsequently arrested by Captain Fergussone of the *Furnace* and taken to London, before eventually receiving a pardon under the 1747 Act of Indemnity. Flora later married Kingsburgh's son Allan MacDonald and together they entertained Dr Johnson and James Boswell at Kingsburgh during their celebrated visit to the Hebrides in 1773.

Cumberland's Cordon Tightens Around the Prince

After all these elaborate and risky arrangements to reach Raasay, the Prince realised when he reached the island that it was too small to hide him if it were searched, so he returned to Skye the next day. Landing just north of Portree, he hid in a cow byre for the night of 2 July, leaving the next evening with MacLeod of Eyre to go south through the hills to Elgol. Next day, MacKinnon of MacKinnon arrange the Prince's escape to the mainland. MacLeod of Eyre returned to Raasay, where he was arrested on 17 September.

The Prince sailed back to the mainland on the night of 4 July with MacKinnon of MacKinnon and Captain John MacKinnon. After landing at Mallaig harbour, then just a rough stretch of coast, he and his companions slept out in the open for the next three nights, before sailing towards the head of Loch Nevis and narrowly avoiding a party of militia. Charles then visited two of his previous supporters to ask for help but was refused by both. Old Clanranald would not provide any more help and neither would MacDonald of Morar. On 10 July, Charles returned to Borrodale, where the MacKinnons now left him. Within twenty-four hours the MacKinnons had been captured.

Charles was now utterly dependent for his safety on the ever-loyal Angus MacDonald of Borrodale and he stayed for a few days in a cave below the burnt-out ruins of Borrodale's house. He then moved four miles east to 'MacLeod's Cave', after news of the MacKinnons' arrest reached him. MacDonald of Glenaladale joined him there on 15 July and the party now began desperately searching for a more secure refuge, having heard from Angus MacEachan that Cumberland's forces already suspected that the Prince was hiding near Borrodale.

The danger was now very real. On 17 July, Borrodale's son was sent out to reconnoitre and he reported that he 'saw the whole coast surrounded by ships-of-war and tenders, as also [was] the country by other military forces'. The Prince rapidly set out for the cave north of Loch Eilt where he had stayed two months previously but, meeting Angus MacEachan on the way, returned with him to his house at Meoble on Loch Morar for the night.

Cumberland's forces now had Clanranald's country virtually surrounded, with a cordon of military posts at intervals of half a mile, between which sentries were stationed within hailing distance of each other. The cordon stretched from the head of Loch Eil as far north as Kinloch Hourn, guarding all the passes through the mountains. Charles's only chance of escape lay in breaking through this cordon, especially as General Campbell now had six men-of-war anchored in Loch Nevis, while Captain Caroline Scott had landed with his forces in Arisaig. The Prince's party spent the next five days probing the cordon to find its weakest point, crossing some of the wildest country in the Scottish Highlands.

The Prince left Meoble on the morning of 18 July with Glenaladale, his brother and Borrodale's son and they headed east through the hills to the north of Loch Eilt. By early afternoon, they had climbed to the summit of Fraoch-bheinne, just north of Glenfinnan, where they heard that government troops were out in force, scouring the surrounding country, with a hundred Argyll militiamen at the very foot of Fraoch-bheinne itself. Their next guide through the hills was to have been Cameron of Glenpean but the proximity of the militiamen meant that they could not risk waiting for him. At nightfall, they moved off north and headed for a previously arranged rendezvous with Glenaladale's brother on the slopes of Sgurr nan Coireachan. However, in the darkness, they managed to miss him. Then, quite by accident, they met Cameron of Glenpean, who led them north and they hid out the next day near the summit of a hill overlooking Loch Arkaig, which had already been searched.

On 19 July, the Prince trekked north across the hills towards the head of Glen Quoich, reaching Coire nan Gall in the small hours. There they hid over the next day in a 'fast place', close to the head of Loch Quoich, although they discovered that a hundred soldiers were camped nearby. But the Prince and his party were undetected and continued north that evening. From the summit of Druim Chosaidh,

> they observed the fires of a camp directly in their front, which they could hardly shun . . . However, being resolved to pass at any rate, they came so near without being observed [by the soldiers] as to hear them talk distinctly; and ascending the next hill, no sooner was his

Royal Highness at the top than he and his small party spied the fires
of another camp at the very foot where they were to descend. But
turning a little westward they passed between two of their guards
betwixt one and two a.m. of 21 July.

They had slipped through the cordon that had been slowly tightening
around the Prince.

After this dramatic escape, the Prince nearly came to grief by stumbling
as he crossed a small stream. He was saved from falling over a cliff by his
companions, who grabbed hold of him, and also by his own quick
reactions, being 'very full of life'. By daybreak, they had reached Coire
Sgoireadail in the hills to the north of Kinloch Hourn. They spent 21 July
hiding in the heather, unaware that two camps of Hanoverian soldiers were
nearby. Once darkness had fallen – and the Prince would later describe it as
'the darkest night ever in my life I have travelled' – they escaped further
north into Seaforth's country, where they hid for the next day in the hills
above Glen Shiel. The Prince had planned to go even farther north, after a
rumour that a French ship had put into Poolewe. But, after news of its
departure, he took refuge in the Braes of Glenmoriston, guided there by
Donald MacDonald, a clansman of Glengarry.

Caves, Shielings and a 'Cage'

The Prince and his companions left Glenshiel after nightfall on 22 July
and Cameron of Glenpean returned home. By early morning, they were
in the hills north of Strathcluanie, but only after a narrow escape from a
Hanoverian officer and two soldiers, who passed close by the Prince's
hiding place after Glenaladale had turned back to find a lost purse. Later
in the day, they made for a high hill between Glen moriston and Glen
Glass, probably Sgurr nan Conbhairean. Hearing gunfire, they spent the
night hiding in a shallow cave. Open to the elements, it made a miserable
shelter and the Prince could not sleep. But next day his luck improved
when he met the 'Seven Men of Glenmoriston', his companions for the
next month.

The Seven Men were also fugitives, who had ambushed a party of seven
redcoats, killing two. They were: Patrick Grant of Craskie (who had served
with Glengarry's Regiment); John MacDonald; Alexander MacDonnell;
Gregor MacGregor; and three Chisholm brothers, Alexander, Donald and
Hugh. After witnessing the atrocities committed by Cumberland's troops,
they had taken a solemn oath with one another, never to submit to the
Hanoverian regime, but to fight to the death for their country. Their refuge
was a roomy cave, high in the hills north of Loch Cluanie, looking out over

Coire Mheadoin on the eastern slopes of Sgurr nan Conbhairean. In the words of Alexander MacDonnell, after

> making a bed for him, his Royal Highness was lulled asleep with the sweet murmurs of the finest purling stream that could be, running by his bedside, within the grotto . . . as comfortably lodged as if he had been in a royal palace . . . in which romantic habitation his Royal Highness passed three days, at the end of which he was so well refreshed that he thought himself able to encounter any hardships.

The next four days and nights were spent in another cave, two miles away in Coire Mheadhoin, 'a grotto no less romantic' than the first.

On 1 August the party heard that the Argyll Militia, under Captain 'Black' Campbell, were camped out only four miles away with a large herd of cattle. The Prince still hoped to find a French ship at Poolewe, so the Men of Glenmoriston now escorted him north into Chisholm's country of Strathglass, keeping to the hills around the head of Glen Affric. He stayed there in a shieling for a few days, before continuing on north, to learn on 7 August that a French vessel had indeed left Poolewe, after landing two officers. They were at that moment making their way south into Lochiel's country, looking for him.

Charles now doubled back south in search of the French officers. At Strathglass, he was told that nearly all of Cumberland's troops had already withdrawn to Fort Augustus after their commander had left for London. They would soon be recalled south to the Lowlands, leaving only Loudon's Regiment and the Independent Companies to continue the search for the Young Pretender. However, troops were still scouring the Braes of Glengarry, so it was not until 12 August that the Prince's party left Strathglass, moving south through the hills west of the Great Glen. At the Braes of Achnasaul at the eastern end of Loch Arkaig, they found a miserable shelter before being taken by Donald Cameron of Clunes to a 'very fast place', just two miles away. This was another cave on the steep wooded slopes overlooking the Dark Mile near Achnacarry.

For the next ten days, Charles was in Lochiel's country around the eastern end of Loch Arkaig, moving between several different hiding places with MacDonald of Lochgarry, Cameron of Clunes and Lochiel's brother Dr Archibald Cameron. Lochiel's other brother Reverend John Cameron has left a description of the Prince when he met him there:

> He was then bare-footed, had an old black kilt coat on, a plaid, a philabeg and waistcoat, a dirty shirt and a long red beard, a gun in his

hand, a pistol and dirk by his side. He was very cheerful and in good
health, and, in my opinion, fatter than when he was at Inverness.

The Prince finally met the French officers who had landed at Poolewe and
was delighted to hear of the determined French efforts to rescue him.
Meanwhile, he sent off a messenger to summon Lochiel, who was
sheltering on Ben Alder with Ewan MacPherson of Cluny.

The Prince was only at risk at this time when a party of Loudon's
Regiment approached his hiding place at Torvault (Torr á Mhuilt). Taking
to the hills, he spent the next night in hiding on Meall an Tagraidh at the
head of Glen Cai-aig, moving even farther west before returning to the
eastern end of Loch Arkaig a few days later. By 28 August, he had
dismissed the Seven Men of Glenmoriston, who made their way back to
their own country, and he had also taken leave of MacDonald of Glenaladale. With Lochgarry, Dr Cameron and Reverend John Cameron, he now
began a long trek across country towards Ben Alder.

Local tradition has it that, after crossing the River Lochy, Charles's party
descended Creag Meagaidh by the valley of Allt Coire Ardair, before
spending the night at Coire an Iubhair Mor south of Loch Laggan. Next
day, they moved to a tiny shieling on the slopes of Meall an Odhar, just
west of Loch Pattack to the north of Ben Alder, where the Prince met
Lochiel, greeting him warmly.

'Gay, hearty and in better spirits than was possible to think he could be',
the Prince sat down with his companions to a feast of 'mutton newly killed,
and an anker of whisky of twenty Scotch pints with some beef sassers
[sausages] made the year before, and plenty of butter and cheese, and
besides, a large well-cured bacon'. He spent the next three nights there
with Lochiel. MacPherson of Cluny joined them on 1 September and the
party moved to 'a little shiel[ing] . . . superlatively bad and smoky', in the
valley of the Allt á Chaoil-réidhe, just north of Ben Alder. They stayed
there for a few nights, before moving finally to Cluny's 'Cage'. Marked on
the OS Map as yet another 'Prince Charlie's Cave', it overlooked Loch
Ericht from the southern slopes of Ben Alder.

According to an account in the Cluny charter-chest, written around
1756, in this cave, Cluny had 'contrived a more comfortable habitation . . .
upon the south face of a mountain, overlooking a beautiful lake of 12 miles
long'. He had woven boughs around a thicket of holly to make

a first and second floor in it, and covered it with moss to defend the
rain. The upper room served for *salle à manger* and bedchamber,
while the lower served for a cave to contain liquors and other
necessaries, at the back part was a proper hearth for cook and baker,

and the face of the mountain had so much the colour and resemblance of a smock, no person could ever discover that there was either fire or habitation in the place. Round this lodge were placed sentries at proper stations, some nearer and some at greater distances, who daily brought them notice of what happened in the country, and even in the enemy camps, bringing them likewise the necessary provisions, while a neighbouring fountain supplied the society with the rural refreshment of pure rock water.

This refuge was sufficiently secure to allow Cluny to spend the next nine years in his own country, moving between this and other hideouts.

The Prince stayed with Cluny for the next eight days. On 12 September, he heard that two French privateers had arrived at Loch nan Uamh. Manned by Irish officers with Jacobite sympathies, they had sailed with the full authority of the French government, on the orders of Louis XV. An Irishman, Colonel Richard Warren, commanded the expedition, having taken back dispatches from the Prince to France after the 'Rout of Moy' in February 1746. Warren had set sail from France after several other attempts to rescue the Prince had failed, and had managed to give the slip to the ever vigilant British navy patrols in the waters around the Western Isles. He had arrived at Loch nan Uamh on 6 September, remaining there at anchor for nearly a fortnight while a fierce gale kept the waters free of British warships.

Leaving Cluny's Cage after midnight on 13 September, the Prince and his companions, began the hazardous journey to Loch nan Uamh, fifty miles away to the west. Joined on the way by John Roy Stewart, they crossed the hills to the north of Glen Spean and passed undetected through Glen Roy the next night. Lying low for a day, they then reached the Great Glen, ferrying themselves by boat across the River Lochy under cover of darkness. After resting near Achnacarry, they started out again at nightfall along the southern shore of Loch Arkaig towards Glen Camgharaidh, where provisions were waiting for them. Pushing farther west over the next day and night, they travelled through the hills towards Borrodale on Loch nan Uamh. By day, the Prince once again disguised himself in women's clothes.

On 19 September, Charles Edward Stuart finally boarded the French ship which would carry him into the melancholy safety of permanent exile. Reaching Loch nan Uamh, he found the two French privateers *L'Heureux* and *Le Conti* still at anchor and boarded *L'Heureux* along with many others, including Lochiel, his brother Dr Archibald Cameron, MacDonald of Lochgarry and John Roy Stewart, apparently 'twenty-three gentlemen and a hundred and seven men of common rank' in all. Before the vessels weighed anchor early next morning, the Prince wrote a letter to Cluny, who had decided to remain in Scotland, confidently awaiting the Prince's return once French help had finally been secured. The letter ordered payments of £150 to Glengarry's clansmen, £300 to Lochiel's clansmen, £200 to be divided equally between the MacGregors and the Stewarts, £100 to Lady Keppoch and £100 to Cluny himself. The Prince had already sent 20 guineas to the Seven Men of Glenmoriston.

Escape to Exile

Charles Edward Stuart sailed into a bitter exile that he had never expected, even in his worst moments of despair, for his actions had been driven by supreme optimism and overweening self-confidence. Despite his defeat, he had brought to Scotland, in the words of David Daiches, 'some glamour and immense suffering, a strange and lingering memory of gaiety and courage, and a sense of a noble cause nobly lost'. Although the darker side of his character would emerge in the years ahead, the Prince returned to France as 'the hero of the century', as Marshal de Saxe described him. Several accounts of the 1745 Rebellion were soon published, including *Ascanius or the Young Adventurer, containing a particular account of all that happened to a certain person during his wanderings in the North from his memorable defeat in April 1746 to his final escape on the 19th of September in the same year*. A bestseller, it was translated into French, Spanish and Italian.

The Prince was lionised by society and his name was known throughout the capitals of Europe. At first he was received with honour by Louis XV at Fontainebleau but he was soon disappointed – Louis would not even contemplate another expedition against Britain on behalf of the Stuarts. After the French conquest of the Austrian Netherlands, the strategic interests of France were no longer served by supporting the Jacobite cause.

This was a devastating blow, made worse by the Treaty of Aix-la-Chapelle, which ended the War of the Austrian Succession in 1748. Britain would only agree to peace with France, already weakened by famine and a financial crisis, if the Prince and his brother Henry left French territory. The Prince refused to comply and, after an acrimonious quarrel had exposed France to ridicule, he was arrested and held prisoner before being expelled from the country. But, having been escorted to the French border with Savoy, he crossed back into France to take refuge in the papal enclave of Avignon. By flaunting the authority of Louis XV, whom he insisted on treating almost as if they were equals, he brought relations with the French king close to breaking point.

In February 1749, Charles secretly left Avignon after only two months and, for the next nine years, he moved incognito between lodgings in Luneville, Ghent, Liege and Basle, returning occasionally in secret to Paris. He even visited London in heavy disguise in September 1750, when it seemed likely that the ailing George II might be ousted in a coup d'état by Cumberland. In London, the Prince renounced Catholicism, rejecting the faith of his father and grandfather at a secret service in an Anglican church in the Strand, although he was later to repent. Although the English Jacobites still refused to risk their lives without foreign assistance, the Prince was sufficiently encouraged to embark on what became known as the Elibank Plot of 1753, once again acting independently of his father.

The English Jacobites were to seize the Tower of London and St James's Palace, holding George II captive, while the Jacobite clans in the Highlands would rise under Lochiel's brother Archibald Cameron and MacDonald of Lochgarry. Among the plan's supporters were George Keith, the Earl Marischal, just appointed Prussian ambassador in Paris, and his brother James Keith, now a field marshal of Prussia, who hinted that Frederick the Great was in approval. However, their plans collapsed when Cameron was arrested near Inversnaid by a government patrol, acting on information supplied by 'Pickle the Spy'. Although the spy's identity has been hotly contested, it is almost certain he was Alasdair Ruadh MacDonald, who became chief of Glengarry on the death of his father John MacDonald in 1754.

Cameron's execution in April 1754 quashed any realistic hope of the throne for James Edward Stuart, as the Prince virtually admitted when he sent word to Ewan MacPherson of Cluny, who was still living in 'Cluny's Cage' on Ben Alder, summoning him to Basle. The Prince's father, however, seems to have already accepted he would never rule over his three kingdoms as James III of Great Britain. In 1747, without consulting Charles, James had persuaded Pope Benedict XIV to promote his younger brother, Henry, as a cardinal of the Catholic Church. Charles was aghast when he heard, knowing that this was a tacit admission by James that he would never be king. But Charles's final blow came when Pope Clement XIII refused to recognise him as King Charles III when his father died in 1766.

The Prince finally emerged from these years of obscurity a broken man. Disappointed in all his hopes, he was now an alcoholic, subject to violent fits of paranoid anger if he could not get his way, interspersed with long periods of melancholy and maudlin self-pity. He enjoyed the favours of several mistresses, including Clementina Walkinshaw, mother of his daughter Charlotte, who had nursed him back to health at Bannockburn in early 1746. But perhaps as a legacy from his own unhappy and traumatic childhood, he proved quite unable to establish a lasting bond with any woman. The only exception was perhaps his daughter Charlotte, who nursed him during his final years as a chronic invalid. His dynastic marriage to Louise of Stolberg, which took place in 1772, ended in divorce after she sought refuge in a convent in 1780.

1745 in Retrospect

Charles Edward Stuart died on 30 January 1788, just a century after William of Orange had landed in England to claim the throne of his grandfather. The Young Pretender's death effectively extinguished any lingering hope that the dynasty he represented might ever again rule over Great Britain. Although his Cardinal brother Henry later took the grandiose title of Henry IX, this was mere bravado. By the time of Henry's death, in 1807, more than sixty years had passed since the Battle of Culloden and its savage aftermath.

During this time, the Highlands had been subject to rapid social and economic change, reaching a climax in the Clearances of the late eighteenth and early nineteenth centuries, when thousands of people were moved off the land to make way for sheep. Long before then, however, the old way of life had virtually disappeared, as Samuel Johnson recognised on his journey to the Hebrides with James Boswell in 1773. Johnson wrote in his *Journal*:

> There was perhaps never any change of national manners so quick, so great, and so general, as that which has operated in the Highlands by the late conquest and the subsequent laws. We came thither too late to see what we expected, a people of peculiar appearance, and a system of antiquated life. The clans retain little now of their original character: their ferocity of temper is softened, their military ardour is extinguished (except it should be admitted in the Highland regiments), their dignity of independence is depressed, their contempt of government subdued, and the reverence for their chiefs is abated.

Government actions after 1745 had fundamentally altered the balance between progressive and reactionary forces within Highland society, as T. C. Smout has emphasised in *A History of the Scottish People: 1560–1830*. Many landowners who, as chiefs of the Jacobite clans, had supported the Prince in 1745, were conservative or even reactionary in their outlook, looking back with favour upon the old days when the clan system had flourished. The abolition of the hereditary jurisdictions, although applied to all of Scotland, meant that Highland chiefs no longer held court over their clansmen, weakening their authority. Moreover, apart from those held prisoner by the government, nearly all had fled abroad in the aftermath of Culloden, leaving their clansmen to fend for themselves as the tenants of forfeited estates.

The more adaptable landowners were left behind in the Highlands by this exodus and had prospered by supporting the Hanoverian regime in 1745 as the chiefs of the Whig clans. They were now free to put their enthusiasm for agricultural improvement into effect upon their estates, in schemes which may have been well intentioned, but which often led to disastrous results. However, it may well be argued that the Acts passed by Parliament after the 1745 Rebellion merely accelerated change. In particular, economic necessity had already driven the former chiefs of the Highland clans to see themselves as mere landowners. By the end of the eighteenth century, they had much more in common with their Lowland counterparts than with their own clansmen, no longer seeing themselves as patriarchal chiefs with the interests of their clansmen at heart.

These changes at the highest levels of Highland society had the effect of destroying the clan system. In 1769, Thomas Pennant wrote of the Highlanders that:

> their character begins to be more faintly marked; they mix more with the world, and become daily less attached to their chiefs; the clans begin to disperse themselves through different parts of the country, finding that their industry and good conduct afford them better protection . . . than any their chieftain can afford; and the chieftain tasting the sweets of advanced rents, and the benefits of industry, dismisses from his table the crowd of retainers, the former instruments of his oppression and freakish tyranny.

Paradoxically, the myth of 'Bonnie Prince Charlie' that arose in the years after his death, gave a romantic aura to the Highland clans who had fought for his cause and then sheltered him for five long months without betraying him to the government, despite the prize of £30,000 on his head. Moreover, the Gaelic-speaking Highlanders, after decades of military service in the British army, were no longer seen as a danger to the Hanoverian dynasty. Instead, the threat now came from the radical forces unleashed on the Continent by the French Revolution and, subsequently, from the territorial ambitions of Napoleon Bonaparte. In 1822, during the period when Highland tenants were being cleared off the land in their thousands, George IV would make his celebrated visit to Edinburgh, appearing in Highland dress. This visit put the stamp upon the Celtic revival, which had started with the publication of the *Poems of Ossian* by James MacPherson in 1765. However the real history of the Highland clans had effectively ended in 1746, leaving their clansmen at the mercy of the social and economic forces that had already transformed the rest of Great Britain.

SELECT BIBLIOGRAPHY

Baynes, J. C. M. (1970), *The Jacobite Rising of 1715*, London: Cassell.

Black, J. (1990), *Culloden and the '45*. Stroud, Gloucestershire: Allan Sutton.

Blaikie, W. B. [1897] (1975), *Itinerary of Prince Charles Edward Stuart*, Edinburgh: Scottish Academic Press for the Scottish History Society.

Blaikie, W. B. (1916), *The Origins of the '45*, Edinburgh: Scottish History Society.

Carmichael, E. K. (1917), 'Jacobitism in the Scottish Commission of Peace, 1707–1760', *Scottish Historical Review, 57*.

Cruikshanks, E. (1979), *Political Untouchables: The Tories and the '45*, London: Duckworth.

Cruikshanks, E. (ed.) (1982), *Ideology and Conspiracy: Aspects of Jacobitism, 1689–1759*, Edinburgh: John Donald.

Cruikshanks, E. and J. Black (eds) (1988), *The Jacobite Challenge*, Edinburgh: John Donald.

Cunningham, A. (1932), *The Loyal Clans*, Cambridge: Cambridge University Press.

Daiches, D. (1973), *Charles Edward Stuart: The Life and Times of Bonnie Prince Charlie*, London: Thames and Hudson.

Dickson, W. K. (ed.) (1895), *The Jacobite Events of 1719*, Edinburgh: Scottish History Society.

Drummond, A. L. and J. Bullock (1973), *The Scottish Church 1688–1843*, Edinburgh: Saint Andrew Press.

Ferguson, J. (1968), *Scotland: 1689 to the Present*, Edinburgh: Mercat Press.

Ferguson of Kilkerran (1951), *Argyll in the Forty-Five*, London: Hutchison.

Gibson, J. S. (1967), *The Ships of the '45: The Rescue of the Young Pretender*, London: Edinburgh University Press.

Gibson, J. S. (1988), *Playing the Scottish Card: the Franco-Jacobite Invasion of 1708*, Edinburgh: Edinburgh University Press.

Gibson, J. S. (1994), *Lochiel of the '45: the Jacobite Chief and the Prince*, Edinburgh: Edinburgh University Press.

Goldie, F. (1976), *A Short History of the Episcopal Church in Scotland (2nd edn)*, Edinburgh: Saint Andrew Press.

Gregg, E. (1972), 'Was Queen Anne a Jacobite?', *History*, 57: pp. 358–75.

Hill, J. M. (1986), *Celtic Warfare: 1595–1763*, Edinburgh: John Donald.

Hook, M. and W. Ross (1995), *The Forty-Five: The Last Jacobite Rebellion*, Edinburgh.

Hutchinson, R. E. (1965), *The Jacobite Rising of 1715*, Edinburgh: Scottish National Portrait Gallery.

Insh, G. P. (1952), *The Scottish Jacobite Movement*, Edinburgh: P. Moray.

Jarvis, R. C. (1971), 'Cope's March North, 1745', in (R. C. Jarvis, ed.) *Collected Papers on the Jacobite Risings (Vol. I)*, Manchester: pub, pp. 3–24.

Lenman, B. (1980), *The Jacobite Risings in Britain, 1689–1746*, London: Methuen.

Lenman, B. (1984), *The Jacobite Clans of the Great Glen 1650–1784*, London: Methuen.

Lenman, B. (1986), *The Jacobite Cause*, Glasgow: Richard Drew, in association with the National Trust for Scotland.

Livingston of Bachuil, A., C. W. H. Aikman and B. S. Hart (eds) (1984), *The Muster Roll of Prince Charles Edward Stuart's Army, 1745–1746*, Aberdeen: Aberdeen University Press.

Lynch, M. (ed) (1980), *Jacobitism and the '45*, London: Historical Society.

MacInnes, A. I. (1996), *Clanship, Commerce and the House of Stuart, 1603–1788*, East Linton: Tuckwell Press.

McLynn, F. J. (1981), *France and the Jacobite Rising of 1745*, Edinburgh: Edinburgh University Press.

McLynn, F. J. (1983), *The Jacobite Army in England 1745: The Final Campaign*, Edinburgh: John Donald.

McLynn, F. J. (1985), *The Jacobites*, London.

McLynn, F. J. (1988), *Charles Edward Stuart: A Tragedy in Many Acts*, London: Routledge.

Menary, G. (1936), *The Life and Letters of Duncan Forbes of Culloden: Lord President of the Court of Session, 1685–1747*, London: Maclehose.

Mitchison, R. (1983), *Lordship to Patronage: Scotland 1603–1745*, Edinburgh: Edward Arnold.

Murray, D. [1883] (1973), *The York Buildings Company*, Edinburgh: Bratton Publishing Ltd.

Petrie, C. (1958), *The Jacobite Movement (3rd edn)*, London: Eyre and Spottiswood.

Philipson, N. T. and R. Mitchison (ed.) (1970), *Scotland in the Age of Improvement*, Edinburgh: Edinburgh University Press.

Pittock, M. G. H. (1995), *The Myth of the Highland Clans*, Edinburgh: Edinburgh University Press.

Pittock, M. G. H. (1998), *The Jacobites*, Basingstoke: Macmillan.

Prebble, J. (1961), *Culloden*, London: Secker and Warburg.

Salmond, J. B. (1934), *Wade in Scotland*, Edinburgh: The Moray Press.

Seton, B. and J. G. Arnot (1928–9), *The Prisoners of the '45*, Scottish History Society: pub.

Simpson, P. (1996), *The Independent Highland Companies: 1603–1760*, Edinburgh: Constable.

Sinclair-Stevenson, C. (1971), *Inglorious Rebellion: The Jacobite Risings of 1708, 1715 and 1719*, London: Hamish Hamilton.

Speck, W. A. (1981), *The Butcher: The Duke of Cumberland and the Suppression of the '45*, Oxford: Blackwell.

Szechi, D. (1994), *The Jacobites: Britain and Europe 1688–1788*, Manchester: Manchester University Press.

Tabraham, C. and D. Grove (1995), *Fortress Scotland and the Jacobites*, London: Batsford.

Tayler A. and H. Tayler (1936), *1715: The Story of the Rising*, London: Nelson.

Tayler A. and H. Tayler (1938), *1745 and After*, London: Nelson.

Tayler, H. (ed.) (1944), *1715: The History of the Rebellion in the Years 1745 and 1746*, Oxford.

Tomasson, K. (1958), *The Jacobite General*, Edinburgh: Blackwood.

Tomasson, K. and F. Buist [1962] (1978), *Battles of the '45*, London: Batsford.

Youngson, A. J. (1985), *The Prince and the Pretender: A Study in the Writing of History*, London: Croom Helm.

INDEX